A DIARY OF READINGS

ALSO BY JOHN BAILLIE:

A Diary of Private Prayer

Available at your local bookstore or from

Collier Books

Macmillan Publishing Company

100K Brown Street

Riverside, New Jersey 08370

A
DIARY
OF
READINGS

BEING AN ANTHOLOGY OF PAGES
SUITED TO ENGAGE SERIOUS THOUGHT
ONE FOR EVERY DAY OF THE YEAR
GATHERED FROM THE WISDOM
OF MANY CENTURIES

JOHN BAILLIE

COLLIER BOOKS
MACMILLAN PUBLISHING COMPANY
New York

Macmillan Publishing Company
866 Third Avenue, New York, N.Y. 10022
Collier Macmillan Canada, Inc.

Library of Congress Cataloging-in-Publication Data
Baillie, John, 1886-1960.
A diary of readings.
(A Scribner classic)
Reprint. Originally published: New York: Scribner, 1955.
1. Devotional calendars.   I. Title.   II. Series.
BV4810.B25 1986   242'.2   86-9534
ISBN 0-02-048360-0

First Collier Books Edition 1986

10 9 8 7 6 5 4 3 2 1

Printed in the United States of America

For
Ian and Sheila

FOREWORD

ANY such selection as this must needs be an individual one, made from those authors, and those of their works, with which the maker is familiar. Another could make as good a selection in which only a few of my authors and books would appear. Also, there are other books as often in my hand which are not here drawn upon because they do not easily lend themselves to quotation within the strait measure of a single page.

So many different traditions, as well as periods, and no doubt tempers of mind, are represented that not everyone, and perhaps no one, can make every page his own. I could not myself do this. But I hope each page may be found worth attending to and thinking about, and that from it something may be learned.

Some pages may be thought difficult, but it does us no hurt to have our minds stretched a little, even when we do not fully comprehend.

I have allowed myself considerable freedom in adjusting the spelling, the punctuation, and the use of capitals and italics to the fashion of our own time.

A table of the sources drawn upon, with some indication of the date of each, will be found at the end of the book.

No particular order is followed in the arrangement of the selections. The reader who puts the book to daily use may begin with the first page on any day of the calendar year.

J. B.

ACKNOWLEDGEMENTS

ACKNOWLEDGEMENT is made to the following publishers, authors, and others for permission to use extracts from the under-mentioned works:

Karl Adam, *Two Essays:* Messrs. Sheed & Ward Ltd.
St. Adamnan, *Life of St. Columba:* Messrs. Routledge & Kegan Paul Ltd.
H.-F. Amiel, *Journal Intime,* trans. Mrs. Humphry Ward: Copyright by The Macmillan Co., N. Y. Used by their permission.
C. F. Andrews, *What I Owe to Christ:* Messrs. Hodder & Stoughton Ltd.
St. Augustine, *City of God,* trans. Marcus Dods: Messrs. T. & T. Clark.
R. W. Barbour, *Thoughts:* Messrs. Wm. Blackwood & Sons Ltd.
Karl Barth, *The Word of God and the Word of Man,* trans. Douglas Horton: The Pilgrim Press, Boston (copyright, the Pilgrim Press). Used by permission.
Nicholas Berdyaev, *The End of the Renaissance (The End of Our Time):* Messrs. Sheed & Ward Ltd.
St. Bernard, *On the Love of God* (Eng. trans. of *De Diligendo Deo*): Messrs. A. R. Mowbray & Co. Ltd.
Dietrich Bonhoeffer, *The Cost of Discipleship* and *Letters and Papers from Prison:* Copyright by The Macmillan Co., N. Y. Used by their permission.
Martin Buber, *Between Man and Man:* Copyright by The Macmillan Co., N. Y. Used by their permission.
Herbert Butterfield, *History and Human Relations:* Copyright by The Macmillan Co. Used by their and the author's permission. *Christianity and History:* the author and Charles Scribner's Sons. Used by permission.
D. S. Cairns, *The Faith that Rebels:* Harper & Brothers.
J. P. de Caussade, *Spiritual Instructions on Prayer* and *Self-Abandonment to Divine Providence* (Eng. trans.): Messrs. Burns Oates & Washbourne Ltd.
A. Clutton-Brock, *Studies in Christianity:* Messrs. Constable & Co. Ltd.
Spiritual Letters of Father Congreve: Messrs. A. R. Mowbray & Co. Ltd.
Archibald C. Craig, *University Sermons:* Messrs. James Clarke & Co. Ltd.
James Denney, *The Way Everlasting:* The Senate of Trinity College, Glasgow, and Messrs. Hodder & Stoughton Ltd.
Gregory Dix, O.S.B., *The Shape of the Liturgy:* Messrs. A. & C. Black Ltd.
Arthur Eddington, *Science and the Unseen World:* Messrs. George Allen & Unwin Ltd.
Erasmus, *Enchiridion* (Eng. trans.): Messrs. Methuen & Co. Ltd.
H. H. Farmer, *The Healing Cross:* Messrs. James Nisbet & Co. Ltd.
Fenelon, *Letters and Reflections* (Eng. trans.): Messrs. A. R. Mowbray & Co. Ltd.
St. Francis de Sales, *On the Love of God,* trans. W. J. Knox Little: Messrs. Methuen & Co. Ltd.; *Introduction to the Devout Life* (Eng. trans.): Messrs. Longmans Green & Co. Ltd.
Erich Frank, *Philosophical Understanding and Religious Truth:* Oxford University Press (copyright 1946 by Oxford University Press, Inc., New York).
Jean Nicolas Grou, *The School of Jesus Christ* (Eng. trans.): Messrs. Burns Oates & Washbourne Ltd.
Donald Hankey, *A Student at Arms:* Messrs. Andrew Melrose Ltd.
J. Rendel Harris, *Memoranda Sacra:* Messrs. Hodder & Stoughton Ltd.
W. E. Hocking, *Human Nature and its Remaking:* the author and Yale University Press.
Leonard Hodgson, *Essays in Christian Philosophy:* Messrs. Longmans Green & Co. Ltd.
Lawrence Hyde, *The Prospects of Humanism:* Mr. Lawrence Hyde.
W. R. Inge, *Personal Religion:* Messrs. Longmans Green & Co. Ltd.
L. P. Jacks, *The Faith of a Worker, The Inner Sentinel:* Harper & Brothers.
William James, *Talks to Teachers and Students* and *The Principles of Psychology:* Messrs. Henry Holt Inc.
St. John of the Cross, *Complete Works,* trans. E. A. Peers: Messrs. Burns Oates & Washbourne Ltd.
Joseph Joubert, *Pensées,* trans. Katherine Lyttelton: Messrs. Gerald Duckworth & Co. Ltd.
Lady Julian, *Comfortable Words for Christ's Lovers* (transcribed by D. Harford): Messrs. Allenson & Co. Ltd.
G. A. Studdert Kennedy, *The New Man in Christ:* Harper & Brothers.
Soren Kierkegaard, *Journals* (trans. A. Dru): Oxford University Press; *For Self-Examination* (trans. W. Lowrie): Princeton University Press.

A DIARY OF READINGS

THAT daily quarter of an hour, for now forty years or more, I am sure has been one of the greatest sustenances and sources of calm for my life. Of course, *such 'reading' is hardly reading in the ordinary sense of the word at all.* As well could you call the letting a very slowly dissolving lozenge melt imperceptibly in your mouth 'eating'. Such reading is, of course, meant as directly as possible to feed the heart, to fortify the will—to put these into contact with God—thus, by the book, to get away from the book to the realities it suggests—the longer the better. And above all, perhaps it excludes, by its very object, all criticism, all going off on one's own thoughts as, in any way, antagonistic to the book's thoughts; and this, not by any unreal (and *most dangerous*) forcing of oneself to swallow, or to 'like', what does not attract one's simply humble self, but (on the contrary) by a gentle passing by, by an instinctive ignoring of what does not suit one's soul. This passing by *should be without a trace of would-be objective judging*; during such reading we are out simply and solely to feed our own poor soul, such as it is *hic et nunc*. What repels or confuses us now may be the very food of angels; it may even still become the light to our own poor souls in this world's dimness. We must exclude none of such possibilities, the 'infant crying for the light' has nothing to do with more than just humbly finding, and then using, the little light that *it* requires.

I need not say that I would not restrict you to only one quarter of an hour a day. You might find two such helpful. But I would not exceed the fifteen minutes *at any one time*; you would sink to ordinary reading, if you did.

BARON FRIEDRICH VON HÜGEL

My dear Godchild,

Years must pass before you will be able to read, with an understanding heart, what I now write. But I trust that the all-gracious God, the Father of our Lord Jesus Christ, the Father of Mercies, who by His only-begotten Son (all mercies in one sovereign mercy!) has redeemed you from the evil ground, and willed you to be born out of darkness, but into light, out of death, but into life, out of sin, but into righteousness, even into the 'Lord our Righteousness'; I trust that He will graciously hear the prayers of your dear parents, and be with you as the Spirit of health and growth in body and mind! . . .

I have known what the enjoyments and advantages of this life are, and what the more refined pleasures which learning and intellectual power can bestow; and with all the experience that more than threescore years can give I now, on the eve of my departure, declare to you . . . that health is a great blessing, competence obtained by honourable industry a great blessing, and a great blessing it is to have kind, faithful, and loving friends and relatives; but that the greatest of all blessings, as it is the most ennobling of all privileges, is to be indeed a Christian. But I have been likewise through a large portion of my later life a sufferer sorely afflicted with bodily pains, languors, and manifold infirmities; and for the last three or four years have, with few and brief intervals, been confined to a sickroom, and at this moment in great weakness and heaviness write from a sick-bed, hopeless of a recovery, yet without prospect of a speedy removal; and I, thus on the very brink of the grave, solemnly bear witness to you that the Almighty Redeemer, most gracious in His promises to them that truly seek Him, is faithful to perform what He hath promised, and has preserved under all my pains and infirmities, the inward peace that passeth all understanding, with the supporting assurance of a reconciled God, who will not withdraw His Spirit from me in the conflict, and in His own time will deliver me from the Evil One!

SAMUEL TAYLOR COLERIDGE

IF we look into our hearts, we shall be filled with confusion when we see there the mean, mercenary ideas that form the bond of our intercourse with God.

Are we not of the number of those who, like the Jews, have no object in their prayers but temporal benefits, those who pray earnestly for the fatness of the earth but never ask for the dew of heaven? Are not our churches full [1795] whenever public calamities overtake us, and quite deserted in times of prosperity? When our domestic affairs are disturbed, or we are involved in a vexatious lawsuit, or are in danger of some serious loss we become very devout, we resort to prayer, and ask our priests and pious friends to help us. When our life, or the life of our husband or a beloved child is in danger, we have Masses said, we begin Novenas and invoke the Saints. Events and circumstances awaken our religion, as though there were no need to pray to God except in illness and sorrow. As soon as affairs take a turn for the better and the danger is past, our devotion vanishes; the most we think of doing is to thank God for the successful end of our troubles; after a short act of gratitude we forget Him, and think of nothing but our pleasures. Speaking generally, it is true to say that the necessities and accidents of life form the main subject and the actuating motive of the prayers of the ordinary Christian.

Do you blame us, they may ask, for thus appealing to God in times of temporal need? I am very far from doing so, since it is God's own intention to call us back to Himself by such needs, and we can do nothing better than appeal to Him on these occasions. What I blame is that He is never invoked except for these needs, as though there were no other blessings and no other evils than those of the present life. What I blame is that God is forgotten as soon as these needs are supplied, as soon as these evils are averted and these blessings secured. Truly it is altogether too material, too carnal, to make piety a matter of such aims and events as these.

JEAN NICOLAS GROU

When I have said my quiet say,
When I have sung my little song,
How sweetly, sweetly dies the day,
The valley and the hill along;
How sweet the summons, 'Come away',
That calls me from the busy throng!

I thought beside the water's flow
Awhile to lie beneath the leaves,
I thought in Autumn's harvest glow
To rest my head upon the sheaves;
But lo! methinks the day was brief
And cloudy; flower, nor fruit nor leaf
I bring, and yet accepted, free
And blest, my Lord, I come to Thee.

What matter now for promise lost
Through blast of spring or summer rains!
What matter now for purpose crost,
For broken hopes and wasted pains!
What if the olive little yields!
What if the grape be blighted! Thine
The corn upon a thousand fields,
Upon a thousand hills the vine.

My spirit bare before Thee stands;
I bring no gift, I ask no sign,
I come to Thee with empty hands,
The surer to be filled from Thine.

DORA GREENWELL

YOUR imagination will wander far and wide, and be affected by the scenes and circumstances in which you are placed: but never mind; the imagination is, as St. Teresa said, the fool of the house, always making a disturbance, misleading the mind and forcing it to heed the images drawn by itself. You cannot help this, but involuntary distraction will not hurt you.

If you are resolved to resist distraction, you will do so successfully; and whenever you discover it, you will recall your mind to God, calmly and without struggling, not delaying to raise your eyes to Him. This faithfulness, in returning to His Presence, will win for you a more abiding sense of it, and thus that Presence will become familiar to you. After a time the practice of speedily returning, the moment you are conscious of distraction, will win for you an habitual easy recollection. But do not suppose you can obtain such by your own efforts; for then you would be perpetually constrained, uneasy, and scrupulous, when you should be free and calm. You would be always fearing that you were losing God's Presence, and striving to retain it, and thus become lost amidst the phantoms of your own imagination; and that Presence, the healing light of which should illumine all around, would only serve to render you confused, and almost incapable of your external duties.

Many persons distract themselves, first by their fear of distraction, and then by their regret of such distraction. What would you think of the traveller who, instead of advancing on his way, was always considering the accidents which he might meet with and, after any accident, returned to contemplate the scene thereof? Would you not urge him rather to go forward? Even so I say to you, Go on without looking back, so that, pleasing God, you may abound more and more. The abundance of His love will do more to correct you than all your anxious self-contemplation.

FÉNELON

LORD, what is my confidence which I have in this life? Or what is the greatest comfort I can derive from anything under heaven? Is it not Thou, O Lord, whose mercies are without number? Where hath it ever been well with me without Thee? Or when could it be ill with me, when Thou wert present?

I had rather be poor for Thee than rich without Thee. I rather choose to be a pilgrim on earth with Thee than without Thee to possess heaven. Where Thou art there is heaven, and where Thou art not there is death and hell. . . .

All men seek their own gain: Thou settest forward my salvation and my profit only, and turnest all things to my good. . . .

In Thee therefore, O Lord God, I place my whole hope and refuge; on Thee I rest my tribulation and anguish; for I find all to be weak and inconstant, whatsoever I behold out of Thee. For many friends cannot profit, nor strong helpers assist, nor prudent counsellors give a profitable answer, nor any precious substance deliver, nor any place, however retired and lonely, give shelter, unless Thou Thyself dost assist, help, strengthen, console, instruct, and guard us.

For all things that seem to belong to the attainment of peace and felicity, without Thee, are nothing, and do bring in truth no felicity at all. Thou therefore art the End of all that is good, the Height of life, the Depth of all that can be spoken; and to hope in Thee above all things is the strongest comfort of Thy servants. To Thee therefore do I lift up mine eyes; in Thee, my God, the Father of mercies, do I put my trust. . . . Protect and keep the soul of me the meanest of Thy servants amidst so many dangers of this corruptible life, and by Thy grace accompanying me direct it along the way of peace to its home of everlasting brightness.

THOMAS À KEMPIS

WHEN we hit a nail with a hammer, the whole of the shock received by the large head of the nail passes into the point without any of it being lost, although it is only a point. If the hammer and the head of the nail were infinitely big it would be just the same. The point of the nail would transmit this infinite shock at the point to which it was applied.

Extreme affliction, which means physical pain, distress of soul, and social degradation, all at the same time, constitutes the nail. The point is applied at the very centre of the soul. The head of the nail is all the necessity which spreads throughout the totality of space and time.

Affliction is a marvel of divine technique. It is a simple and ingenious device which introduces into the soul of a finite creature the immensity of force, blind, brutal, and cold. The infinite distance which separates God from the creature is entirely concentrated into one point to pierce the soul in its centre. . . .

He whose soul remains ever turned in the direction of God while the nail pierces it, finds himself nailed on to the very centre of the universe. It is the true centre, it is not in the middle, it is beyond space and time, it is God. In a dimension which does not belong to space, which is not in time, which is indeed quite a different dimension, this nail has pierced a hole through all creation, through the thickness of the screen which separates the soul from God. In this marvellous dimension the soul, without leaving the place and the instant where the body to which it is united is situated, can cross the totality of space and time and come into the very presence of God.

It is at the intersection of creation and its Creator. This point of intersection is the point of intersection of the branches of the Cross.

SIMONE WEIL

SUPPOSE I were to say to you that if you were to go down to Hastings you would be able to see the French coast clearly and distinctly, you would say, 'Impossible even to the longest-sighted person; it is more than fifty miles away'; and yet, as you may see in the Philosophical Transactions for 1798, the coast of France was so visible, without a telescope, from Calais to St. Valery, with the fishing-boats and the colour of the houses clearly perceived. When you hear this, you say, 'Well, if it is in the Philosophical Transactions, it must be true, and if it happened once, it may happen again.' Good enough reasoning; and the Scriptures are the Spiritual Transactions, the record of God's dealings with and revealings to men of old time. If they are true, He has unveiled the hidden mysteries not once or twice to waiting souls; and what He has done, He not only may do again, but will do, wherever He finds a truly humble heart in which to work and rest. If He stood by Paul, saying 'Fear not', just as really and maybe as evidently will He stand by you. If He guided him in his work, restraining him from preaching here, and calling him to service there, He will give you also leadings just as certain and maybe as distinct. But do you say, 'Are we then to seek for signs and wonders, to fast and pray, ardently longing for the divine revelation, until the vision dawns?' I do not say so; but rather add unto your faith virtue; and to virtue knowledge; and to knowledge temperance; and to temperance patience; and to patience godliness; and to godliness brotherly kindness; and to brotherly kindness love: for if ye do these things ye shall never fall, and an entrance shall be abundantly ministered unto you into the everlasting kingdom of our Lord Jesus Christ.

J. RENDEL HARRIS

No lofty reasonings about God and about His relations to us and ours will do away with the obstinate fact that if we love Him really, and not in our reveries alone, we must love our neighbour too, really, and not in theory alone. It is no use at all to see (as who can fail to see?) that He is in all things and persons and consequently is to be found and loved in them and they in Him, unless our belief flows over into action and in the practical affairs of daily life we do thus see Him and them too and do act upon what we see. Few things are more disconcerting than the oft-recurring phenomenon of high ideals and fine and subtle speculations upon the nature of God and of the spiritual life—much devotion too, and even austerity—in combination with an almost total insensibility to the duty of charity to others. In such persons one is sometimes bewildered to find a sort of contempt for this realized charity, as if it were an inferior, elementary, unintelligent kind of thing. Or perhaps, by a remarkable obliquity of judgement, they will consider that their superior perceptions somehow absolve them from deference to this Commandment, or at least from anything so coarse as putting it into vulgar practice. But though one may be a competent art critic without having ever handled a brush or a chisel, and may legitimately pass judgement upon a book which one could not have written oneself, in the life of the soul there are no such privileges: knowledge there is no knowledge at all unless it is also and equally action, and if it is not that, then it is worse than ignorance.

R. H. J. STEUART

It is quite clear that the whole teaching of Jesus Christ about God, expressed alike in His words and in the whole fashion and mould of His character, implies that God is always nearer, mightier, more loving, and more free to help every one of us than any one of us ever realizes. This alone is what makes His incessant summons to faith, and to more faith, coherent and reasonable. This again seems to me to imply that mankind generally is under a kind of hypnotic spell about God, which is always contracting and chilling their thoughts of Him, and leading to all kinds of depressing and terrifying illusions about Him. The story of the growth of the disciples' faith is the story of the breaking of that evil spell. If we transport ourselves in imagination into the little company of His disciples, it is not difficult to imagine what the effect upon them of His continual demand for faith in God must have been. Taken along with His own unbroken confidence of God's presence, power, and love, He must have seemed like one holding a continued dialogue with the Unseen One. Yet a doubt must have sometimes crept in. Was it not rather a monologue? No man but He heard the other Voice.... Was He mad?... The issue, as He meant that it should, gradually became inevitable. Either He was a dreamer, or they and all other men were dreamers, walking in the darkness and deeming it to be light....

Such, I doubt not, was the early struggle of faith. The issue does not seem to me vitally different today.... We are all alike wrapped up in the great earth-dream, and He alone was fully awake of all the sons of men; or we men and women of the twentieth century are broad awake to the reality, and He was dreaming His solitary dream.

D. S. CAIRNS

WELL, you are going to pack, pack and unpack, unpack for a fortnight. What is it that I would have you quietly set your mind and heart on, during that in itself lonesome and dreary bit of your road, Child? Why, *this!* You see, all we do has a *double-relatedness.* It is a link or links of a chain that stretches back to our birth and on to our death. It is part of a long train of cause and effect, of effect and cause, in your own chain of a life—this chain variously intertwisted with, variously affecting, and affected by, numerous other chains and other lives. It is certainly your duty to do quietly your best that these links may help on your own chain and those other chains, by packing well, by being a skilful packer.

Yes, but there is also, all the time, another, a far deeper, a most darling and inspiring relation. Here you have no slow succession, but you have each single act, each single moment joined directly to God—Himself not a chain, but one great Simultaneity. True, certain other acts, at other moments, will be wanted, of a kind more intrinsically near to God—Prayer, Quiet, Holy Communion. Yet not even these other acts could unite you as closely to God as can do this packing, if and when the packing is the duty of certain moments, and if, and as often as, the little daughter does this her packing with her heart and intention turned to God her Home, if she offers her packing as her service, the service which is perfect liberty.

Not even a soul already in Heaven, not even an angel or archangel, can take your place there; for what God wants, what God will love to accept, in those rooms, in those packing days, and from your packing hands, will be just this little packing performed by you in those little rooms.

BARON FRIEDRICH VON HÜGEL

To consider the world in its length and breadth, its various history, the many races of man, their starts, their fortunes, their mutual alienation, their conflicts; and then their ways, habits, governments, forms of worship; their enterprises, their aimless courses, their random achievements and acquirements, the impotent conclusion of long-standing facts, the tokens so faint and broken of a superintending design, the blind solution of what turn out to be great powers or truths, the progress of things, as if from unreasoning elements, not towards final causes, the greatness and littleness of man, his far-reaching aims, his short duration, the curtain hung over his futurity, the disappointments of life, the defeat of good, the success of evil, physical pain, mental anguish, the prevalence and intensity of sin, the pervading idolatries, the corruptions, the dreary hopeless irreligion, that condition of the whole race, so fearfully yet exactly described in the Apostle's words, 'having no hope and without God in the world'—all this is a vision to dizzy and appal; and inflicts upon the mind the sense of a profound mystery, which is absolutely beyond human solution.

What shall be said to this heart-piercing, reason-bewildering fact? I can only answer that either there is no Creator, or this living society of men is in a true sense discarded from His presence. Did I see a boy of good make and mind, with the tokens on him of a refined nature, cast upon the world without provision, unable to say whence he came, his birth-place or his family connexions, I should conclude that there was some mystery connected with his history, and that he was one, of whom, for one cause or another, his parents were ashamed. Thus only should I be able to account for the contrast between the promise and the condition of his being. And so I argue about the world;—*if* there be a God, *since* there is a God, the human race is implicated in some terrible aboriginal calamity. It is out of joint with the purposes of its Creator. This is a fact, a fact as true as the fact of its existence; and thus the doctrine of what is theologically called original sin becomes to me almost as certain as that the world exists, and as the existence of God. JOHN HENRY NEWMAN

If as a flower doth spread and die,
    Thou would'st extend me to some good,
Before I were by frost's extremity
                Nipt in the bud;

The sweetness and the praise were Thine;
    But the extension and the room,
Which in Thy garland I should fill, were mine,
                At Thy great doom.

For as Thou dost impart Thy grace,
    The greater shall our glory be.
The measure of our joys is in this place,
                The stuff with Thee.

Let me not languish then, and spend
    A life as barren to Thy praise
As is the dust, to that which life doth tend,
                But with delays.

All things are busy; only I
    Neither bring honey with the bees,
Nor flowers to make that, nor the husbandry
                To water these.

I am no link of Thy great chain,
    But all my company is a weed,
Lord! place me in Thy concert; give one strain
                To my poor reed.

                                    GEORGE HERBERT

1. To love God's will in *consolations* is a good love, when indeed it is God's will that is loved, and not the consolation which is the form it takes; nevertheless, this is a love without contradiction, repugnance, or effort; for who would not love so worthy a will, in a form so agreeable?

2. To love God's will in His *commandments*, counsels, and inspirations, is a second degree of love, and much more perfect, for it leads us to renounce and forsake our own will, and makes us abstain from, and forbear some, though not all, pleasures.

3. To love *sufferings* and afflictions for the love of God is the highest point of most holy charity; for in this there is nothing lovable save the love of God only; there is a great contradiction on the part of our nature; and not only do we forsake all pleasures, but we embrace torments and labours. Our mortal enemy knew well what was the farthest and finest act of love when, having heard from the mouth of God that 'Job was a perfect and upright man, one that feareth God, and escheweth evil', he made no account of this in comparison with bearing afflictions, by which he made the last and surest trial of this great servant of God; and to make these afflictions extreme he formed them out of the loss of all his goods, and of all his children, abandonment by all his friends, an arrogant contradiction by his most intimate associates, . . . to which he added a collection of almost all human diseases, and particularly a universal, cruel, infectious, and horrible plague. And yet there is the great Job, king of all miserable creatures, seated upon a dunghill as upon the throne of misery, covered with sores, ulcers, and corruption, as with royal robes suitable to the quality of his royalty, with such great abjection and annihilation that, if he had not spoken, it could scarcely have been discovered if Job were a man reduced to a dunghill or the dunghill a corruption in the form of a man. Now, say I, hear the great Job crying out: 'Shall we receive good at the hand of God, and shall we not receive evil?'

ST. FRANCIS DE SALES

WITHOUT voice and without opening of lips was formed in my soul this word: 'Herewith is the fiend overcome.' This word said our Lord, meaning His Passion. In this our Lord brought to my mind and showed me a part of the fiend's malice and the whole of his weakness; and for that He showed me that His Passion is the overcoming of the fiend. God showed me that he has now the same malice that he had before the Incarnation. And however sore he travails, and however continually, yet he sees that all chosen souls escape him worshipfully; and that is all his sorrow. For all that God suffers him to do turns us to joy, and him to pain and shame. And he has as much sorrow when God gives him leave to work, as when he works not; and that is because he may never do as ill as he would; for his might is all locked in God's hand. Also I saw our Lord scorn his malice and set him at naught; and He will that we do the same.

For this sight I laughed mightily, and that made them to laugh that were about me. And their laughing was pleasing to me. I thought I would mine even-Christians had seen as I saw; then should they all have laughed with me. But I saw not Christ laugh. Nevertheless, He is pleased that we laugh in comforting of us, and are joying in God that the fiend is overcome.

And after this I fell into seriousness and said: 'I see, I see three things—game, scorn, and earnest.

'I see game, that the fiend is overcome.

'And I see scorn, that God scorns him, and he shall be scorned.

'And I see earnest, that he is overcome by the Passion of our Lord Jesus Christ, and by His Death that was done full earnestly and with sad travail.'

After this our Lord said: 'I thank thee for thy service, and for thy travail, and especially in thy youth.'

LADY JULIAN OF NORWICH

NOW, when we set out to seek for anything that we have lost, we do not go gaping about anywhere and everywhere. We go straight to the place where we lost it. We retrace our steps to the exact spot where we wakened up to miss the thing we now value and miss so much. Go back, then, to that sad house where God, in His anger at you, forsook you. On what day? At what hour? On what occasion was it? Was it when you were sitting at table, and forgetting yourself? Was it during that ever-to-be-lamented and never-to-be-recalled conversation? Was it at that moment when the golden rule leapt too late into your mind? You would not have believed it beforehand that Almighty God would have descended to take notice of such trifles. That He would have taken a passing indiscretion in eating, and drinking, and conversation, so much to heart! and would have kept it up so long against you— you would not have believed it, if you had not yourself experienced it. No! But He has taken you this time out of all men's hands into His own hands. And, on your own admission, He is teaching you a lesson, this time, that you will not soon forget. . . .

Would you know, then, where you may have any hope to find Him? Would you come this day to His seat? Would you have it again, between Him and you, as it was in months past, and as it was in days when God preserved you? Well—come this way. Try this door. . . . Take up your cross daily in that thing concerning which God has had a controversy with you in your conscience secretly ever since. Was it in eating and drinking? Was it in bad temper? Was it in envy and ill will? Was it in that sweet conversation in which you sat and spoke such unanimous things to the depreciation and damage of your brother? If it was, try this. I have known this work well. I have known it work an immediate miracle. Go straight to your brother today: or take pen and ink, and tell him that you have not had a dog's life with God ever since.

ALEXANDER WHYTE

Now if they ask, Why then did He not appear by means of other and nobler parts of creation, and use some nobler instrument, as the sun, or moon, or stars, or fire, or air, instead of man merely? let them know that the Lord came not to make a display, but to heal and teach those who were suffering. For the way for one aiming at display would be just to appear and to dazzle the beholders; but for one seeking to heal and teach the way is, not simply to sojourn here, but to give himself to the aid of those in want, and to appear as they who need him can bear it; that he may not, by exceeding the requirements of the sufferers, trouble the very persons that need him, rendering God's appearance useless to them. Now nothing in God's creation had gone astray with regard to their notions of God save man only. Why, neither sun nor moon nor heaven nor the stars nor water nor air had swerved from their order: but knowing their Artificer and Sovereign, the Word, they remain as they were made. But men alone, having rejected what was good, then devised things of nought instead of the truth and have ascribed the honour due to God and their knowledge of Him to demons and men in the shape of stones. With reason, then, since it were unworthy of the Divine Goodness to overlook so grave a matter, while yet men were not able to recognize Him as ordering and guiding the whole, He takes to Himself as an instrument a part of the whole, the human body, and unites Himself with that, in order that since men could not recognize Him in the whole, they should not fail to know Him in the part; and since they could not look up to His invisible power, might be able at any rate, from what resembled themselves, to reason to Him and to contemplate Him.

ST. ATHANASIUS

IN the acquisition of a new habit, or the leaving off of an old one, we must take care to *launch ourselves with as strong and decided an initiative as possible*. Accumulate all the possible circumstances which shall re-enforce the right motives; put yourself assiduously in conditions that encourage the new way; make engagements incompatible with the old. . . .

The second maxim is: *Never suffer an exception to occur until the new habit is securely rooted in your life*. Each lapse is like the letting fall of a ball of string which one is carefully winding up; a single slip undoes more than a great many turns will wind again. . . .

A third maxim may be added to the preceding pair: *Seize the very first possible opportunity to act on every resolution you make, and on every emotional prompting you may experience in the direction of the habits you aspire to gain*. . . .

As a final practical maxim . . . we may offer something like this: *Keep the faculty of effort alive in you by a little gratuitous exercise every day*. That is, be systematically ascetic or heroic in little unnecessary points, do every day or two something for no other reason than that you would rather not do it, so that when the hour of dire need draws nigh, it may find you not unnerved and untrained to stand the test. . . .

Could the young but realize how soon they will become mere walking bundles of habits, they would give more heed to their conduct while in the plastic state. We are spinning our own fates, good or evil, and never to be undone. . . . The drunken Rip van Winkle, in Jefferson's play, excuses himself for every fresh dereliction by saying, 'I won't count this time!' Well! he may not count it, and a kind Heaven may not count it; but it is being counted none the less. Down among his nerve-cells and fibres the molecules are counting it, registering it, and storing it up to be used against him when the next temptation comes.

WILLIAM JAMES

BUT we must not disguise from ourselves that God's dealings with this world are still a very difficult problem. After reading the Old Testament we have no right to think that what perplexed the chosen people for so many centuries will all be plain to us even with the New Testament to guide us. There is a great deal of shallow optimism which 'heals too slightly' the wounds which experience inflicts upon Faith and Hope. It is useless to say, 'God's in His heaven; All's right with the world', when many things are obviously all wrong in the world. It is vain to argue, as Emerson does, that divine justice is an automatic self-adjusting machine, so that all get their deserts (not of course in a grossly material sense) in this life. Eminent literary men in the last century were too secure and comfortable to see what a rough place the world is for the majority of those who live in it. It was only after long travail of soul that the Jews learned their lesson; we shall not learn ours by turning epigrams. Remember that complacent optimism, no less than pessimism, is treason against Hope. The world, as it is, is not good enough to be true. We ought not to be satisfied with it. 'God has prepared some better thing.' . . .

This world exists for the realization in time of God's eternal purposes. Some of these are bound up with individual lives, for God intended each one of us to do and to be something; others have a far wider scope, and require far more time for their fulfilment. The manifold evils in the world are allowed to exist because only through them can the greater good be brought into activity. This greater good is not any external achievement, but the love and heroism and self-sacrifice which the great conflict calls into play. We must try to return to the dauntless spirit of the early Christians. . . . And let us remember, when we are inclined to be disheartened, that the private soldier is a poor judge of the fortunes of a great battle.

W. R. INGE

CONCERNING the fittest place for heavenly meditation it is sufficient to say that the most convenient is some private retirement. Our spirits need every help, and to be freed from every hindrance in the work. If in private prayer, Christ directs us to 'enter into our closet and shut the door', that 'our Father may see us in secret'; so should we do in this meditation. How often did Christ Himself retire to some mountain, or wilderness, or other solitary place! I give not this advice for occasional meditation, but for that which is set and solemn. Therefore withdraw thyself from all society, even the society of godly men, that thou mayest awhile enjoy the society of the Lord. If a student cannot study in a crowd, who exerciseth only his invention and memory, much less shouldst thou be in a crowd, who art to exercise all the powers of thy soul, and upon an object so far above nature. . . .

But observe for thyself what place best agrees with thy spirit; whether within doors, or without. Isaac's example in 'going out to meditate in the field' will, I believe, best suit with most. Our Lord so much used a solitary garden that even Judas, when he came to betray Him, knew where to find Him: and though He took His disciples thither with Him, yet He was 'withdrawn from them' for more secret devotions. . . . So that Christ had His accustomed place, and consequently accustomed duty, and so must we; He hath a place that is solitary, whither He retireth Himself, even from His own disciples, and so must we; His meditations go farther than His words, they affect and pierce His heart and soul, and so must ours. Only there is a wide difference in the object: Christ meditates on the sufferings that our sins had deserved, so that the wrath of His Father passed through all His soul; but we are to meditate on the glory He hath purchased, that the love of the Father, and the joy of the Spirit, may enter at our thoughts, revive our affections, and overflow our souls.

RICHARD BAXTER

To pray 'in the name of Jesus' may perhaps be explained most simply in this way. A magistrate orders this and the other thing *in the name of the King*. What does that mean? In the first place it means: I myself am nothing. I have no power, nothing to say for myself—but it is in the name of the King. Thus to pray in the name of Christ means: I dare not approach God without a mediator; if my prayer is to be heard, then it will be in the name of Jesus; what gives it strength is that name. Next, when a magistrate gives a command in the name of the King it naturally follows that what he commands must be the King's will, he cannot command his own will in the King's name. The same thing is true of praying in the name of Jesus, to pray in such a way that it is in conformity with the will of Jesus. I cannot pray in the name of Jesus to have my own will; the name of Jesus is not a signature of no importance, but the decisive factor; the fact that the name of Jesus comes at the beginning is not prayer in the name of Jesus; but it means to pray in such a manner that I dare name Jesus in it, that is to say think of Him, think His holy will together with whatever I am praying for. Finally, when a magistrate gives an order in the name of the King it means that the King assumes the responsibility. So too with prayer in the name of Jesus, Jesus assumes the responsibility and all the consequences, He steps forward for us, steps into the place of the person praying.

*   *   *

Father in Heaven, when the thought of Thee wakes in our hearts, let it not awaken like a frightened bird that flies about in dismay, but like a child waking from its sleep with a heavenly smile.

SÖREN KIERKEGAARD

As to those things which it still remains to say or do, we will think of those in their proper time, and God will provide for all; sufficient unto the day is the evil thereof; will not tomorrow and the next day bring with them their peculiar graces? Let us then think only of the present and follow the order of God, let us leave the past to His mercy, the future to Providence, striving peaceably all the time and without anxiety, first of all for salvation; and for the rest, let us leave its success entirely to God, casting on His parental bosom all our vain anxieties. . . . Let us then often say by a simple reflection of confidence and surrender, that can do more for us and better remedy all our ills than our own most anxious cares: 'O Lord, while I do not wish to neglect anything of what Thou ordainest for me, for the good of my soul or my body, I hope that in due time and place Thou wilt grant me the thought, the movement, and the facility to undertake and carry out such and such things which come so often and at such inappropriate times to present themselves to my spirit. I give them all up to Thee with their various outcomes, in the intention of occupying myself more freely with Thee, of waiting patiently and with complete resignation for everything to happen at the will of Thy wise Providence.' By means of this holy preparation of the spirit and the heart, and all the sacrifices which it involves, this adorable Providence, which is always attentive to the needs and conduct of certain souls, disposes and arranges things in their favour to the very smallest event, which is only fortuitous in appearance; it is also by the frequent experiences of these happy and divine arrangements that their confidence and abandonment grows continually. Happy the persons who, in order to become more recollected in God and more disposed to prayer, are able to banish constantly all this waste of the spirit, retaining only what is in the strictest sense necessary for the present which so soon passes, and for the future which will not be what one imagines and perhaps will never come.

J. P. DE CAUSSADE

SINCE I have learnt to know Christ afresh in this Eastern setting, it has been easy for me to point out the weakness of the portraiture when His character has been depicted with only Western ideals to draw from, as though these comprehended the 'fullness of the Christ'. For in such pictures the true proportion has not been kept. Some of the marked traits of His character have not appeared at all. Much has been lost. Some day I would like to draw His likeness anew, with the colour of the Eastern sky added to the scene.

In the same way, no doubt, the proportion would have been lost in due time, if Christianity had spread only in Asia in the first century, instead of passing on into Europe. Then, after many generations of Christian culture, we should have had an Oriental Christ, whom the West would rightly recognize as inadequate, and wish to draw over again.

For the supreme miracle of Christ's character lies in this: that He combines within Himself, as no other figure in human history has ever done, the qualities of every race. His very birthplace and home in childhood were near the concourse of the two great streams of human life in the ancient world, that flowed East and West. Time and place conspired, but the divine spark came down from above to mould for all time the human character of the Christ, the Son of Man.

This is a tremendous claim to set forward. In all other ages of mankind verification would have been impossible, because the world of men had not yet been fully explored. But in our own generation the claim may at last be made, and may be seen to correspond with the salient facts of human history. For those who, through intimate contact with other races, have gained the right to be heard, have borne witness that each race and region of the earth responds to His appeal, finding in the Gospel record that which applies specially to themselves. His sovereign character has become the one golden thread running through mankind, binding the ages and the races together.

C. F. ANDREWS

IT takes a long time for the average over-intellectualized person to realize that in this particular sphere of reality he must be prepared to receive illumination from the most unexpected quarters, to learn his lessons in completely unfamiliar terms, to strain his ear to catch overtones to which he previously paid little attention, to abandon some of his most cherished preconceptions, to bare himself to truths which he has not hitherto been prepared to face. Yet only at this price can spiritual be substituted for merely intellectual knowledge. . . .

The point is that the particular kind of awareness which the educated derive from dealing with experience in its more intellectual aspects hardly comes into play at all when it is a question of the deeper laws of life. The attention then becomes concentrated upon a certain type of datum which the unsophisticated person can identify and handle just as effectively as can any other —often more effectively, indeed, than the person who is highly educated. We find ourselves in a region in which the vital issues are brought into focus by such factors as acts of devotion, simplicity of behaviour, humbleness of spirit. . . .

We may draw from this an important conclusion. If anything in the nature of a religious revival ever takes place in this country . . ., we shall be prudent not to expect the educated classes to play any more important a part in it than that which is played by people of quite humble origin and pretensions. Spiritual power, insight, and authority—these things are apt at such an epoch to manifest themselves in the most unexpected places, to the confusion of the orthodox. A tram-driver who has been spiritually quickened in the way in which certain slaves were once quickened at the beginning of the Christian era, or as certain Quakers were quickened in the seventeenth century, is a figure to be reckoned with—particularly in a society which, like our own, is beginning to regard the capacities of its intelligentsia with distrust.

LAWRENCE HYDE

SOME desire to live that they may see more of that glorious work of God for His Church, which they believe He will accomplish. So Moses prayed that he might not die in the wilderness, but go over Jordan, and see the good land, and that goodly mountain and Lebanon, the seat of the Church and of the worship of God; which yet God thought meet to deny unto him. And this denial of the request of Moses, made on the highest consideration possible, is instructive unto all in the like case. Others may judge themselves to have some work to do in the world, wherein they suppose that the glory of God and good of the Church are concerned; and therefore would be spared for a season. Paul knew not clearly whether it were not best for him to abide a while longer in the flesh on this account; and David often deprecates the present season of death because of the work which he had to do for God in the world. Others rise no higher than their own private interests or concerns with respect unto their persons, their families, their relations, and goods in this world. They would see these things in a better or more settled condition before they die, and then they shall be most willing so to do. But it is the love of life that lies at the bottom of all these desires in men; which of itself will never forsake them. But no man can die cheerfully or comfortably who lives not in a constant resignation of the time and season of his death unto the will of God, as well as himself with respect unto death itself. Our times are in His hand, at His sovereign disposal; and His will in all things must be complied withal. Without this resolution, without this resignation, no man can enjoy the least solid peace in this world.

JOHN OWEN

THERE is a sphere in the life of everyone, except the child, in which he is appointed to *rule*, and to exercise some functions by the methods of his own will. From the monitor in a school to the minister of an empire, there are gradations of authority that leave no one without a place. Would you know the real worth of any soul, be it another's or your own, *that* is the sphere on which you must fix your eye. It is little that a man goes right under orders and when he is obliged to serve: you may always make a good soldier by sufficient drill; and amid the pressure of custom and beneath the light of the public gaze, even a passive and pliant conscience may be shaped into good looks and wear a gloss. But how is it with you in your place of power—among the servants whom you govern, the children whom you train, the companions who place you at their head? Do you take liberties there, as if there were nothing to restrain, and fling about your self-will as if it were free of all the field? Do you profane the law of duty by making it a homage to yourself, instead of letting its authority pass through you, as yourself chief captive of the will of God? Do you grant exemptions to yourself, exemptions of sloth, exemptions of temper, exemptions of truth, as if it were given you to loose as well as bind? There is no surer mark of a low and unregenerate nature than this tendency of power to loudness and wantonness instead of quietude and reverence. To souls baptized in Christian nobleness the largest sphere of command is but a wider empire of obedience, calling them, not into escape from holy rule, but to its full impersonation. Only now that no outer rule is given them by another, and they have nothing to copy with painful imitation, have they to bring forth the interpretation from within, and set themselves at one with the will of God by a heart of self-renunciation—a love that seizes all divine ends, and in expressing itself realizes them.

JAMES MARTINEAU

O MOST high, almighty, good Lord God, to Thee belong praise, glory, honour, and all blessing!

Praised be my Lord God with all His creatures; and specially our brother the sun, who brings us the day, and who brings us the light; fair is he, and shining with a very great splendour: O Lord, to us he signifies Thee!

Praised be my Lord for our sister the moon, and for the stars, the which He has set clear and lovely in heaven.

Praised be my Lord for our brother the wind, and for air and cloud, calms and all weather, by the which Thou upholdest in life all creatures.

Praised be my Lord for our sister water, who is very serviceable unto us, and humble, and precious, and clean.

Praised be my Lord for our brother fire, through whom Thou givest us light in the darkness; and he is bright, and pleasant, and very mighty, and strong.

Praised be my Lord for our mother the earth, the which doth sustain and keep us, and bringeth forth divers fruits, and flowers of many colours, and grass.

Praised be my Lord for all those who pardon one another for His love's sake, and who endure weakness and tribulation; blessed are they who peaceably shall endure, for Thou, O most Highest, shalt give them a crown.

Praised be my Lord for our sister, the death of the body, from whom no man escapeth. Woe to him who dieth in mortal sin! Blessed are they who are found walking by Thy most holy will, for the second death shall have no power to do them harm.

Praise ye, and bless ye the Lord, and give thanks unto Him, and serve Him with great humility.

ST. FRANCIS

THE persistent refusal to criticize or to retaliate can be a sign of more life, rather than less, *only when it is a response to a greater degree of truth*. It must mean that the self which has defects or which does injury is seen to be other than the real self; and the non-resistance constitutes an appeal from the apparent self to the real self, or from the actual self to the self that may be. In this case, it is not injustice, but it is justice to the living and the changeable. It is a type of justice undiscovered by the Greek, for it is based neither on equity nor on proportionality to any self that exists. Greek justice, distributive or retributive, took men statically, as they presented themselves. This type of justice refuses to take a man at his own estimate of himself; it insists on the self of a more nearly absolute estimate, the self that *must be*, and which this resolve of the non-resisting will will help to bring into being. It is a justice done for the first time to the plasticity and responsiveness of human nature toward our own wills: it is an absolute, or creative, justice. . . .

The creative attitude is not meant to displace but to subordinate the critical attitude, and its varieties, the competitive, the punitive, the warlike attitudes. . . .

Amenity without opposition becomes empty; even lovers weary of it. The force of the rule of love in common social interchange is directed, not to eliminating the critical judgement, but rather to making firm that prior understanding according to which we unite in the will to stand or fall by the rules of the proposed contest.

W. E. HOCKING

As Jesus Christ does not only teach humility, but also bestows it, let us begin by asking Him to give us a love for that virtue. . . . No prayer could be more pleasing to Jesus Christ; we can feel sure of that; He will infallibly grant our request if we sincerely wish it to be granted. But many who pray for humility would be extremely sorry if God were to grant it to them. This is one of the points on which people are most easily deluded. Some book, or meditation, or Communion touches their heart; they feel the attraction of this virtue, and ask God to give it to them; but they forget that to love, desire, and ask for humility is loving, desiring, and asking for humiliations, for these are the companions, or rather the food of humility, and without them it is no more than a beautiful but meaningless idea. Now, if the bare thought of humiliation fills us with horror; if we repel it with our whole strength; if pride and self-love get the better of us on every occasion; and if, instead of stiffening ourselves against them, we yield to them and cannot for a moment endure anything that wounds them, we are flattering ourselves if we think we love humility. The fact is that we dislike it, and our prayer is a delusion. We shall do well, then, to examine ourselves a little on this point before offering our petition to God; and instead of giving rein to our imagination, and making proposals that we are too weak to carry out, see whether we be resolved and prepared to bear the lightest and most ordinary humiliations. Otherwise such a prayer can have no result except self-deception; for our inmost feelings would nullify it if we were really abhorring what we seemed to be asking for.

But there are truly those, though not very many, who ask God in all sincerity to grant them humility and offer themselves to carry all the humiliating crosses that He is pleased to send them. This offer on their part is a real consecration. From that moment they should feel that they are not their own, but belong to Jesus Christ and are fighting under His standard.

JEAN NICOLAS GROU

THE human value is not the ultimate, but only the penultimate value; the last, the highest value is God the Father. He alone is the cause and the measure of all things, cause and measure of all valuations, cause and measure of all love. Because this Father loves men—no matter whether they are good or bad—and because we prove ourselves His children precisely by showing that same love, are we to love men. My relation to men has therefore its ultimate roots in a transcendental fact, namely in that fundamental relation of love in which God includes men, all men. Man is a mystery. He is the culmination-point of an eternal love which issues from God; a point in the actuality of the world where, as nowhere else, the love of God burns. That is the reason why man is worth loving: not by reason of what he is in himself or for himself, but by reason of what he is for God; or in the language of theology: not for a natural but for a supernatural reason. I shall never reach man by starting from the earth; I must first reach to heaven to find man through God. The floodstream of the love of man passes through the heart of God. I must first have God before I can have man. God is the way to man. . . .

The lover can reach his beloved only through God. God alone can carry him over that dead point which lies between the *ego* and the *alter* and cannot be transcended by mere logic. . . . Thus in every genuine, unselfish, serious love belief in God is contained, even really presupposed. No one has expressed this truth with greater profundity than the apostle of love, St. John: 'Everyone that loveth is born of God and knoweth God.'

KARL ADAM

BEGIN the day by offering it and yourself to God. Look at the day as an individual thing that begins and ends with completeness in itself; then take this thing, this day, and offer it to God to be a day for His use. . . . The day at once becomes a unity and life becomes unified. However many distracting details come into the day, both mind and emotion are dominated, not by them, but by the sense that you have only one thing to do—namely, to act in obedience to God with regard to them.

*   *   *

At the end of a common day's life, with all care, and no deliberate handling of unclean things, our hands are soiled. Life in this world is like that. Even our bodies, clothed and covered from contact with the outside world, are soiled. Living in the world we know inevitably brings defiling. So it is with soul and spirit. The day's living, in contact with much that is stained with evil, in the common world we know, brings its own soiling and weakening. At the close of the day, even where no deliberate sin appears, we ask for cleansing from the dust of the way, the soil of the day's life with all its contacts. And God gives it, with refreshing and renewal and rest in His gift. Truly we need this. It is no shame to a man to come home from his day's work with soiled hands. They have been soiled in the inevitable contact with soiling things, and are more honourable in their stain than hands that have kept their whiteness by withdrawal from the world's life. Yet they are soiled and unclean. It is shame to him if he leaves them so, and eats and sleeps without the washing he should give. Then he becomes truly a dirty person. This is true of the spiritual life also. It is no disgrace that the soiling of the day's life affects our souls; it is disgrace if we suffer it to remain uncleansed and accept the defilement. So we ask God for cleansing from 'the dust of the way'. How willingly Christ washed His disciples' feet!

GEORGE S. STEWART

WE all know the curiosity that comes over us when from a window we see the people in the street suddenly stop and look up—shade their eyes with their hands and look straight up into the sky toward something which is hidden from us by the roof. Our curiosity is superfluous, for what they see is doubtless an aeroplane. But as to the sudden stopping, looking up, and tense attention characteristic of the people of the Bible, our wonder will not be so lightly dismissed. To me personally it came first with Paul: this man evidently sees and hears something which is above everything, which is absolutely beyond the range of my observation and the measure of my thought. Let me place myself as I will to this coming something that in enigmatical words he insists he sees and hears, I am still taken by the fact that he, Paul, or whoever it was who wrote the Epistle to the Ephesians, for example, is eye and ear in a state which expressions such as inspiration, alarm, or stirring or overwhelming emotion, do not satisfactorily describe. I seem to see within so transparent a piece of literature a personality who is actually thrown out of his course by seeing and hearing what I for my part do not see and hear—who is, so to speak, captured, in order to be dragged as a prisoner from land to land for strange, intense, uncertain, and yet mysteriously well-planned service.

And if ever I come to fear lest mine is a case of self-hallucination, one glance at the secular events of those times, one glance at the widening circle of ripples in the pool of history, tells me of a certainty that a stone of unusual weight must have been dropped into deep water somewhere—tells me that, among all the hundreds of peripatetic preachers and miracle-workers from the Near East who in that day must have gone along the same Appian Way into imperial Rome, it was this one Paul, seeing and hearing what he did, who was the cause, if not of all, yet of the most important developments in that city's future.

KARL BARTH

GODHEAD here in hiding, whom I do adore
Masked by these bare shadows, shape and nothing more,
See, Lord, at thy service low lies here a heart
Lost, all lost in wonder at the God thou art.

Seeing, touching, tasting are in thee deceived;
How says trusty hearing? that shall be believed;
What God's Son has told me, take for true I do;
Truth himself speaks truly or there's nothing true.

On the cross thy godhead made no sign to men;
Here thy very manhood steals from human ken:
Both are my confession, both are my belief,
And I pray the prayer of the dying thief.

I am not like Thomas, wounds I cannot see,
But can plainly call thee God and Lord as he:
This faith each day deeper be my holding of,
Daily make me harder hope and dearer love.

O Thou our reminder of Christ crucified,
Living Bread the life of us for whom he died,
Lend this life to me then: feed and feast my mind,
There be thou the sweetness man was meant to find.

Bring the tender tale true of the Pelican;
Bathe me, Jesu Lord, in what thy bosom ran—
Blood that but one drop of has the world to win
All the world forgiveness of its world of sin.

Jesu, whom I look at shrouded here below,
I beseech thee send me what I thirst for so,
Some day to gaze on thee face to face in light,
And be blest for ever with thy glory's sight.

ST. THOMAS AQUINAS

15 October 1914.—Religion means being aware of God as a factor in one's environment: perfect religion is perceiving the true relative importance of God and the rest.

5 December 1914.—Almost all men are slaves: they are mastered by foolish ambitions, vile appetites, jealousies, prejudices, the conventions and opinions of other men. These things obsess them, so that they cannot see anything in its right perspective.

For most men the world is centred in self, which is misery: to have one's world centred in God is the peace that passeth understanding.

This is liberty: to know that God alone matters.

25 May 1915.—It is blessed to give: blessed is he of whom it is said that he so loved giving that he was glad to give his life.

Death is a great teacher: from him men learn what are the things they really value.

Men live for eating and drinking, position and wealth: they die for honour and for friendship.

True religion is betting one's life that there is a God.

1 June 1915.—I have seen with the eyes of God. I have seen the naked souls of men, stripped of circumstance. Rank and reputation, wealth and poverty, knowledge and ignorance, manners and uncouthness, these I saw not. I saw the naked souls of men. I saw who were slaves and who were free; who were beasts and who were men; who were contemptible and who honourable. I have seen with the eyes of God. I have seen the vanity of the temporal and the glory of the eternal. I have despised comfort and honoured pain. I have understood the victory of the Cross. O Death, where is thy sting? *Nunc dimittis, Domine. . . .*

DONALD HANKEY

WHILE contemporary historians took great pains in recounting the noisy deeds of the Caesars, they failed to notice that in a far corner of the world, among people who hardly seemed worth the attention of the educated, certain things were taking place that were of an entirely different nature and of far greater importance for the history of the world than anything they had written in their books. The modern historian who, following these ancient authors, understands the history of that age merely as the reign of the Caesars and the decline of ancient civilization, similarly fails to understand the significance of those events that were to shake the world to its foundations.

These happenings cannot indeed be grasped in the same categories of national historical interpretation as the deeds of the emperors. . . . As long as we see Christ only as an historical figure of the past, like Socrates or Caesar, we do not have the right approach. Even to the Apostles, Christ during his lifetime was not the same as He was afterwards, namely the Spirit that was present with them, that guided them 'into all truth'.

This experience is beyond the reach of historical method. It is an experience of the soul, of the spirit, accessible only to him who holds the belief that in all those events which seemed of little importance a new truth had come into the world, a truth through which he who has faith in it may become a new man. It is the nature of religion that through it man experiences the presence of God, who, being the absolute truth, determines his whole existence. To consider this experience as a merely human and subjective phenomenon and seek to explain it historically or psychologically means to deny its truth. But the belief in that truth which was revealed through Christ—whether man is passionately opposed to it, or whether he makes every effort to realize it as his own destiny—has been *the* driving force of history ever since.

ERICH FRANK

MOST of us die *of* something; of disease, accident, old age. But occasionally there appears in our midst a man who resolves to die *for* something, like Winkelried when he gathered the spears of the Austrians into his breast at the battle of Sempach. This dying *for* something, instead of waiting to die *of* something, as most of us do, this deliberate dying for something deemed worthy of it, is the strongest form of self-affirmation I know of. The power and vitality of it are tremendous, and the stamp that it leaves on the world is indelible. The Christian religion is an example of it.

*   *   *

The conquest of death is the final achievement of religion. No religion is worth its name unless it can prove itself more than a match for death; hence the need for valour at the heart of it. It is often said, by those who would domesticate religion to the service of man's temporal interests, that religion has to do exclusively with *life*. . . . It is true that religion has to do with 'life', but the 'life' in question is known to be death-ended. . . . And is not the life of society itself death-ended? They reckon ill who leave that out.

Christianity, now debased almost beyond recognition in secularized versions of it, came into the world as a death-conquering religion. It centred in the figure of a death conqueror, 'declared to be the Son of God with power by the resurrection from the dead'. Its power through the ages is derivative from that; like a tree severed from the roots its vitality declines the instant the connexion is broken. Christianity will never revive until it rises to its original height; perhaps in a transfigured form. The last enemy it has to destroy is death.

L. P. JACKS

THE God of Christians is not a God who is simply the author of mathematical truths, or of the order of the elements, as is the god of the pagans and of Epicureans. Nor is He merely a God who providentially disposes the life and fortunes of men, to crown His worshippers with length of happy years. Such was the portion of the Jews. But the God of Abraham, the God of Isaac, the God of Jacob, the God of Christians, is a God of love and consolation, a God who fills the souls and hearts of His own, a God who makes them feel their inward wretchedness and His infinite mercy, who unites Himself to their inmost spirit, filling it with humility and joy, with confidence and love, rendering them incapable of any end other than Himself.

All who seek God apart from Jesus Christ, and who rest in nature, either find no light to satisfy them, or form for themselves a means of knowing God and serving Him without a Mediator. Thus they fall either into atheism or into deism, two things which the Christian religion almost equally abhors.

The God of Christians is a God who makes the soul perceive that He is her only good, that her only rest is in Him, her only joy in loving Him; who makes her at the same time abhor the obstacles which withhold her from loving Him with all her strength. Her two hindrances, self-love and lust, are insupportable to her. This God makes her perceive that the root of self-love destroys her, and that He alone can heal.

The knowledge of God without that of our wretchedness creates pride. The knowledge of our wretchedness without that of God creates despair. The knowledge of Jesus Christ is the middle way, because in Him we find both God and our wretchedness.

                                                        BLAISE PASCAL

FIVE years ago I came to believe in Christ's teaching, and my life suddenly changed; I ceased to desire what I had previously desired, and began to desire what I formerly did not want. What had previously seemed to me good seemed evil, and what had seemed evil seemed good. It happened to me as it happens to a man who goes out on some business and on the way suddenly decides that the business is unnecessary and returns home. All that was on his right is now on his left, and all that was on his left is now on his right; his former wish to get as far as possible from home has changed into a wish to be as near as possible to it. The direction of my life and my desires became different, and good and evil changed places. . . .

I, like that thief on the cross, have believed Christ's teaching and been saved. And this is no far-fetched comparison, but the closest expression of the condition of spiritual despair and horror at the problem of life and death in which I lived formerly, and of the condition of peace and happiness in which I am now. I, like the thief, knew that I had lived and was living badly. . . . I, like the thief, knew that I was unhappy and suffering. . . . I, like the thief to the cross, was nailed by some force to that life of suffering and evil. And as, after the meaningless sufferings and evils of life, the thief awaited the terrible darkness of death, so did I await the same thing.

In all this I was exactly like the thief, but the difference was that the thief was already dying, while I was still living. The thief might believe that his salvation lay there beyond the grave, but I could not be satisfied with that, because besides a life beyond the grave life still awaited me here. But I did not understand that life. It seemed to me terrible. And suddenly I heard the words of Christ and understood them, and life and death ceased to seem to me evil, and instead of despair I experienced happiness and the joy of life undisturbed by death.

COUNT LEO TOLSTOY

THERE is no sickness so great but children endure it, and have natural strengths to bear them out quite through the calamity, what period soever nature hath allotted it. Indeed they make no reflections upon their sufferings, and complain of sickness with an uneasy sigh or a natural groan, but consider not what the sorrows of sickness mean; and so bear it by a direct sufferance. . . .

If we consider how much men can suffer if they list, and how much they do suffer for greater and little causes, and that no causes are greater than the proper causes of patience in sickness (that is, necessity and religion) we cannot, without huge shame to our nature, to our persons, and to our manners, complain of this tax and impost of nature. . . .

Sickness is the more tolerable, because it cures very many evils, and takes away the sense of all the cross fortunes, which amaze the spirits of some men, and transport them certainly beyond all the limits of patience. Here all losses and disgraces, domestic cares and public evils, the apprehensions of pity and a sociable calamity, the fears of want and the troubles of ambition, lie down and rest upon the sick man's pillow. . . .

And yet, after all this, sickness leaves in us appetites so strong, and apprehensions so sensible, and delights so many, and good things in so great a degree, that a healthless body and a sad disease do seldom make men weary of this world, but still they would fain find an excuse to live. . . .

All impatience, howsoever expressed, is perfectly useless to all purposes of ease, but hugely effective to the multiplying of trouble; and the impatience and vexation is another, but the sharper disease of the two. . . .

Remember that this sickness is but for a short time: if it be sharp, it will not last long; if it be long, it will be easy and very tolerable.

JEREMY TAYLOR

WE are in 1903 and I am nearly seventy-one years old. I always thought I should love to grow old, and I find it is even more delightful than I thought. It is so delicious to be *done* with things, and to feel no need any longer to concern myself much about earthly affairs. I seem on the verge of a most delightful journey to a place of unknown joys and pleasures, and things here seem of so little importance compared to things there, that they have lost most of their interest for me.

I cannot describe the sort of done-with-the-world feeling I have. It is not that I feel as if I was going to die at all, but simply that the world seems to me nothing but a passage way to the real life beyond; and passage ways are very unimportant places. It is of very little account what sort of things they contain, or how they are furnished. One just hurries through them to get to the place beyond.

My wants seem to be gradually narrowing down, my *personal* wants, I mean, and I often think I could be quite content in the Poor-house! I do not know whether this is piety or old age, or a little of each mixed together, but honestly the world and our life in it does seem of too little account to be worth making the least fuss over, when one has such a magnificent prospect close at hand ahead of one; and I am tremendously content to let one activity after another go, and to await quietly and happily the opening of the door at the end of the passage way, that will let me in to my real abiding place. So you may think of me as happy and contented, surrounded with unnumbered blessings, and delighted to be seventy-one years old.

MRS. PEARSALL SMITH

I

THE Lord is my Shepherd, I shall not want,
   I lie down in his meadows so green,
I follow his lead where the low winds chant
   By the softly stealing stream;
And I seek to obey whate'er he saith
   Because he is my Lord;
Though I grope through the Vale of the Shadow of Death
   He draws near me, my friend and adored.
For his rod and his staff are so comforting,
   Director, and comrade, and priest;
When my foemen are boasting and trumpeting
   He leads me awhile to his Feast.
O, surely his mercy and kindness
   Shall abide after seeing is dim!
He is everlasting divineness,
   I will house me in Him.

II

Come, little David, come now down,
   Quit for awhile the skies;
Run through the streets of London Town,
   Lend unto all your eyes.
Come with the waters the angels quaff
   From the rivers beyond the moon,
Come with your bright harp and shepherding staff
   Soon . . . Soon!

                                   HERBERT E. PALMER

WHOSOEVER would fully and feelingly understand the words of Christ must endeavour to conform his life wholly to the life of Christ.

What will it avail thee to dispute profoundly of the Trinity if thou be void of humility and art thereby displeasing to the Trinity?

Surely high words do not make a man holy and just; but a virtuous life maketh him dear to God.

I had rather feel compunction than understand the definition thereof.

*   *   *

How much the more thou knowest, and how much the better thou understandest, so much the more grievously shalt thou therefore be judged, unless thy life be also more holy.

Be not therefore extolled in thine own mind for any art or science, but rather let the knowledge given thee make thee more humble and cautious.

If thou thinkest that thou knowest much, know also that there be many things more which thou knowest not.

*   *   *

All perfection in this life hath some imperfection mixed with it; and no knowledge of ours is without some darkness.

An humble knowledge of thyself is a surer way to God than a deep search after learning.

Yet learning is not to be blamed, nor the mere knowledge of anything whatsoever to be disliked, it being good in itself, and ordained of God; but a good conscience and a virtuous life is always to be preferred before it. . . .

Truly at the day of judgement we shall not be examined on what we have read, but what we have done; not how well we have spoken, but how religiously we have lived.

THOMAS À KEMPIS

THERE is a story of a man who prayed earnestly one morning for grace to overcome his besetting sin of impatience. A little later he missed a train by half a minute and spent an hour stamping up and down the station platform in furious vexation. Five minutes before the next train came in he suddenly realized that here had been the answer to his prayer. He had been given an hour to practise the virtue of patience; he had missed the opportunity and wasted the hour. There are also many stories of men who have similarly missed trains which have been wrecked, and who ascribe their escape to Providence. If they are combining the thought of God as the celestial chess-player with the thought of God as preeminently concerned in their enjoyment of earthly life at the expense of others, there is not much to be said for their point of view. But if they are humbly acknowledging a call to further service on earth before they pass beyond, they are rightly interpreting their escape. In all probability all the events which led up to all these men missing their various trains could be adequately accounted for in terms of the interaction of natural law, human freedom, and divine grace. But at every point within the interaction God sees what are its possibilities for good, and the man who shares His enlightenment and His power and gives himself to make that good come true, has found the meaning of that moment and his 'special providence'. The gates of the future are indeed open, the universe is in the making. But only if made aright can the making stand. . . . The end is sure, for He who at every moment in the process sees its possibilities for good is God omnipotent—omnipotent to turn all circumstances to good account, to turn today's defeat into tomorrow's victory. But this omnipotence will never be so exercised as to substitute the external compulsion of men for the internal eliciting of their freedom.

LEONARD HODGSON

To Milan I came, to Ambrose the Bishop, known to the whole
world as among the best of men, Thy devout servant whose elo-
quent discourse did then plentifully dispense unto Thy people
the flour of Thy wheat, the gladness of Thine oil, and the sober
inebriation of Thy wine. To him was I unknowing led by Thee,
that by him I might knowingly be led to Thee. That man of God
received me as a father, and showed me on my coming an epis-
copal kindness. Thenceforth I began to love him; at first indeed
not as a teacher of the truth (which I utterly despaired of in Thy
Church), but as a person kind towards myself. And I listened diligently to him preaching to the people, not with that intent I ought
but, as it were, trying his eloquence, whether it answered the
fame thereof, or flowed fuller or lower than was reported; and I
hung on his words attentively; but of the matter I was as a careless
and scornful looker on; and I was delighted with the sweetness of
his discourse, more recondite, yet in manner less winning and
harmonious, than that of Faustus. Of the matter, however, there
was no comparison; for the one was wandering among Mani-
chaean delusions, the other teaching salvation most soundly. But
salvation is far from sinners, such as I then stood before him, and
yet I was drawing nearer by little and little, and unconsciously.

For though I took no pains to learn what he spake, but only to
hear how he spake (for that empty care alone was left to me,
despairing of a way, open to man, to Thee), yet together with the
words I cherished there came also into my mind the things I would
reject; for I could not separate them. And while I opened my heart
to admit how eloquently he spake, there also entered in how truly
he spake; but this only by degrees.

ST. AUGUSTINE

WHEN I look back upon my early days I am stirred by the thought of the number of people whom I have to thank for what they gave me or for what they were to me. At the same time I am haunted by an oppressive consciousness of the little gratitude I really showed them when I was young.... For all that, I think I can say with truth that I am not ungrateful. I did occasionally wake up out of that youthful thoughtlessness. ... But down to my twentieth year, and even later still, I did not exert myself sufficiently to express the gratitude which was really in my heart. I valued too low the pleasure felt at receiving real proofs of gratitude. Often, too, shyness prevented me from expressing the gratitude I felt.

As a result of this experience with myself I refuse to think that there is so much ingratitude in the world as is commonly maintained. I have never interpreted the parable of the Ten Lepers to mean that only one was grateful. All the ten, surely, were grateful, but nine of them hurried home first . . . One of them, however, had a disposition which made him act at once as his feelings bade him; he sought out the person who had helped him, and refreshed his soul with the assurance of his gratitude.

In the same way we ought all to make an effort to act on our first thoughts and let our unspoken gratitude find expression. Then there will be more sunshine in the world, and more power to work for what is good. But as concerns ourselves, we must all of us take care not to adopt as part of a theory of life all people's bitter sayings about the ingratitude of the world. A great deal of water is flowing underground which never comes up as a spring. In that thought we may find comfort. But we ourselves must try to be the water which does find its way up; we must become a spring at which men can quench their thirst for gratitude.

ALBERT SCHWEITZER

ALAS! we cannot here think of Christ but we are quickly ashamed of and troubled at our own thoughts: so confused are they, so unsteady, so imperfect. Commonly they issue in a groan or a sigh: 'Oh when shall we come unto Him? When shall we be ever with Him? When shall we see Him as He is?' And if at any time He begins to give more than ordinary evidences and intimations of His glory and love unto our souls, we are not able to bear them, so as to give them any abiding residence in our minds. But ordinarily this trouble and groaning is amongst our best attainments in this world, a trouble which, I pray God, I may never be delivered from until deliverance do come at once from this state of mortality. Yea, the good Lord increase this trouble more and more in all that believe.

The heart of a believer affected with the glory of Christ is like the needle touched with the lodestone. It can no longer be quiet, no longer be satisfied in a distance from Him. It is put into a continual motion towards Him. The motion indeed is weak and tremulous. Pantings, breathings, sighings, groanings, in prayer, in meditations, in the secret recesses of our minds, are the life of it. However, it is continually pressing towards Him. But it obtains not its point, it comes not to its centre and rest in this world.

But now above, all things are clear and serene, all plain and evident in our beholding the glory of Christ; we shall be ever with Him, and see Him as He is. This is heaven, this is blessedness, this is eternal rest. . . .

But alas! here at present our minds recoil, our meditations fail, our hearts are overcome, our thoughts confused, and our eyes turn aside from the lustre of this glory. But there, an immediate, constant view of it will bring in everlasting refreshment and joy unto our whole souls.

JOHN OWEN

WHAT is the fundamental nature of envy? It may be described as hunger without humility, the perversion of that true poverty of spirit which Christ exalts, the blind and barren attempt of emptiness to justify itself over against fullness. Sometimes a man will be envious of that in others which he himself lacks, but which may be his for the taking if he will only stoop to take it, acknowledging his poverty or pretence of wealth, and becoming a learner where he has loved to be a leader. In the realm of morals there is only one thing harder than climbing up: it is climbing down from a false peak. The most bitterly envious people are often those who have toiled up to some respectable height only to find that the true summit of the mountain lies on the other side of a ravine, and that to reach it they must descend and start again from a new angle of approach. But, concealing from themselves this humbling knowledge, they will sometimes hold to their station on the false peak, and try to justify themselves by defaming more successful climbers. Is not this the situation of many of us when men and movements put a formidable mark of interrogation over against our achievements, and challenge us to new beginnings? Sometimes a man will be envious of that in others which will never be his, and can never be his. One who, in the providence of God, is only averagely endowed in respect of physique or intellect, or whom misfortune has gravely handicapped, may never settle down to accept his limitations and serve God gladly within them, but may go about all his life in a state of resentful bitterness and envy. All the while it is open to him, the second-rater, to be first-rate in magnanimity, to honour and love those who eclipse him in every respect, and who will eclipse him to the end of the chapter.

A. C. CRAIG

How happy is he born and taught
That serveth not another's will;
Whose armour is his honest thought,
And simple truth his utmost skill!

Whose passions not his masters are;
Whose soul is still prepared for death,
Untied unto the world by care
Of public fame or private breath.

Who envies none that chance doth raise,
Nor vice; who never understood
How deepest wounds are given by praise;
Nor rules of state, but rules of good.

Who hath his life from rumours freed;
Whose conscience is his strong retreat;
Whose state can neither flatterers feed,
Nor ruin make oppressors great;

Who God doth late and early pray
More of His grace than gifts to lend;
And entertains the harmless day
With a religious book or friend;

This man is freed from servile bands
Of hope to rise or fear to fall:
Lord of himself, though not of lands,
And having nothing, yet has all.

SIR HENRY WOTTON

CLEMENS has his head full of imaginary piety. He is often proposing to himself what he would do if he had a great estate. He would outdo all charitable men that are gone before him, he would retire from the world, he would have no equipage, he would allow himself only necessaries, that widows and orphans, the sick and distressed, might find relief out of his estate. He tells you that all other way of spending an estate is folly and madness. Now, Clemens has at present a moderate estate, which he spends upon himself in the same vanities and indulgences as other people do. He might live upon one-third of his fortune and make the rest the support of the poor; but he does nothing of all this that is in his power, but pleases himself with what he would do if his power was greater. Come to thy senses, Clemens. Do not talk what thou wouldst do if thou wast an angel, but consider what thou canst do as thou art a man. Make the best use of thy present state, do now as thou thinkest thou wouldst do with a great estate, be sparing, deny thyself, abstain from all vanities, that the poor may be better maintained, and then thou art as charitable as thou canst be in any estate. Remember the poor widow's mite.

WILLIAM LAW

SHAMEFUL my sloth, that have deferred my night prayer till I am in bed. This lying along is an improper posture for piety. Indeed there is no contrivance of our body but some good man in Scripture hath hanselled it with prayer. The publican standing, Job sitting, Hezekiah lying on his bed, Elijah with his face between his legs. But of all gestures give me St. Paul's: For this cause I bow my knees to the Father of my Lord Jesus Christ. Knees, when they may, then they must be bended.

I have read a copy of a grant of liberty from Queen Mary to Henry Ratcliffe, Earl of Sussex, giving him leave to wear a night-cap or coif in Her Majesty's presence, counted a great favour, because of his infirmity. I know in case of necessity God would graciously accept my devotion, bound down in a sick dressing; but now whilst I am in perfect health it is inexcusable. Christ commanded some to take up their bed in token of their full recovery; my laziness may suspect lest thus my bed taking me up prove a presage of my ensuing sickness. But may God pardon my idleness this once, I will not again offend in the same kind, by His grace hereafter.

THOMAS FULLER

IT daily becomes more apparent that God's respect for the freedom of our affections, thoughts, and purposes is complete. It is part of that respect for our freedom that He never forces upon us His own gifts. He offers them, but unless we actively accept them, they remain ineffective as far as we are concerned. 'Behold, I stand at the door and knock'—that is always the relation of God our Redeemer to our souls. He has paid the whole price; He has suffered the atoning Death; yet still He waits till we open the door of our hearts to let in His love which will call our love out. He never breaks down that door. He stands and knocks. And this is true not only of His first demand for admission to the mansion of the soul; it is true also of every room within that mansion. There are many of us who have opened the front door to Him, but have only let Him into the corridors and staircases; all the rooms where we work or amuse ourselves are still closed against Him. There are still greater multitudes who have welcomed Him to some rooms, and hope that He will not ask what goes on behind the doors of others. But sooner or later He asks; and if we do not at once take Him to see, He leaves the room where we were so comfortable with Him, and stands knocking at the closed door. And then we can never again have the joy of His presence in the first room until we open the door at which He is now knocking. We can only have Him with us in the room that we choose for Him, if we really make Him free of all the house.

                                                  WILLIAM TEMPLE

'As he that taketh away a garment in cold weather, and as vinegar upon nitre, so is he that singeth songs to a heavy heart' (Proverbs xxv. 20). Worldly mirth is so far from curing spiritual grief, that even worldly grief, where it is great and takes deep root, is not allayed but increased by it. A man who is full of inward heaviness, the more he is encompassed about with mirth, it exasperates and enrages his grief the more; like ineffectual weak physic, which removes not the humour, but stirs it and makes it more unquiet. But spiritual joy is seasonable for all estates; in prosperity it is pertinent to crown and sanctify all other enjoyments with this which so far surpasses them; and in distress it is the only Nepenthe, the cordial of fainting spirits. This mirth makes way for itself, which other mirth cannot do. These songs are sweetest in the night of distress.

There is something exquisitely beautiful and touching in the first of these similes: and the second, though less pleasing to the imagination, has the charm of propriety and expresses the transition with equal force and liveliness. A grief of recent birth is a sick infant that must have its medicine administered in its milk, and sad thoughts are the sorrowful heart's natural food. This is a complaint that is not to be cured by opposites, which for the most part only reverse the symptoms while they exasperate the disease—or like a rock in the mid-channel of a river swoln by a sudden rain-flush from the mountains, which only detains the excess of waters from their proper outlet, and makes them foam, roar, and eddy. The soul in her desolation hugs the sorrow close to her, as her sole remaining garment: and this must be drawn off so gradually, and the garment to be put in its stead so gradually slipt on and feel so like the former, that the sufferer shall be sensible of the change only by the refreshment.

SAMUEL TAYLOR COLERIDGE

WHEN I was of the age to receive confirmation and full member-ship of the Church, I was told to choose a passage from the Bible as the expression of my personal approach to the Biblical message and to the Christian Church. Every confirmand was obliged to do so, and to recite the passage before the congregation. When I chose the words, 'Come unto me, all ye that labour and are heavy laden', I was asked with a kind of astonishment and even irony why I had chosen that particular passage. For I was living under happy conditions and, being only fifteen years old, was without any apparent labour and burden. I could not answer at that time; I felt a little embarrassed, but basically right. And I was right, indeed; every child is right in responding immediately to those words; every adult is right in responding to them in all periods of his life, and under all the conditions of his internal and external history. These words of Jesus are universal, and fit every human being and every human situation. They are simple; they grasp the heart of the primitive as well as that of the profound, disturbing the mind of the wise. Practically every word of Jesus had this character, sharing the difference between Him as the originator and the dependent interpreters, disciples and theologians, saints and preachers. Returning for the first time in my life to the passage of my early choice, I feel just as grasped by it as at that time, but infinitely more embarrassed by its majesty, profundity, and in-exhaustible meaning.

PAUL TILLICH

Lazarus

WHEN Lazarus left his charnel-cave,
  And home to Mary's house returned,
  Was this demanded—if he yearned
To hear her weeping by his grave?

'Where wert thou, brother, these four days?'
  There lives no record of reply,
  Which telling what it is to die
Had surely added praise to praise.

From every house the neighbours met,
  The streets were filled with joyful sound
  A solemn gladness even crowned
The purple brows of Olivet.

Behold a man raised up by Christ!
  The rest remaineth unrevealed;
  He told it not; or something sealed
The lips of that Evangelist.

*   *   *

Her eyes are homes of silent prayer,
  Nor other thought her mind admits
  But, he was dead, and there he sits,
And he that brought him back is there.

Then one deep love doth supersede
  All other, when her ardent gaze
  Roves from the living brother's face,
And rests upon the Life indeed.

All subtle thought, all curious fears,
  Borne down by gladness so complete,
  She bows, she bathes the Saviour's feet
With costly spikenard and with tears.

                              ALFRED TENNYSON

READER, heaven is above thee, and dost thou think to travel this steep ascent without labour and resolution? Canst thou get that earthly heart to heaven, and bring that backward mind to God, while thou liest still and takest thine ease? If lying down at the foot of a hill, and looking toward the top and wishing we were there, would serve the turn, then we should have daily travellers for heaven. But 'the kingdom of heaven suffereth violence, and violent men take it by force'. There must be violence used to get these first-fruits, as well as to get the full possession. Dost thou not feel it so, though I should not tell thee? Will thy heart get upwards, except thou drive it? Thou knowest that heaven is all thy hopes; that nothing below can yield thee rest; that a heart seldom thinking of heaven can fetch but little comfort thence; and yet dost thou not lose thy opportunities, and lie below, when thou shouldst walk above and live with God? Dost thou not commend the sweetness of a heavenly life, and judge those the best Christians who use it, and yet never try it thyself? As the sluggard that stretches himself on his bed and cries, O that this were working! so dost thou talk, and trifle, and live at thine ease and say, O that I could get my heart to heaven! How many read books and hear sermons, expecting to hear of some easier way, or to meet with a shorter course to comfort than they are ever likely to find in Scripture? Or they ask for directions for a heavenly life, and if the hearing them will serve, they will be heavenly Christians; but if we show them their work, and tell them they cannot have these delights on easier terms, then they leave us, as the young man left Christ, sorrowful.

RICHARD BAXTER

THEY waste their energies in unrewarding efforts; yet they accomplish nothing, for, setting their affections on created things, they try them all in turn before they dream of trying God from whom all things proceed. Suppose they did get everything they wanted, what would happen then? One treasure after another would fail to satisfy, and then the only object of desire left would be the Cause of all. It is our nature's law that makes a man set higher value on the things he has not got than upon those he has, so that he loathes his actual possessions for longing for the things that are not his. And this same law, when all things else in earth and heaven have failed, drives him at last to God, the Lord of all, whom hitherto alone he has not had.

It is, however, a practical impossibility to make such trial of all other things before we turn to God. Life is too short, our strength too limited, the number of competitors for this world's goods too great; so long a journey, such unfruitful toil, would wear us out. We want to satisfy all our desires, and find we cannot get possession of all desirable things. Much wiser would we be to make the choice not by experiment but by intelligence; for this we could do easily and not without result. . . . Indeed God gives us reason for this very purpose, that it may guide the senses in their choice and see to it that they be not satisfied except by that which reason has approved. . . . There will therefore be no ascent to God for you, the gift of reason will have been bestowed on you in vain if, like the beasts, you let yourself be guided by your senses, while reason just looks on. They run indeed whose steps are not controlled by reason, but not along the track. . . . How can they win, seeing they want the prize only when they have tried all else and failed? Theirs is an endless road, a hopeless maze, who seek for goods before they seek for God.

ST. BERNARD OF CLAIRVAUX

WE should hardly remain within the limits of Biblical promise if we expected that within this sinful world the nations of the earth could ever be a perfectly harmonious family of nations, entirely governed by the spirit of love. But we do believe that, even in the hard impersonal world of states, certain basic principles can and should be the standards of order and conduct. Among these principles must be included *the equal dignity of all men, respect for human life, acknowledgement of the solidarity for good and evil of all nations and races of the earth, respect for the plighted word, and the recognition that power of any kind, political or economic, must be co-extensive with responsibility*. It is true that the proclamation and the acknowledgement of these principles does not as such solve any one single concrete political problem. Nevertheless these principles, if Christians are resolved to make them the basis of their political action, may have much effect and meaning in the present chaotic situation where all such standards are being abandoned.

While it is our Christian faith which urges us to adhere to these principles, they are of such a character that many who do not profess the Christian faith, but are equally bewildered by the openly proclaimed moral anarchy, will respond with cordial assent.

We do not forget that the Church can never be satisfied with urging such directions upon all its members. It has a greater message for the world, the word of redemption and eternal life. But this message will not be taken seriously if the Church does not earnestly impress upon its members the standards of political conduct which are derived from Christianity.

                                                            EMIL BRUNNER

FORTUNE is like the market; where many times, if you can stay a little, the price will fall. And again, it is sometimes like Sibylla's offer; which at first offereth the commodity at full, then consumeth part and part, and still holdeth up the price. For occasion (as it is in the common verse) turneth a bald noddle, after she hath presented her locks in front, and no hold taken; or at least turneth the handle of the bottle to be received, and after the belly, which is hard to clasp. There is surely no greater wisdom than well to time the beginnings and onsets of things. Dangers are no more light, if they once seem light; and more dangers have deceived men than forced them. Nay, it were better to meet some dangers half-way, though they came nothing near, than to keep too long a watch upon their approaches; for if a man watch too long, it is odds he will fall asleep. On the other side, to be deceived with too long shadows (as some have been when the moon was low and shone on their enemies' back), and so to shoot off before the time; or to teach dangers to come on, by over early buckling towards them; is another extreme. The ripeness or unripeness of the occasion (as we said) must ever be well weighed; and generally it is good to commit the beginnings of all great actions to Argos with his hundred eyes, and the ends to Briareus with his hundred hands; first to watch, and then to speed. For the helmet of Pluto, which maketh the politic man go invisible, is secrecy in the counsel and celerity in the execution. For when things are once come to the execution, there is no secrecy comparable to celerity; like the motion of a bullet in the air, which flieth so swift as it outruns the eye.

FRANCIS BACON

YOUNG men are perpetually told that the first of duties is to render oneself independent. But the phrase, unless it mean that the first of duties is to avoid hanging, is unhappily chosen; saying what it ought not to say, and leaving unsaid what it ought to say.

It is true that, in a certain sense, the first of duties is to become free; because freedom is the antecedent condition for the fulfilment of every other duty, the only element in which a reasonable soul can exist. Until the umbilical cord is severed, the child can hardly be said to have a separate life. So long as the heart and mind continue in slavery, it is impossible for a man to offer up a voluntary and reasonable sacrifice of himself. Now in slavery, since the Fall, we are all born; from which slavery we have to emancipate ourselves by some act of our own, half-conscious it may be, or almost unconscious. By some act of our own, I say; not indeed unassisted; for every parent, every friend, every teacher is a minister ordained to help us in this act. But though we cannot by our own act lift ourselves out of the pit, we must by an act of our own take hold of the hand which offers to lift us out of it. . . .

Hence we perceive that the true motive for our striving to set ourselves free is to manifest our freedom by resigning it through an act to be renewed every moment, ever resuming and ever resigning it; to the end that our service may be entire, that the service of the hands may likewise be the service of the will; even as the Apostle, *being free from all, made himself servant to all.* This is the accomplishment of the great Christian paradox, *Whosoever will be great, let him be a minister; and whosoever will be chief, let him be a servant.*

J. C. and AUGUSTUS HARE

CHARITY does not demand of us that we should not see the faults of others; we must in that case shut our eyes. But it commands us to avoid attending unnecessarily to them, and that we be not blind to the good, while we are so clear-sighted to the evil that exists. We must remember too God's continual kindness to the most worthless creature, and think how many causes we have to think ill of ourselves; and finally we must consider that charity embraces the very lowest human being. It acknowledges that in the sight of God the contempt that we indulge for others has in its very nature a harshness and arrogance opposed to the spirit of Jesus Christ. The true Christian is not insensible to what is contemptible; but he bears with it.

Because others are weak, should we be less careful to give them their due? You who complain so much of what others make you suffer, do you think that you cause others no pain? You who are so annoyed at your neighbour's defects, are you perfect?

How astonished you would be if those whom you cavil at should make all the comments that they might upon you. But even if the whole world were to bear testimony in your favour, God, who knows all, who has seen all your faults, could confound you with a word; and does it never come into your mind to fear lest He should demand of you why you had not exercised towards your brother a little of that mercy which He, who is your Master, so abundantly bestows on you?

FÉNELON

STRANGE reminiscence! At the end of the terrace of La Treille, on the eastern side, as I looked down the slope, it seemed to me that I saw once more in imagination a little path which existed there when I was a child, and ran through the bushy underwood, which was thicker then than it is now. It is at least forty years since this impression disappeared from my mind. The revival of an image so dead and so forgotten set me thinking. Consciousness seems to be like a book in which the leaves turned by life successively cover and hide each other in spite of their semi-transparency; but although the book may be open at the page of the present, the wind, for a few seconds, may blow back the first pages into view.

And at death will these leaves cease to hide each other, and shall we see all our past at once? Is death the passage from the successive to the simultaneous—that is, from time to eternity? Shall we then understand, in its unity, the poem or mysterious episode of our existence, which till then we have spelled out phrase by phrase? And is this the secret of that glory which so often enwraps the brow and countenance of those who are newly dead? If so, death would be like the arrival of a traveller at the top of a great mountain, whence he sees spread out before him the whole configuration of the country, of which till then he had had but passing glimpses. To be able to overlook one's own history, to divine its meaning in the general concert and in the divine plan, would be the beginning of eternal felicity. Till then we had sacrificed ourselves to the universal order, but then we should understand and appreciate the beauty of that order. We had toiled and laboured under the conductor of the orchestra; and we should find ourselves become surprised and delighted hearers. We had seen nothing but our own little path in the mist; and suddenly a marvellous panorama and boundless distances would open before our dazzled eyes. Why not?

HENRI-FRÉDÉRIC AMIEL

THE mere swallowing of food is not enough unless it be assimilated and digested; yet it is a necessary condition of digestion. So with our beliefs; we swallow them wholesale by an act of extrinsic faith based on the word of others; and such faith is like the prop that supports a plant till it strikes root downwards and becomes self-supporting. They are not ours fully save in the measure that we have worked them into the fabric of our life and thought. Thus the collective mind; the corporate experience and reflection of the society into which we are born, does not live in us fully except so far as it has ceased to be an external rule of faith and has reproduced itself in our own mind and drawn it into living and active conformity with itself. So too with divine revelation whose mysteries are obscure, not because God wants to hide truth from us, but because we are not educated sufficiently, either mentally or morally, to apprehend them aright. Its purpose is to enlighten us, not to puzzle us; to improve our mind, not to stultify it. Our intelligence should, so to say, eat its way gradually into the meaning of what at first we hold to merely by obedient assent. Yet there is ever a Beyond of mystery; for the more we know, the more we wonder. It needs understanding to understand the extent of our ignorance. It is precisely as being beyond us that revelation provokes the growth of our mind. We strain upwards and find the outlook ever widening around us; and from each question answered a new brood of doubt is born.

Let us not then imagine that we have finished our duty by swallowing revelation wholesale in submission to external authority; we swallow that we may digest, and we digest that we may live the eternal life of the mind and heart by an intelligent sympathy with the mind and heart of God.

GEORGE TYRRELL

BUT one day, as I was passing in the field, and that too with some dashes on my conscience, fearing lest yet all was not right, suddenly this sentence fell upon my soul, *Thy righteousness is in heaven*; and methought withal, I saw, with the eyes of my soul, Jesus Christ at God's right hand. There, I say, was my righteousness; so that wherever I was, or whatever I was adoing, God could not say of me, *He wants my righteousness*, for that was just before Him. I also saw, moreover, that it was not my good frame of heart that made my righteousness better, nor yet my bad frame that made my righteousness worse; for my righteousness was Jesus Christ Himself, *the same yesterday, and today, and for ever*.

Now did my chains fall off my legs indeed; I was loosed from my affliction and irons; my temptations also fled away; now went I also home rejoicing, for the grace and love of God. So when I came home, I looked to see if I could find that sentence, *Thy righteousness is in heaven*, but could not find such a saying; wherefore my heart began to sink again; only that was brought to my remembrance, *He is made unto us of God wisdom, and righteousness, and sanctification and redemption*; by this word I saw the other sentence true.

For by this Scripture I saw that the Man Christ Jesus, as He is distinct from us, as touching His bodily presence, so He is our righteousness and sanctification before God. Here, therefore, I lived for some time, very sweetly at peace with God through Christ. Oh methought, Christ! Christ! there was nothing but Christ that was before my eyes: I was not now only for looking upon this and the other benefits of Christ apart, as of His blood, burial, or resurrection, but considered Him as a whole Christ; as He in whom all these, and all other His virtues, relations, offices, and operations met together, and that as He sat on the right hand of God in heaven.

JOHN BUNYAN

To those who know a little of Christian history probably the most moving of all the reflections it brings is not the thought of the great events and the well-remembered saints, but of those innumerable millions of entirely obscure faithful men and women, every one with his or her own individual hopes and fears and joys and sorrows and loves—and sins and temptations and prayers—once every whit as vivid and alive as mine are now. They have left no slightest trace in the world, not even a name, but have passed to God utterly forgotten by men. Yet each of them once believed and prayed as I believe and pray, and found it hard and grew slack and sinned and repented and fell again. Each of them worshipped at the eucharist, and found their thoughts wandering and tried again, and felt heavy and unresponsive and yet knew—just as really and pathetically as I do these things. There is a little ill-spelled ill-carved rustic epitaph of the fourth century from Asia Minor:—'Here sleeps the blessed Chione, who has found Jerusalem, for she prayed much.' Not another word is known of Chione, some peasant woman who lived in that vanished world of Christian Anatolia. But how lovely if all that should survive after sixteen centuries were that one had prayed much, so that the neighbours who saw all one's life were sure one must have found Jerusalem! What did the Sunday eucharist in her village church every week for a lifetime mean to the blessed Chione—and to the millions like her then, and every year since? The sheer stupendous *quantity* of the love of God which this ever repeated action has drawn from the obscure Christian multitudes through the centuries is in itself an overwhelming thought. (All that going with one to the altar every morning.)

GREGORY DIX

A SIBYL came to Tarquinius Superbus, king of Rome, and offered to sell unto him three tomes of her oracles: but he, counting the price too high, refused to buy them. Away she went and burnt one tome of them. Returning, she asketh him whether he would buy the two remaining at the same rate: he refused again, counting her little better than frantic. Thereupon she burns the second tome; and peremptorily asked him whether he would give the sum demanded for all the three for the one tome remaining: otherwise she would burn that also, and he would dearly repent it. Tarquin, admiring at her constant resolution, and conceiving some extraordinary worth contained therein, gave her her demand.

There are three volumes of man's time; youth, man's estate, and old age; and ministers advise them to redeem this time. But men conceive the rate they must give to be unreasonable, because it will cost them the renouncing of their carnal delights. Hereupon one-third of their life (youth) is consumed in the fire of wantonness. Again, ministers counsel men to redeem the remaining volumes of their life. They are but derided for their pains. And man's estate is also cast away in the smoke of vanity. But preachers ought to press peremptorily on old people to redeem, now or never, the last volume of their life. Here is the difference; the sibyl still demanded but the same rate for the remaining book; but aged folk (because of their custom in sinning) will find it harder and dearer to redeem this, the last volume, than if they had been chapmen for all three at first.

THOMAS FULLER

In the hour of death, after this life's whim,
When the heart beats low, and the eyes grow dim,
And pain has exhausted every limb—
    The lover of the Lord shall trust in Him.

When the will has forgotten the life-long aim,
And the mind can only disgrace its fame,
And a man is uncertain of his own name—
    The power of the Lord shall fill this frame.

When the last sigh is heaved, and the last tear shed,
And the coffin is waiting beside the bed,
And the widow and child forsake the dead—
    The angel of the Lord shall lift this head.

For even the purest delight may pall,
And power must fail, and the pride must fall,
And the love of the dearest friends grow small—
    But the glory of the Lord is all in all.

                                        R. D. BLACKMORE

ONE of the most solemn facts in all history—one of the most significant for anybody who cares to ponder over it—is the fact that Jesus Christ was not merely murdered by hooligans in a country road; He was condemned by everything that was most respectable in that day, everything that pretended to be most righteous—the religious leaders of the time, the authority of the Roman government, and even the democracy itself which shouted to save Barabbas rather than Christ. . . . In a profound sense we may say that the Crucifixion, however else we may interpret it, accuses human nature, accuses all of us in the very things that we think are our righteousness. If we followed the twentieth-century forms of moralizing, which have run so quickly to the national sort, we might imagine that the Jews of the time of Christ were particularly bad sinners, worse than the rest of human nature. Our attitude to the Crucifixion must be that of self-identification with the rest of human nature—we must say '*We* did it'; and the inability to adopt something of the same attitude in the case of twentieth-century events has caused our phenomenal failure to deal with the problem of evil in our time. So the Crucifixion challenges the prestige and power of the Pharisaical notion of upright living, challenges the old Roman respectabilities, and supersedes the pre-Christian notion of a righteous man. In the light of it the claim that '*our* conscience is clear' is the ugliest pretence of all. Indeed, if we call to mind that high-and-mighty kind of righteousness which congeals into moral rectitude and seems to close up the windows of the soul and sometimes makes good men so intolerable—in all the world's literature there is no place where it is attacked more persistently and more profoundly than in the Bible.

HERBERT BUTTERFIELD

I TAKE it for granted that every Christian that is in health is up early in the morning; for it is much more reasonable to suppose a person up early because he is a Christian than because he is a labourer or a tradesman or a servant or has business that wants him. We naturally conceive some abhorrence of a man that is in bed when he should be at his labour or in his shop. We cannot tell how to think any good thing of him who is such a slave to drowsiness as to neglect his business for it. Let this therefore teach us to conceive how odious we must appear in the sight of heaven if we are in bed, shut up in sleep and darkness, when we should be praising God, and are such slaves to drowsiness as to neglect our devotions for it. For if he is to be blamed as a slothful drone that rather chooses the lazy indulgence of sleep than to perform his proper share of worldly business, how much is he to be reproved that had rather lie folded up in a bed than be raising up his heart to God in acts of praise and adoration? Prayer is the noblest exercise of the soul, the most exalted use of our best faculties, and the highest imitation of the blessed inhabitants of heaven. . . . On the other hand, sleep is the poorest, dullest refreshment of the body, that is so far from being intended as an enjoyment that we are forced to receive it either in a state of insensibility or in the folly of dreams. Sleep is such a dull, stupid state of existence that even amongst mere animals we despise them most which are most drowsy. He therefore that chooses to enlarge the slothful indulgence of sleep rather than be early at his devotions to God, chooses the dullest refreshment of the body before the highest, noblest employment of the soul; he chooses a state which is a reproach to mere animals rather than that exercise which is the glory of angels.

WILLIAM LAW

WHAT an unfortunate task it would be for a charioteer who had harnessed a set of horses, however strong, if he could not make them draw together; if, while one of them would go forward, another was restiff, another struggled backward, another started aside. If even one of the four were unmanageably perverse, while the three were tractable, an aged beggar with his crutch might leave Phaeton behind. So in a human being, unless the chief forces act consentaneously, there can be no inflexible vigour, either of will or execution. *One* dissentient principle in the mind not only deducts so much from the strength and mass of its agency, but counteracts and embarrasses all the rest. If the judgement holds in low estimation that which the passions incline to pursue, the pursuit will be irregular and inconstant, though it may have occasional fits of animation, when those passions happen to be highly stimulated. If there is an opposition between judgement and habit, though the man will probably continue to act mainly under the sway of habit in spite of his opinions, yet sometimes the intrusion of these opinions will have for the moment an effect like that of Prospero's wand on the limbs of Ferdinand; and to be alternately impelled by habit and checked by opinion will be a state of vexatious debility. If two principal passions are opposed to each other, they will utterly distract the mind, whatever might be the force of its faculties if acting without embarrassment. The one passion may be somewhat stronger than the other, and therefore just prevail barely enough to give a feeble impulse to the conduct of a man; a feebleness which will continue till there be a greater disparity between these rivals. . . . The disparity must be no less than an absolute predominance of the one and subjection of the other, before the prevailing passion will have at liberty from the intestine conflict any large measure of its force to throw actively into the system of conduct.

JOHN FOSTER

THERE seems to me to be a very surprising feature in most of the books that I have read and the sermons that I have heard on this subject. Over and over again it is said that Our Lord promises forgiveness to those who repent; there is often some discussion of the question how far His Death was a necessary condition of forgiveness on the side of God; but there is almost complete agreement that the one condition required on our side is repentance. Of course there is in the Gospels an immense insistence on the need for repentance. Also there is the reference to repentance in Our Lord's teaching about our duty to forgive others. But when He is actually speaking about God's forgiveness of us it is not 'repentance' that He mentions; it is our own forgiveness of those who have injured us. Only one petition in the Lord's prayer has any condition attached to it: it is the petition for forgiveness; and the condition attached to it is this. No doubt if by repentance we mean all that the word means in the New Testament, it will include a forgiving spirit; for to repent is to change one's outlook and to regard men and the world as God regards them. But everyone can feel that the emphasis would be quite different if the words were, 'Forgive us our trespasses, for we do truly repent of them.' This would be like saying, 'I am so sorry; and I won't do it again; do forgive me.' In other words, the plea for forgiveness would rest on an apology and a promise made to God; and that is not the basis on which Our Lord bids us rest our plea. It is to rest on our attitude, not towards God, but towards His other children. He is always ready and eager to forgive; but how can He restore us to the freedom and intimacy of the family life if there are other members of the family towards whom we refuse to be friendly?

WILLIAM TEMPLE

My friends, do you remember that old Scythian custom, when the head of a house died? How he was dressed in his finest dress, and set in his chariot, and carried about to his friends' houses; and each of them placed him at his table's head, and all feasted in his presence? Suppose it were offered to you in plain words, as it *is* offered to you in dire facts, that you should gain this Scythian honour, gradually, while you yet thought yourself alive. Suppose the offer were this: You shall die slowly; your blood shall daily grow cold, your flesh petrify, your heart beat at last only as a rusted group of iron valves. Your life shall fade from you, and sink through the earth into the ice of Caina; but, day by day, your body shall be dressed more gaily, and set in higher chariots, and have more orders on its breast—crowns on its head, if you will. Men shall bow before it, stare and shout round it, crowd after it up and down the streets; build palaces for it, feast with it at their tables' heads all the night long; your soul shall stay enough within it to know what they do, and feel the weight of the golden dress on its shoulders, and the furrow of the crown-edge on the skull; —no more. Would you take the offer, verbally made by the death-angel? Would the meanest among us take it, think you? Yet practically and verily we grasp at it, every one of us, in a measure; many of us grasp at it in its fullness of horror. Every man accepts it who desires to advance in life without knowing what life is; who means only that he is to get more horses, and more footmen, and more fortune, and more public honour, and—*not* more personal soul. He only is advancing in life whose heart is getting softer, whose blood warmer, whose brain quicker, whose spirit is entering into living peace.

JOHN RUSKIN

WHEN for the thorns with which I long, too long,
With many a piercing wound,
My Saviour's head have crown'd,
I seek with garlands to redress that wrong:
Through every garden, every mead,
I gather flow'rs (my fruits are only flow'rs),
Dismantling all the fragrant towers
That once adorn'd my shepherdesse's head:
And now, when I have summ'd up all my store,
Thinking (so I my self deceive)
So rich a chaplet thence to weave
As never yet the King of Glory wore:
Alas! I find the Serpent old,
That, twining in his speckled breast,
About the flowers disguis'd, does fold
With wreaths of fame and interest.

    Ah! foolish man, that would'st debase with them,
And mortal glory, Heaven's diadem!
But Thou who only could'st the Serpent tame,
Either his slipp'ry knots at once untie,
And disentangle all his winding snare;
Or shatter too with him my curious frame
And let these wither—so that he may die—
Though set with skill, and chosen out with care:
That they, while Thou on both their spoils dost tread,
May crown Thy feet, that could not crown Thy head.

ANDREW MARVELL

I THINK it was about five this morning that I opened my Testament on those words, 'There are given unto us exceeding great and precious promises, even that ye should be partakers of the divine nature.' Just as I went out, I opened it again on those words, 'Thou art not far from the kingdom of God.' In the afternoon I was asked to go to St. Paul's. The anthem was, 'Out of the deep have I called unto thee, O Lord. O let thine ears consider well the voice of my complaint. If thou, Lord, wilt be extreme to mark what is done amiss, O Lord, who may abide it? For there is mercy with thee; therefore shalt thou be feared. O Israel, trust in the Lord: for with the Lord there is mercy, and with him is plenteous redemption. And he shall redeem Israel from all his sins.'

In the evening I went very unwillingly to a society in Aldersgate Street, where one was reading Luther's preface to the Epistle to the Romans. About a quarter before nine, while he was describing the change which God works in the heart through faith in Christ, I felt my heart strangely warmed. I felt I did trust in Christ, Christ alone, for my salvation; and an assurance was given me that He had taken away my sins, even mine, and saved me from the law of sin and death.

I began to pray with all my might for those who had in a more especial manner despitefully used me and persecuted me. I then testified openly to all there what I now first felt in my heart. But it was not long before the enemy suggested, 'This cannot be faith; for where is thy joy?' Then was I taught that peace and victory over sin are essential to faith in the Captain of our salvation; but that, as to the transports of joy that usually attend the beginning of it, especially in those who have mourned deeply, God sometimes giveth, sometimes withholdeth them, according to the counsels of His own will.

JOHN WESLEY

WE are full of inconsistencies, and so is all around us. But those inconsistencies are the mark of the passage from the lower consistency of unconscious animal life to the higher consistency of spiritual life, preserving and perfecting every element of the animal life, yet transforming it by the new creation. To go back now to the lower consistency means to choose chaos, darkness, death. Each noble inconsistency results from some one fragment of discipleship, some accepted task of sonship. Yet we ought never to be satisfied with inconsistency. We must struggle forward toward a rational and effectual unity. The conditions of that unity are, the Gospel tells us, to be found only in Christ the Son of God. We want a principle of conduct, a truth which will satisfy reason, a flow of inward life. We want all these, each for its own sake, and each for the sake of the others; yet for the sake of one we are constantly driven to sacrifice the rest. There is but one perfect unity, and that is in the heavens: yet it came down from the heavens that we might be raised into fellowship with it. Daily taking up the cross and following Jesus the Christ as Lord, daily turning and becoming as little children in the Sonship of the Heavenly Father, are the means by which it is attained. So with all our inconsistencies and weaknesses and sins we are kept in the one Way, the one Truth, and the one Life; and each step that we take brings us nearer to the one Father above.

F. J. A. HORT

YEARS ago a small party of us crossed the Alps into Italy by the Pass of Mount St. Gotthard. . . .

At a certain point of the ascent the mountain bloomed into an actual garden of forget-me-nots.

Unforgotten and never to be forgotten that lovely lavish efflorescence which made earth cerulean as the sky.

Thus I remember the mountain. But without that flower of memory could I have forgotten it?

Surely not: yet there, not elsewhere, a countless multitude of forget-me-nots made their home.

Such oftentimes seems the principle of allotment (if reverently I may term it so) among the human family. Many persons whose chief gifts taken one by one would suffice to memorialize them, engross not those only but along with them the winning graces which endear. Forget-me-nots enamel the height.

And what shall they do who display neither loftiness nor love-liness? If 'one member be honoured, all the members rejoice with it'.

Or, if this standard appears too exalted for frail flesh and blood to attain, then send thought onwards.

The crowning summit of Mount St. Gotthard abides invested, not with flowers, but with perpetual snow: not with life, but with lifelessness.

In foresight of the grave, whither we all are hastening, is it worth while to envy any? 'There is no work, nor device, nor know-ledge, nor wisdom, in the grave whither thou goest.' 'Grudge not one against another, brethren, lest ye be condemned: behold the Judge standeth before the door.'

CHRISTINA ROSSETTI

M. LEPEAUX on one occasion confided to Talleyrand his disappointment at the ill success with which he had met in his attempt to bring into vogue a new religion which he regarded as an improvement on Christianity. He explained that despite all the efforts of himself and his supporters his propaganda made no way. He asked Talleyrand's advice as to what he was to do. Talleyrand replied that it was indeed difficult to found a new religion, more difficult indeed than could be imagined, so difficult that he hardly knew what to advise. 'Still', he said—after a moment's reflection, 'there is one plan which you might at least try. I should recommend you to be crucified and to rise again on the third day.' . . .

Whether we are prepared or no to accept the occurrence of the Resurrection as a fact of history, we cannot deny the influence which a belief in it has exercised in the world. We cannot deny that it has brought life and immortality to light as no other belief could conceivably have done; that it has substituted for the fear of death, for a large portion of the human race, that sure and certain knowledge of God which is eternal life; that it has permeated our customs, our literature, and our language with a glory and a hope which could have been derived from no other source.

C. H. ROBINSON

WE tremble at the thought of eternity, and well we may; but if the fear was turned to good account, we should soon learn to rejoice in trembling. To those who yield unrestrainedly to their passions, the thought of eternity must needs be terrible. Yet they too might well pause and think whether they do well to sacrifice an eternal future to the moment of time now passing. Those too who cling tightly to the hopes and joys of this life may tremble to feel that what they cherish most is gliding from beneath their grasp, and eternity alone remains. But then arises the question, If all this is so soon to pass away, why should I cleave so closely to it? Why not seek that which endureth for ever rather than that which is but as foam upon the sea, as lightning in the midnight sky? Again, some timid souls shrink from the thought of the possible condemnation, and loss of that blessed eternity promised to the faithful. But let such remember that God loves them better than they love themselves; that He desires their salvation more earnestly than they desire it, that He has given them unfailing means of salvation, if they will but use such means. What more need they save faith and trust? Their overweening fearfulness comes of self—from measuring God by their own poor standard, rather than themselves by His boundless greatness. They have not looked chiefly at His Glory, His Will, His Love, but at themselves. Let them look higher, and fear will yield to love; peace will come to their souls, and Eternity will cease to dismay them.

It must do more;—it must become a source of abiding rest and joy. Hear St. Paul telling us that 'our light affliction, which is but for a moment, worketh for us a far more exceeding and eternal weight of glory!' Will not this thought carry you over many waves of this troublesome life, through many heartaches, and wearinesses, and sorrows?

JEAN NICOLAS GROU

ALL creatures are living in the hand of God; the senses only perceive the action of the creature, but faith sees the divine action in everything; faith believes that Jesus Christ is alive in everything and operates throughout the whole extent of the centuries; faith believes that the shortest moment and the tiniest atom contain a portion of His hidden life and His mysterious action. The action of creatures is a veil concealing the profound mysteries of the divine action. Jesus Christ after His resurrection took His disciples by surprise in His appearances, He presented Himself to them under symbols which disguised Him; and as soon as He manifested Himself, He disappeared. This very same Jesus, always living and active, still takes by surprise souls whose faith is not sufficiently pure and penetrating.

There is no moment at which God does not present Himself under the guise of some suffering, some consolation, or some duty. All that occurs within us, around us, and by our means covers and hides His divine action. His action is there, most really and certainly present, but in an invisible manner, the result of which is that we are always being taken by surprise and that we only recognize His action after it has passed away. Could we pierce the veil, and were we vigilant and attentive, God would reveal Himself continuously to us and we should rejoice in His action in everything that happened to us. At every occurrence we should say: *Dominus est*—it is the Lord; and in all circumstances we should find a gift from God; we should consider creatures as very feeble instruments in the hands of an almighty worker, and we should recognize without difficulty that nothing is lacking to us and that God's constant care leads Him to give us each instant what is suited to us. If we had faith, we should welcome all creatures; we should, as it were, caress them interiorly for contributing so favourably to our perfection when applied by the hand of God.

J. P. DE CAUSSADE

To keep God's door—
I am not fit.
I would not ask for more
Than this—
    To stand or sit
Upon the threshold of God's House
Out of the reach of sin,
To open wide His door
To those who come,
To welcome Home
His children and His poor:
To wait and watch
The gladness on the face of those
That are within:
Sometimes to catch
A glimpse or trace of those
I love the best, and know
That all I failed to be,
And all I failed to do,
Has not sufficed
To bar them from the Tree
Of Life, the Paradise of God,
The Face of Christ.

JOHN W. TAYLOR

JESUS did love a man who was able, sometimes, to be reckless. He did not care for the rulers as a class, but when one of them forgot his dignity, and ran after a peasant teacher and fell on the road at His feet, we read that 'Jesus, seeing him, loved him.' He did not choose for His disciples discreet and futile persons, but a man whose temper was not always under control, and whose tongue was rough when he was roused, and another who might have been a saint, but his life got twisted and he betrayed his Lord. He saw a widow flinging into the treasury all that she had, which no doubt was a very foolish action, but it stirred His heart with gladness to see somebody venturing herself simply upon God. He wanted life in men, energy, impulse; and in His Church He has often found nothing but a certain tame decorum, of which even He can make little.

* * *

He sought out in the world all people of affluent nature, not chilled by learning or manners, but with some voice of the heart in them, and where He found such He had hope. I wish His Church could learn the lesson from Him, and could make access easier for the multitude of enjoying natures in whose companionship He found such pleasure. For about them He held the conviction that, even though they may have fallen to be last, it is in them by His grace to be first, true saints, the splendour and light of His kingdom.

W. M. MACGREGOR

THERE is a place in front of the Royal Exchange where the wide pavement reaches out like a promontory. It is in the shape of a triangle with a rounded apex. A stream of traffic runs on either side, and other streets send their currents down into the open space before it. Like the spokes of a wheel converging streams of human life flow into this agitated pool. Horses and carriages, carts, vans, omnibuses, cabs, every kind of conveyance cross each other's course in every possible direction. Twisting in and out by the wheels and under the horses' heads, working a devious way, men and women of all conditions wind a path over. . . . Now the tide rises and now it sinks, but the flow of these rivers always continues. Here it seethes and whirls, not for an hour only, but for all present time, hour by hour, day by day, year by year.

Here it rushes and pushes, the atoms triturate and grind and, eagerly thrusting by, pursue their separate ends. . . . Yet the agitated pool is stonily indifferent, the thought is absent or preoccupied, for it is evident that the mass are unconscious of the scene in which they act.

But it is more sternly real than the very stones, for all these men and women that pass are driven on by the push of accumulated circumstances; they cannot stay, they must go, their necks are in the slave's ring, they are beaten like seaweed against the solid walls of fact. In ancient time Xerxes, the king of kings, looking down upon his myriads, wept to think that in a hundred years not one of them would be left. Where will be these millions of today in a hundred years? But, further than that, let us ask, where then will be the sum and outcome of their labour? If they wither away like summer grass, will not at least a result be left which those of a hundred years hence may be the better for? No, not one jot! There will not be any sum or outcome or result of this ceaseless labour and movement; it vanishes in the moment that it is done, and in a hundred years nothing will be there, for nothing is there now.

RICHARD JEFFERIES

To a man of middle life existence is no longer a dream but a reality. He has not much more new to look forward to, for the character of his life is generally fixed by that time. His profession, his home, his occupations, will be for the most part what they are now. He will make few new acquaintances—no new friends. It is the solemn thought connected with middle age that life's last business is begun in earnest; and it is then, midway between the cradle and the grave, that a man begins to look and marvel with a kind of remorseful feeling that he let the days of youth go by so half enjoyed. It is the pensive autumn feeling that we experience when the longest day of the year is past, and every day that follows is shorter, and the lights fainter, and the feebler shadows tell that nature is hastening with gigantic footsteps to her winter grave. So does man look back upon his youth. When the first grey hairs become visible—when the unwelcome truth fastens itself upon the mind that a man is no longer going up the hill, but down, and that the sun is already westering, he looks back on things behind. Now this is a natural feeling, but is it the high Christian tone of feeling? ... We may assuredly answer, No. We who have an inheritance incorruptible and undefiled, and that fadeth not away, what have we to do with things past? When we were children we thought as children. But now there lies before us manhood, with its earnest work: and then old age, and then the grave, and then home.

And so manhood in the Christian life is a better thing than boyhood, because it is a riper thing; and old age ought to be a brighter, and a calmer, and a more serene thing than manhood.

F. W. ROBERTSON

FOR disappointments that come not by our own folly, they are the trials or corrections of heaven: and it is our own fault if they prove not to our advantage.

To repine at them does not mend the matter: it is only to grumble at our Creator. But to see the hand of God in them, with a humble submission to His will, is the way to turn our water into wine and engage the greatest love and mercy on our side.

We must needs disorder ourselves if we look only at our losses. But if we consider how little we deserve what is left, our passion will cool, and our murmurs will turn into thankfulness.

If our hairs fall not to the ground, less do we or our substance without God's providence.

Nor can we fall below the arms of God, how low soever it be we fall.

For though our Saviour's passion is over, His compassion is not. That never fails His humble, sincere disciples. In Him they find more than all that they lose in the world.

Is it reasonable to take it ill that anybody desires of us that which is their own? All we have is the Almighty's: and shall not God have His own when He calls for it?

Discontentedness is not only in such a case ingratitude, but injustice. For we are both unthankful for the time we had it, and not honest enough to restore it, if we could keep it.

But it is hard for us to look on things in such a glass, and at such a distance from this low world; and yet it is our duty, and would be our wisdom and our glory to do so.

WILLIAM PENN

CHRISTIANA. What was the matter that you did laugh in your sleep tonight? I suppose you was in a dream? . . .

MERCY. I was a-dreamed that I sat all alone in a solitary place and was bemoaning the hardness of my heart. Now I had not sat there long, but methought many were gathered about me, to see me and to hear what it was that I said. So they hearkened, and I went on bemoaning the hardness of my heart. At this some of them laughed at me, some called me fool, and some began to thrust me about. With that methought I looked up and saw one coming with wings towards me. So he came directly to me and said, Mercy, what aileth thee? Now when he had heard me make my complaint, he said, Peace be to thee: he also wiped mine eyes with his handkerchief and clad me in silver and gold; he put a chain about my neck and ear-rings in mine ears, and a beautiful crown upon my head. Then he took me by the hand and said, Mercy, come after me. So he went up, and I followed, till we came at a golden gate. Then he knocked, and when they within had opened, the man went in and I followed him up to a throne, upon which one sat, and he said to me, Welcome, daughter. . . . So I awoke from my dream. But did I laugh?

CHRISTIANA. Laugh! Ay, and well you might to see yourself so well. For you must give me leave to tell you that I believe it was a good dream, and that as you have begun to find the first part true, so you shall find the second at last. 'God speaketh once, yea twice, yet man perceiveth it not. In a dream, in a vision of the night, when deep sleep falleth upon men, in slumberings upon the bed.' We need not, when a-bed, lie awake to talk with God. He can visit us while we sleep, and cause us then to hear His voice. Our heart oft times wakes when we sleep, and God can speak to that, either by words, by proverbs, by signs and similitudes, as well as if one was awake.

MERCY. Well, I am glad of my dream, for I hope ere long to see it fulfilled, to the making of me laugh again.

JOHN BUNYAN

HE to whom human life is to appear as vain, must possess in his consciousness the idea of a true life, and this idea itself will give to human life a real worth and value.

*   *   *

He who sincerely takes life in earnest finds it quite natural and a matter of course so to do, and does not, therefore, make any great noise about it.

*   *   *

The contemplation of our earthly life as a 'vale of tears' is a natural consequence of that life being considered exclusively as that of the individual, not as also that of the race. How can *love* obtain its rights if we look upon the matter thus?

*   *   *

Human life includes so much real gold, so many precious jewels, that he who knows these will not be tempted to set it off with gewgaws.

*   *   *

The most pressing necessity for a Christian man, I mean for one who really believes in Christ, even simply in the salvation of his soul, is that he shall have some good work to do.

*   *   *

God does not require that each individual shall have capacity for everything.

*   *   *

One lesson which it costs us all much trouble to learn, but which we all must learn, if we are to prosper and do good to others, is to desire to be nothing more and nothing different, in regard to an individual personality, from that which God has really given us capacity to become.

RICHARD ROTHE

WHAT is this heart of Nature, if it exist at all? Is it, according to the conventional doctrine derived from Wordsworth and Shelley, a heart of love, according with the heart of man, and stealing out to him through a thousand avenues of mute sympathy? No; in this sense. . . . Nature has no heart.

I sit now, alone and melancholy, with that melancholy which comes to all of us when the waters of sad knowledge have left their ineffaceable delta in the soul. As I write, a calm, faint-tinted evening sky sinks like a nestward bird to its sleep. At a little distance is a dark wall of fir-wood; while close at hand a small group of larches rise like funeral plumes against that tranquil sky, and seem to say, 'Night cometh'. They alone are in harmony with me. All else speaks to me of a beautiful, peaceful world in which I have no part. And did I go up to yonder hill, and behold at my feet the spacious amphitheatre of hill-girt wood and mead, overhead the mighty aerial *velarium*, I should feel that my human sadness was a higher and deeper and wider thing than all. O Titan Nature! a petty race, which has dwarfed its spirit in dwellings, and bounded it in selfish shallows of art, may find you too vast, may shrink from you into its earths; but though you be a very large thing, and my heart a very little thing, yet Titan as you are, my heart is too great for you. . . . Absolute Nature lives not in our life, nor yet is lifeless, but lives in the life of God; and in so far, and so far merely, as man himself lives in that life, does he come into sympathy with Nature, and Nature with him. She is God's daughter, who stretches her hand only to her Father's friends. Not Shelley, not Wordsworth himself, ever drew so close to the heart of Nature as did the Seraph of Assisi, who was close to the Heart of God.

FRANCIS THOMPSON

THE assent which is ordinarily given to divine truths is very faint and languid, very weak and uneffectual, flowing only from a blind inclination to follow that religion which is in the fashion, or a lazy indifference and unconcernedness whether they be so or not. Men are unwilling to quarrel with the religion of their country, and since all their neighbours are Christians, they are content to be so too. But they are seldom at the pains to consider the evidences of those truths, or to ponder the importance and tendency of them; and thence it is that they have so little influence on their affections and practice. Those spiritless and paralitick thoughts (as one doth rightly term them) are not able to move the will and direct the mind. We must therefore endeavour to work up our minds to a serious belief and full persuasion of divine truths, unto a sense and feeling of spiritual things. Our thoughts must dwell upon them till we be both convinced of them and deeply affected with them. Let us urge forward our spirits, and make them approach the invisible world, and fix our mind upon immaterial things, till we clearly perceive that these are no dreams, nay, that all things are dreams and shadows besides them. When we look about us and behold the beauty and magnificence of this goodly frame, the order and harmony of the whole creation, let our thoughts from thence take their flight toward that omnipotent Wisdom and Goodness which did at first produce, and doth still establish and uphold the same. When we reflect upon ourselves, let us consider that we are not a mere piece of organized matter, a curious and well-contrived engine, that there is more in us than flesh and blood and bones, even a divine sparkle, capable to know and love and enjoy our Maker.

HENRY SCOUGAL

I MET a traveller from an antique land
Who said: Two vast and trunkless legs of stone
Stand in the desert. . . . Near them, on the sand,
Half sunk, a shatter'd visage lies, whose frown
And wrinkled lip, and sneer of cold command,
Tell that its sculptor well those passions read
Which yet survive, stamp'd on these lifeless things,
The hand that mock'd them, and the heart that fed:
And on the pedestal these words appear:
'My name is Ozymandias, king of kings:
Look on my works, ye Mighty, and despair!'
Nothing beside remains. Round the decay
Of that colossal wreck, boundless and bare
The lone and level sands stretch far away.

*　　　　*　　　　*

The One remains, the many change and pass:
Heaven's light for ever shines, Earth's shadows fly;
Life, like a dome of many-coloured glass,
Stains the white radiance of Eternity,
Until Death tramples it to fragments. . . .

PERCY BYSSHE SHELLEY

GOD certainly is well within His rights in claiming to Himself the works of His own hands, the gifts Himself has given! How should the thing made fail to love the Maker, provided that it have from Him the power to love at all? How should it not love Him with all its powers, since only by His gift has it got anything? Man, called into being out of nothing by God's free act and raised to such high honour, how patent is his debt of love to God's most just demand! How vastly God has multiplied His mercy too, in saving man and beast in such a way! Why, we had turned our glory into the likeness of a calf that eateth hay; our sin had brought us to the level of the beasts that know not God at all! If then I owe myself entire to my Creator, what shall I give my Re-creator more? The means of our remaking too, think what they cost! It was far easier to make than to redeem; for God had but to speak the word and all things were created, I included; but He who made me by a word, and made me once for all, spent on the task of my re-making many words and many marvellous deeds, and suffered grievous and humiliating wrongs.

What reward therefore shall I give the Lord for all the benefits that He has done to me? By His first work He gave me to myself; and by the next He gave Himself to me. And when He gave Himself, He gave me back myself that I had lost. Myself for myself, given and restored, I doubly owe to Him. But what shall I return for Himself? A thousand of myself would be as nothing in respect of Him.

ST. BERNARD OF CLAIRVAUX

THE Church has a demand upon your allegiance because it is an essential part of Christ's gospel. Christ wills through His members, that is through the Christians, to create a new community in the world . . . a community which in its corporate life and action expresses and bears witness to those eternal values and ends which constitute God's purpose for the world. . . . This is what the Church is for, and this is in fact what the Church has been doing all through history, though with lamentable apostasies and capitulations.

But in spite of those, and in spite of that mortal tendency to corruption and decay which besets all institutions in the world, the Church has shown a power of vitality and a renewal of its first love which, in spite of everything that may appear to the contrary, is as marked today as ever. It is the Church of the saints and martyrs and prophets, who have been the light of the world in their several generations, that has the demand upon your allegiance—not the Church which has been corrupted by wealth and worldly power. But the true Church is embedded in the existing Churches —you will not find it elsewhere, though I agree that it is tempting to look for it elsewhere.

Across the Churches today there is happening a real renewal of faith and insight and courage, which I believe holds more promise for the future than anything else in the world.

It may be that a lot of superstition, it may be that a lot of conservative prejudice, clings to the historic Churches; but superstition and prejudice are the grime upon the pavement of what is still a *sacred* building; and he who would wash that pavement clean should be willing to get down on his knees to his work inside the Church.

                                                      A. R. VIDLER

IT is a thing far too precarious, vexatious, and unsafe, if I must be obliged to place my salvation, or my being kept and preserved therein, upon any outward circumstance whatsoever. If I am to place my salvation, and my being kept therein, upon the good and sound understanding God almighty has endowed me with; then, as long as God lets me have the use of my understanding, I shall entertain no other conceptions; but how if I should lose my understanding? As long as I can make use of my five senses I shall never have any other sentiments in regard to these matters; but how shall I do when the use of them is taken from me? As long as I have the Bible, God's word, in my hands I would thereby always have its consolation in my eye; but how when I have the Bible no more? Yet the great, important, and profound words thereof will be always remaining in my memory; but how if I lose my memory? As long as I have a friend left, he will be reminding me of it, and doubtless I shall always have one person at least who will be concerned for me; but how if there should be nobody? Why then I will meditate and recollect my thoughts again; but how when the capacity of thinking and reflecting is gone? Now, all these are not only suppositions possible in themselves, but such as do actually happen. To suppose the defect of any of these things has the most lamentable effect, it renders the whole business of religion an unsafe, uncertain, and precarious thing. . . . Are these cases absolutely necessary? Are these unavoidable mischiefs? In effect they are, but they have no foundation in the nature of the thing. For were but souls acquainted with this point, viz. to cleave to their only, inward, true, chosen, and necessary friend, who is to them on their side indispensably necessary, and who again for His person neither can nor will subsist without them, who is so captivated with them that He cannot leave the souls, that He cannot do without souls, whom He bought at the price of His own blood and life, and who must forget and deny Himself if He would deny and lose the pains He has been at on their account; did they, I say, cleave to Him, they would be in safety.

ZINZENDORF

SELF-GOVERNMENT with tenderness—here you have the condition of all authority over children. The child must discover in us no passion, no weakness of which he can make use; he must feel himself powerless to deceive or to trouble us; then he will recognize in us his natural superiors, and he will attach a special value to our kindness, because he will respect it. The child who can arouse in us anger or impatience or excitement, feels himself stronger than we, and a child respects only strength. The mother should consider herself as her child's sun, a changeless and ever radiant world whither the small restless creature, quick at tears and laughter, light, fickle, passionate, full of storms, may come for fresh stores of light, warmth, and electricity, of calm and of courage. The mother represents goodness, providence, law; that is, the divinity, under that form of it which is accessible to childhood. If she is passionate, she will inculcate on her child a capricious and despotic God. The religion of a child depends on what its mother and father are, and not on what they say. The inner and unconscious ideal which guides their life is precisely what touches the child; their words, their remonstrances, their bursts of feeling even, are for him merely thunder and comedy; what they worship—this it is which his instinct divines and reflects.

The child sees what we are, behind what we wish to be. Hence his reputation as a physiognomist. He extends his power as far as he can with each of us; he is the most subtle of diplomatists. Unconsciously he passes under the influence of each person about him, and reflects it while transforming it after his own nature. He is a magnifying mirror. This is why the first principle of education is: train yourself; and the first rule to follow if you wish to possess yourself of a child's will is: master your own.

HENRI-FRÉDÉRIC AMIEL

I T is not possible to make a simple separation between the creative and destructive elements in anxiety; and for that reason it is not possible to purge moral achievement of sin as easily as moralists imagine. The same action may reveal a creative effort to transcend natural limitations, and a sinful effort to give an unconditioned value to contingent and limited factors in human existence. Man may, in the same moment, be anxious because he has not become what he ought to be; and also anxious lest he cease to be at all....

The statesman is anxious about the order and security of the nation. But he cannot express this anxiety without an admixture of anxiety about his prestige as a ruler, and without assuming unduly that only the kind of order and security which he establishes is adequate for the nation's health. The philosopher is anxious to arrive at the truth; but he is also anxious to prove that his particular truth is the truth. He is never as completely in possession of the truth as he imagines. That may be the error of being ignorant of one's ignorance. But it is never simply that. The pretensions of final truth are always partly an effort to obscure a darkly felt consciousness of the limits of human knowledge. Man is afraid to face the problem of his limited knowledge lest he fall into the abyss of meaninglessness. Thus fanaticism is always a partly conscious, partly unconscious, attempt to hide the fact of ignorance and to obscure the problem of scepticism.

REINHOLD NIEBUHR

Partly to Will, Partly to Nill

So many things then I did, when to will was not in itself to be able; and I did not what both I longed incomparably more to do and which soon after, when I should will, I should be able to do; because soon after, when I should will, I should will thoroughly. For in these things the ability was one with the will, and to will was to do; and yet it was not done: and more easily did my body obey the weakest willing of my soul, in moving its limbs at its nod, than the soul obeyed itself to accomplish her transcendent purposes by a simple act of will.

Whence is this anomaly, and to what end?. . . The mind commands the body, and it obeys instantly; the mind commands itself, and is resisted. The mind commands the hand to be moved, and such readiness is there that command is scarce distinct from obedience. Yet the mind is mind, the body is body. The mind commands the mind, its own self, to will, and yet it doth not. Whence this anomaly, and to what end? It commands itself, I say, to will, and would not command unless it willed, and what it commands is not done. But it willeth not entirely, therefore it doth not command entirely. For so far forth it commandeth, as it willeth, and so far forth is the thing commanded not done, as it willeth not. For the will commandeth that there be a will; not another but itself. But it doth not command entirely, therefore what it commandeth is not. For were the will entire, it would not even command it to be, because it would already be. It is therefore no anomaly partly to will, partly to nill; but a disease of the mind that it doth not wholly rise by truth up-borne, but is by custom down-borne. And therefore are there two wills, for the one of them is not entire: and what the one lacketh, the other hath.

ST. AUGUSTINE

ONE other thing stirs me when I look back at my youthful days, viz. the fact that so many people gave me something or were something to me without knowing it. Such people, with whom I never perhaps exchanged a word, yes, and others about whom I merely heard things by report, had a decisive influence on me; they entered into my life and became powers within me. Much that I should otherwise not have felt so clearly or done so effectively was felt or done as it was, because I stand, as it were, under the sway of these people. Hence I always think that we all live, spiritually, by what others have given us in the significant hours of our life. These significant hours do not announce themselves as coming, but arrive unexpected. Nor do they make a great show of themselves; they pass almost unperceived. Often, indeed, their significance comes home to us first as we look back, just as the beauty of a piece of music or of a landscape often strikes us first in our recollection of it. Much that has become our own in gentleness, modesty, kindness, willingness to forgive, in veracity, loyalty, resignation under suffering, we owe to people in whom we have seen or experienced these virtues at work, sometimes in a great matter, sometimes in a small. A thought which had become act sprang into us like a spark, and lighted a new flame within us. . . .

If we had before us those who have thus been a blessing to us, and could tell them how it came about, they would be amazed to learn what passed over from their life into ours.

ALBERT SCHWEITZER

ROWING on the Thames, the waterman confirmed me in what formerly I had learnt from the maps; how that river, westward, runs so crooked as likely to lose itself in a labyrinth of its own making. From Reading to London by land, thirty; by water a hundred miles. So wantonly that stream disporteth itself, as if as yet unresolved whether to advance to the sea or retreat to its fountain.

But the same being past London (as if sensible of its former laziness, and fearing to be checked of the ocean, the mother of rivers, for so long loitering; or else, as if weary with wandering, and loth to lose more way; or lastly, as if conceiving such wildness inconsistent with the gravity of his channel, now grown old, and ready to be buried in the sea), runs in so direct a line that from London to Gravesend the number of the miles are equally twenty both by land and by water.

Alas! how much of my life is lavished away! Oh the intricacies, windings, wanderings, turnings, tergiversations, of my deceitful youth! I have lived in the midst of a crooked generation, and with them have turned aside unto crooked ways. High time it is now for me to make straight paths for my feet, and to redeem what is past by amending what is present and to come. Flux, flux (in the German tongue, quick, quick) was a motto of Bishop Jewel's, presaging the approach of his death. May I make good use thereof; make haste, make haste, God knows how little time is left me, and may I be a good husband to improve the short remnant thereof.

THOMAS FULLER

IT is advised by the guides of souls, wise men and pious, that all persons should communicate very often, even as often as they can do it without excuse and delays. Everything that puts us from so holy an employment, when we are moved to it, being either a sin or an imperfection, an infirmity or indevotion, and an inactiveness of spirit. All Christian people must come. They, indeed, that are in the state of sin must not come so, but yet they must come. First they must quit their state of death, and then partake of the bread of life. They that are at enmity with their neighbours must come; that is no excuse for their not coming; only they must not bring their enmity along with them, but leave it, and then come. They that have variety of secular employment must come; only they must leave their secular thoughts and affections behind them, and then come and converse with God. If any man be well grown in grace, he must needs come, because he is so excellently disposed to so holy a feast: but he that is but in the infancy of piety had need to come, that so he may grow in grace. The strong must come, lest they become weak; and the weak that they may become strong. The sick must come to be cured, and the healthful to be preserved. They that have leisure must come, because they have no excuse; they that have no leisure must come hither, that by so excellent religion they may sanctify their business. The penitent sinners must come, that they may be justified; and they that are justified, that they may be justified still. They that have fears and great reverence to these mysteries, and think no preparation to be sufficient, must receive, that they may learn how to receive the more worthily; and they that have a less degree of reverence must come often to have it heightened: that as those creatures that live amongst the snows of the mountains turn white with their food and conversation with such perpetual whitenesses, so our souls may be transformed into the similitude and union with Christ by our perpetual feeding on Him, and conversation not only in His courts, but in His very Heart, and most secret affections, and incomparable purities.

                                                   JEREMY TAYLOR

THE proper and natural effect, and in the absence of all disturbing and intercepting forces, the certain and inevitable accompaniment of peace (or reconcilement) with God is our own inward peace, a calm and quiet temper of mind. . . . Still we must be cautious not to transfer to the Object the defects of the organ, which must needs partake of the imperfections of the imperfect beings to whom it belongs. Not without the co-assurance of other senses and of the same sense in other men, dare we affirm that what our eye beholds is verily there to be beholden. Much less may we conclude negatively, and from the inadequacy or the suspension, or from any other affection, of sight infer the non-existence or departure or changes of the thing itself. The chameleon darkens in the shade of him who bends over it to ascertain its colours. In like manner, but with yet greater caution, ought we to think respecting a tranquil habit of inward life, considered as a spiritual *sense*, as the medial organ in and by which our peace with God, and the lively working of His grace in our spirit, are perceived by us. This peace which we have with God in Christ, is inviolable; but because the sense and persuasion of it may be interrupted, the soul that is truly at peace with God may for a time be disquieted in itself, through weakness of faith, or the strength of temptation, or the darkness of desertion, losing sight of that grace, that love and light of God's countenance, on which its tranquillity and joy depend. But when these eclipses are over, the soul is revived with new consolation, as the face of the earth is renewed and made to smile with the return of the sun in the spring; and this ought always to uphold Christians in the saddest times, namely, that the grace and love of God towards them depend, not on their sense, nor upon anything in them, but is still in itself, incapable of the smallest alteration.

SAMUEL TAYLOR COLERIDGE

'I LOVE and love not: Lord, it breaks my heart
   To love and not to love.
Thou veiled within Thy glory, gone apart
   Into Thy shrine which is above,
Dost Thou not love me, Lord, or care
   For this mine ill?'—

'I love thee here or there,
   I will accept thy broken heart—lie still.'

'Lord, it was well with me in time gone by
   That cometh not again,
When I was fresh and cheerful, who but I?
   I fresh, I cheerful: worn with pain
Now, out of sight and out of heart;
   O Lord, how long?'

'I watch thee as thou art,
   I will accept thy fainting heart—be strong.'

'Lie still, be strong, today: but, Lord, tomorrow,
   What of tomorrow, Lord?
Shall there be rest from toil, be truce from sorrow,
   Be living green upon the sward,
Now but a barren grave to me,
   Be joy for sorrow?'

'Did I not die for thee?
   Do I not live for thee? Leave me tomorrow.'

CHRISTINA ROSSETTI

GREAT virtues are rare: the occasions for them are very rare; and when they do occur, we are prepared for them, we are excited by the grandeur of the sacrifice, we are supported either by the splendour of the deed in the eyes of the world or by the self-complacency that we experience from the performance of an uncommon action. Little things are unforeseen; they return every moment; they come in contact with our pride, our indolence, our haughtiness, our readiness to take offence; they contradict our inclinations perpetually. We would much rather make certain great sacrifices to God, however violent and painful they might be, upon condition that we should be rewarded by liberty to follow our own desires and habits in the detail of life. It is, however, only by fidelity in little things that a true and constant love to God can be distinguished from a passing fervour of spirit.

All great things are only a great number of small things that have been carefully collected together. He who loses nothing will soon grow rich. Besides, let us remember that God looks in our actions only for the motive. The world judges us by appearance; God counts for nothing what is most dazzling to men. What He desires is a pure intention, true docility, and a sincere self-renunciation. All this is exercised more frequently, and in a way that tries us more severely, on common than on great occasions. Sometimes we cling more tenaciously to a trifle than to a great interest. It would give us more pain to relinquish an amusement than to bestow a great sum in charity. We are more easily led away by little things, because we believe them more innocent and imagine that we are less attracted to them; nevertheless, when God deprives us of them, we soon discover, from the pain of deprivation, how excessive and inexcusable was our attachment to them.

FÉNELON

But why do I exercise my meditation so long upon this, of having plentiful help in time of need? Is not my meditation rather to be inclined another way, to condole and commiserate their distress who have none? How many are sicker (perchance) than I, and laid in their woeful straw at home (if that corner be a home), and have no more hope of help, though they die, than of preferment, though they live! Nor do more expect to see a physician then, than to be an officer after; of whom, the first that takes knowledge, is the sexton that buries them, who buries them in oblivion too! For they do but fill up the number of the dead in the bill, but we shall never hear their names till we read them in the book of life with our own. How many are sicker (perchance) than I, and thrown into hospitals where (as a fish left upon the sand must stay the tide), they must stay the physician's hour of visiting, and then can be but visited! How many are sicker (perchance) than all we, and have not this hospital to cover them, not this straw to lie in, to die in, but have their gravestone under them, and breathe out their souls in the ears and in the eyes of passengers, harder than their bed, the flint of the street! that taste of no part of our physic, but a sparing diet, to whom ordinary porridge would be julap enough, the refuse of our servants bezoar enough, and the off-scouring of our kitchen tables cordial enough. O my soul, when thou art not enough awake to bless thy God enough for His plentiful mercy, in affording thee many helpers, remember how many lack them, and help them to them, or to those other things which they lack as much as them.

JOHN DONNE

HE told me that God always gave us light in our doubts when we had no other design but to please Him and to act for His love.

That our sanctification did not depend upon changing our works, but in doing that for God's sake which commonly we do for our own. That it was lamentable to see how many people mistook the means for the end, addicting themselves to certain works, which they performed very imperfectly, by reason of their human or selfish regards.

That the most excellent method which he had found of going to God was that of doing our common business without any view of pleasing men, and (as far as we are capable) purely for the love of God. . . .

That his view of prayer was nothing else but a sense of the Presence of God, his soul being at that time insensible to everything but Divine Love. That when the appointed times of prayers were passed, he found no difference, because he still continued with God, praising and blessing Him with all his might, so that he passed his life in continual joy; yet hoped that God would give him somewhat to suffer, when he should have grown stronger. . . .

That we ought not to be weary of doing little things for the love of God, for He regards not the greatness of the work, but the love with which it is performed. . . .

'The time of business', said he, 'does not with me differ from the time of prayer, and in the noise and clatter of my kitchen, while several persons are at the same time calling for different things, I possess God in as great tranquillity as if I were upon my knees at the Blessed Sacrament.'

BROTHER LAWRENCE

THERE is only one way of following Jesus and of worshipping God, and that is to be reconciled with our brethren. If we come to hear the word of God and receive the sacrament without first being reconciled with our neighbours, we shall come to our own damnation. In the sight of God we are murderers. Therefore 'go thy way, first be reconciled with thy brother, and then come and offer thy gift'. This is a hard way, but it is the way Jesus requires if we are to follow Him. It is a way which brings much personal humiliation and insult, but it is indeed the way to Him, our crucified Brother, and therefore a way of grace abounding. In Jesus the service of God and the service of the least of the brethren were one. He went His way and became reconciled with His brother and offered Himself as the one true sacrifice to His Father.

We are still living in the age of grace, for each of us still has a brother, we are still 'with him in the way'. The court of judgement lies ahead, and there is still a chance for us to be reconciled with our brother and pay our debt to him. The hour is coming when we shall meet the judge face to face, and then it will be too late. We shall then receive our sentence and be made to pay the last farthing. But do we realize that at this point our brother comes to us in the guise not of law, but of grace? It is grace that we are allowed to find favour with our brother, and pay our debt to him; it is grace that we are allowed to become reconciled with him. In our brother we find grace before the seat of judgement.

Only He can speak thus to us, who as our Brother has Himself become our grace, our atonement, our deliverance from judgement. The humanity of the Son of God empowers us to find favour with our brother. May the disciples of Jesus think upon this grace aright!

DIETRICH BONHOEFFER

WHAT is Paradise? All things that are; for all are goodly and pleasant, and therefore may fitly be called a Paradise. It is said also that Paradise is an outer court of Heaven. Even so this world is verily an outer court of the Eternal, or of Eternity; and specially is this true of whatever in time, of whatever temporal thing or creature, manifesteth or remindeth us of God or Eternity; for the creatures are a guide and a path unto God and Eternity. Thus this world is an outer court of Eternity, and therefore it may well be called a Paradise, for it is such in truth. And in this Paradise all things are lawful save one tree and the fruits thereof. That is to say: of all things that are, nothing is forbidden and nothing is contrary to God but one thing only: that is, self-will, or to will otherwise than as the Eternal Will would have it. For God saith to Adam, that is, to every man, 'Whatever thou art, or doest, or leavest undone, or whatever cometh to pass, is all lawful and not forbidden if it be not done from or according to thy will, but for the sake of and according to My Will. But all that is done from thine own will is contrary to the Eternal Will.'

It is not that every work which is thus wrought is in itself contrary to the Eternal Will, but in so far as it is wrought from a different will, or otherwise than from the Eternal and Divine Will.

THEOLOGIA GERMANICA

MOST people really believe that the Christian commandments (e.g. to love one's neighbour as oneself) are intentionally a little too severe—like putting the clock on half an hour to make sure of not being late in the morning.

✻   ✻   ✻

The remarkable thing about the way in which people talk about God, or about their relation to God, is that it seems to escape them completely that God hears what they are saying. A man says: 'At the moment I have not the time or the necessary recollection to think about God, but later on perhaps.' Or better still: a young man says: 'I am too young now; first of all I will enjoy life—and then.' Would it be possible to talk like that if one realized that God heard one?

✻   ✻   ✻

The world has often seen examples of the presumptuous religious individual who is perfectly secure in his own God-relationship, flippantly assured of his own salvation, but self-importantly engaged in doubting the salvation of others and in offering to help them. However, I believe it would be a fitting expression for a genuinely religious attitude if the individual were to say: 'I do not doubt the salvation of any human being; the only one I have fears about is myself. Even when I see a man sink very low, I should never presume to doubt his salvation; but if it were myself, I should doubtless have to suffer this terrible thought.' A genuine religious personality is always mild in his judgement of others, and only in his relation to himself is he cold and strict as a master inquisitor. His attitude towards others is like that of a benevolent patriarch to the younger generation; in relation to himself he is old and incorruptible.

SÖREN KIERKEGAARD

I STATED to him an anxious thought, by which a sincere Christian might be disturbed, even when conscious of having lived a good life, so far as is consistent with human infirmity; he might fear that he should afterwards fall away, and be guilty of such crimes as would render all his former religion vain. Could there be, upon this awful subject, such a thing as balancing of accounts? Suppose a man who has led a good life for seven years, commits an act of wickedness, and instantly dies; will his former good life have any effect in his favour? JOHNSON. 'Sir, if a man has led a good life for seven years, and then is hurried by passion to do what is wrong, and is suddenly carried off, depend upon it he will have the reward of his seven years' good life; God will not take a catch of him. Upon this principle Richard Baxter believes that a suicide may be saved. "If", says he, "it should be objected that what I maintain may encourage suicide, I answer, I am not to tell a lie to prevent it."' BOSWELL. 'But does not the text say, "As the tree falls, so must it lie?"' JOHNSON. 'Yes, Sir; as the tree falls: but—(after a little pause)—that is meant as to the general state of the tree, not what is the effect of a sudden blast.' In short, he interpreted the expression as referring to condition, not to position. The common notion, therefore, seems to be erroneous; and Shen-stone's witty remark on divines trying to give the tree a jerk upon the death-bed, to make it lie favourably, is not well founded. . . .

Talking of devotion, he said, 'Though it be true that "God dwelleth not in temples made with hands", yet in this state of being, our minds are more piously affected in some places appro-priated to divine worship than in others. Some people have a particular room in their house, where they say their prayers; of which I do not disapprove, as it may animate their devotion.'

JAMES BOSWELL

THEY might have sat quietly at home, watching, let us say, cricket matches and other spectacles beloved of most of the young men of their generation. There are those who have the effrontery to sneer at their sacrifice as 'fun' and to suggest that they would have been better advised to indulge in safer recreations than climbing. A more perverted view of what makes life worth living could hardly be conceived. In this country especially, which owes its very existence and its vast empire to the adventurous spirit of its sons, there should be no room for such feeble reflections. It is largely because there is no personal or material gain to be found at the summit of Everest that it is worth while trying to get there. No one with vision can read the accounts of the acts of devotion and daring of each individual member of the party without not only a glow of pride, but a feeling that it is worth while to do hard things just because they are hard.

THE TIMES

*　　*　　*

When we are tempted to cry out upon the loss of two such lives, it is well for us to try and see Everest as Mallory saw it. To him the attempt was not just an adventure, still less was it an opportunity for record-breaking. The climbing of the mountain was an inspiration, because it signified the transcendence of mind over matter. Nowhere as among the high snow and ice is the utter insignificance of man's bodily presence so overwhelming, nowhere as among those mighty masses do his desires and aspirations seem, by comparison, so triumphant. Those two black specks, scarcely visible among the vast eccentricities of nature but moving up slowly, intelligently, into regions of unknown striving, remain for us a symbol of the invincibility of the human spirit.

DAVID PYE

Dear Sister,

One line to thank you for your letter. I think we often fail by our own foolishness, impulsiveness, or selfishness, and hurt people needlessly (some are called to punish as a duty, that is another matter), and still God may overrule it; yet that will be no excuse for our self-confidence, or rudeness, or hastiness, or lack of humility, or whatever the fault was. I must humble myself before God for the fault; but then it is very pride and a still worse fault to go on fidgeting about the forgiven fault, calling myself all the bad names in the dictionary. It may be quite true in fact, but it is not true in humility and gratitude for God's love of me a sinner, to go on dwelling upon my badness, the obstinate contemplation of which shuts out the sight of God's goodness and beauty. . . .

I am very glad if it may possibly be that my fault may do good somehow to someone else, because God overrules evil for good; but the evil is not God's work but mine. But if I am sorry and own it, I will not dwell on it as if evil were the victorious power, but will thank God for His pardoning love, and try to be more humble and simple, and to keep my spirit in obedience to the Spirit of Christ for the future. It is possible to go on simply, and avoid a thousand perplexing questions, pains and doubts, which are unnecessary and unreal. It is possible because we can learn to abide in Christ more closely, and so to be subject to His wise and gracious inspiration, instead of at the mercy of our own tempests.

God bless you always.
Yours sincerely in Christ,
G. CONGREVE

A Contrite Heart

THE Lord will happiness divine
    On contrite hearts bestow;
Then tell me, gracious God, is mine
    A contrite heart, or no?

I hear, but seem to hear in vain,
    Insensible as steel;
If aught is felt, 'tis only pain
    To find I cannot feel.

I sometimes think myself inclined
    To love Thee, if I could;
But often feel another mind,
    Averse to all that's good.

My best desires are faint and few,
    I fain would strive for more;
But when I cry, 'My strength renew!'
    Seem weaker than before.

Thy saints are comforted, I know,
    And love Thy house of prayer;
I therefore go where others go,
    But find no comfort there.

O make this heart rejoice or ache;
    Decide this doubt for me;
And if it be not broken, break—
    And heal it if it be.

                              WILLIAM COWPER

THERE is another very safe and simple way of escape when the dull mood begins to gather round one, and that is to turn as promptly and as strenuously as one can to whatever work one can at the moment do. If the energy, the clearness, the power of intention, is flagging in us, if we cannot do our best work, still let us do what we can—for we can always do something; if not high work, then low work; if not vivid and spiritual work, then the plain, needful drudgery.

When it is dull and cold and weary weather with us, when the light is hidden, and the mists are thick, and the sleet begins to fall, still we may get on with the work which can be done as well in the dark days as in the bright; work which otherwise will have to be hurried through in the sunshine, taking up its happiest and most fruitful hours. When we seem poorest and least spiritual, when the glow of thankfulness seems to have died quite away, at least we can go on with the comparatively featureless bits of work, the business letters, the mechanism of life, the tasks which may be almost as well done then as ever. And not only, as men have found and said in every age, is the activity itself a safeguard for the time, but also very often, I think, the plainer work is the best way of getting back into the light and warmth that are needed for the higher. Through humbly and simply doing what we can, we retrieve the power of doing what we would. It was excellent advice of Mr. Keble's, 'When you find yourself overpowered as it were by melancholy, the best way is to go out, and do something kind to somebody or other.'

FRANCIS PAGET

Do you habitually thus unlock your hearts and subject your thoughts to Almighty God? Are you living in this conviction of His Presence? And have you this special witness that that Presence is really set up within you unto your salvation, namely, that you live in the sense of it? Do you believe, and act on the belief, that His light penetrates and shines through your heart, as the sun's beams through a room? You know how things look when the sun's beams are on it—the very air then appears full of impurities which, before it came out, were not seen. So it is with our souls. We are full of stains and corruptions, we see them not, they are like the air before the sun shines; but though we see them not, God sees them: He pervades us as the sunbeam. Our souls, in His view, are full of things which offend, things which must be repented of, forgiven, and put away. He, in the words of the Psalmist, 'has set our misdeeds before Him, our secret sins in the light of His countenance'. This is most true, though it be not at all welcome doctrine to many. We cannot hide ourselves from Him; and our wisdom, as our duty, lies in embracing this truth, acquiescing in it, and acting upon it. Let us then beg Him to teach us the Mystery of His Presence in us, that, by acknowledging it, we may thereby possess it fruitfully. Let us confess it in faith, that we may possess it unto justification. Let us so own it as to set Him before us in everything. 'I have set God always before me', says the Psalmist, 'for He is on my right hand, therefore I shall not fall.' Let us in all circumstances thus regard Him. Whether we have sinned, let us not dare keep from Him, but, with the prodigal son, rise up and go to Him. Or, if we are conscious of nothing, still let us not boast in ourselves or justify ourselves, but feel that 'He who judgeth us is the Lord'. . . . Let us have no secret apart from Him.

JOHN HENRY NEWMAN

IN this world, full of crude self-assertion and of feeble conformity, in this society where men invade each other's lives, and yet where, if one man stands out and claims his own life, his claim seems arrogant and harsh and makes a discord in the feeble music to which alone it seems as if the psalm of life could be sung—how sometimes we have dreamed of a better state of things in which each man's independence should make the brotherhood of all men perfect; where the more earnestly each man claimed his own life for himself, the more certainly other men should know that that life was given to them. Must we wait for such a society as that until we get to heaven? Surely not! Even here every man may claim his own life, not for himself but for his Lord. Belonging to that Lord, this life then must belong through Him to all His brethren. And so all that the man plucked out of their grasp, to give to Christ, comes back to them freely, sanctified and ennobled by passing through Him who is the Lord and Master of them all.

For such a social life as that we have a right to pray. But we may do more than pray for it. We may begin it in ourselves. Already we may give ourselves to Christ. We may own that we are His. We may see in all our bodily life—in the strength and glory of our youth if we are young and strong, in the weariness and depression of our age or feebleness if we are old and feeble—the marks of His ownership, the signs that we are His. We may wait for His coming to claim us, as the marked tree back in the woods waits till the ship-builder who has stuck his sign into it with his axe comes by and by to take it and make it part of the great ship that he is building. And while we wait we may make the world stronger by being our own, and sweeter by being our brethren's; and both, because and only because we are really not our own nor theirs, but Christ's.

PHILLIPS BROOKS

BUT indeed Conviction, were it never so excellent, is worthless till it convert itself into Conduct. Nay properly Conviction is not possible till then; inasmuch as all Speculation is by nature endless, formless, a vortex amid vortices: only by a felt indubitable certainty of Experience does it find any centre to revolve round, and so fashion itself into a system. Most true is it, as a wise man teaches us, that 'Doubt of any sort cannot be removed except by Action.' On which ground, too, let him who gropes painfully in darkness or uncertain light, and prays vehemently that the dawn may ripen into day, lay this other precept well to heart, which to me was of invaluable service: '*Do the Duty which lies nearest thee*', which thou knowest to be a Duty! Thy second Duty will already have become clearer.

May we not say, however, that the hour of Spiritual Enfranchisement is even this: When your Ideal World, wherein the whole man has been dimly struggling and inexpressibly languishing to work, becomes revealed, and thrown open; and you discover, with amazement enough, like the Lothario in *Wilhelm Meister*, that your 'America is here or nowhere'? The Situation that has not its Duty, its Ideal, was never yet occupied by man. Yes here, in this poor, miserable, hampered, despicable Actual, wherein thou even now standest, here or nowhere is thy Ideal: work it out therefrom; and working, believe, live, be free. Fool, the Ideal is in thyself, the impediment too is in thyself: thy Condition is but the stuff thou art to shape that same Ideal out of: what matter whether such stuff be of this sort or that, so the Form thou givest it be heroic, be poetic. O thou that tirest in the imprisonment of the Actual, and criest bitterly to the gods for a Kingdom wherein to rule and create, know this of a truth: the thing thou seekest is already with thee, 'here or nowhere', couldst thou only see!

THOMAS CARLYLE

WHAT, I ask, is the truth of water? Is it that it is formed of hydrogen and oxygen?... Is it for the sake of the fact that hydrogen and oxygen combined form water that the precious thing exists? Is oxygen-and-hydrogen the divine idea of water?.... The water itself, that dances, and sings and slakes the wonderful thirst— symbol and picture of that draught for which the woman of Samaria made her prayer to Jesus—this lovely thing itself, whose very wetness is a delight to every inch of the human body in its embrace—this water is its own self its own truth, and is therein a truth of God. Let him who would know the love of the maker become sorely athirst and drink of the brook by the way—then lift up his heart—not at that moment to the maker of oxygen and hydrogen, but to the inventor and mediator of thirst and water, that man might foresee a little of what his soul may find in God.... As well may a man think to describe the joy of drinking by giving thirst and water for its analysis, as imagine he has revealed anything about water by resolving it into its scientific elements. Let a man go to the hillside and let the brook sing to him till he loves it, and he will find himself far nearer the fountain of Truth than the triumphal car of the chemist will ever lead the shouting crew of his half-comprehending followers. He will draw from the brook the water of joyous tears, 'and worship Him that made heaven, and earth, and the sea, and the fountains of waters'.

The truth of a thing, then, is the blossom of it, the thing it is made for, the topmost stone set on with rejoicing; truth in a man's imagination is the power to recognize this truth of a thing; and wherever, in anything that God has made, in the glory of it, be it sky or flower or human face, we see the glory of God, there a true imagination is beholding a truth of God.

                                        GEORGE MACDONALD

In my drives I generally go out towards the west, and of course return with my face towards the east. During the winter I was attracted and interested by the frequent recurrence of the same natural phenomenon. The moon rose a little before the sun set, and had just the appearance of a thin bit of fleecy cloud, like a great many others, for in the hazy atmosphere its outline was not at all distinct. I was not looking out for the moon, and so it was often a good while before I identified it as the moon. I saw it simply as a bit of cloud floating about along with many others of a like tissue and even a like form. At last it gradually distinguished itself from the rest by having always the same shape and the same place. It got occasionally covered over or merged in the other fleecy things; but still it never failed to reassert its own individuality. It was evidently a permanent thing amongst changeable things—an objective thing amongst subjective things, shall I say? For I felt that these clouds were exhalations from myself (I being the earth), suggestions of my own mind, continually liable to change through the modifications which they suffered from other thoughts; they were all decidedly subjective. At the same time they bore witness not unfrequently to the existence of an objective, just as the clouds bear witness to the existence of the sun by the glory which they receive from him. But I wanted and needed to have the consciousness of the actual presence of the great Objective in me,—not thoughts about Him, but Himself, or at least something which I was sure did not depend upon myself, but would always assert its own distinct independent reality, and which could not possibly be my own imagination, having this personal power and life in it, unmistakably.

ERSKINE OF LINLATHEN

MANY of the things that we most desire can be obtained only if we do not aim directly at them. They are as it were by-products of something else. Happiness is one of these things. If you go after it directly and of set purpose you miss it entirely. You may of course have what you are pleased to call a good time, but that is quite a different thing and it does not last long. Goodness is another of these by-products. You cannot attain it either by aiming at it. That is what the Pharisees tried to do and tried very earnestly. Yet Jesus said of them, 'Except your righteousness exceed the righteousness of the scribes and Pharisees, ye shall in no wise enter the kingdom of heaven.' For the pride of the good man is the deadliest sin of all, and for that reason in the parable of the Prodigal Son the virtuous brother who stayed at home (the Pharisee) was all the time farther away from the father's house than the younger son returning from the far country with nothing but a broken and a contrite heart. You cannot read the Gospels without seeing that Jesus did not tell men how to be good in the manner of the moralists of every age; he told them how to be happy. The Sermon on the Mount, for instance, contains among other things a series of recipes for happiness: they are called the beatitudes and they suggest that happiness is a by-product of some other things, such as simplicity and humility and mercy and purity of heart and being persecuted for righteousness' sake. These sound like paradoxes, for it is by no means self-evident that the meek shall inherit the earth or that it is better to give than to receive—to take another saying of Jesus reported by St. Paul. I am pretty sure that we err in treating these sayings as paradoxes. It would be nearer the truth to say that it is life itself which is paradoxical and that the sayings of Jesus are simply a recognition of that fact.

T. M. TAYLOR

A YEAR ago I was ill in a New Jersey hospital and my doctor (who
had been a missionary) was talking with me about the difference,
as he saw it, between the all-out keenness with which medical
resources were mobilized for the very humblest and the apathy of
Christians in the Christian cause. He said that a few nights before
a negro had come into the hospital, dangerously wounded after a
drunken fracas. He was a known bully, and dying of a knife-
wound in his belly. But the hospital, though it had no hope of
saving him and though he was a drunken ne'er-do-well of whom
society might deem itself well rid, used its most expensive methods
for him and did for him all that it could have done for anyone—
and this out of professional loyalty and keenness. My doctor
wished that Christians and Churches were as unlimited in their
sacrifice and their commitment.

Of course, the reason is that we do not really believe. We assent,
but we do not *believe*. When men really believe that the Son of
God died for the sins of men and that through Him we are brought
into that kind of family relation to the Creator of all the worlds
which is typified in Christ's use of the word 'Abba', they do not
keep the news to themselves.

WILLIAM PATON

INQUIRE often, but judge rarely, and thou wilt not often be mistaken.

It is safer to learn than to teach; and who conceals his opinion has nothing to answer for.

Vanity or resentment often engage us, and 'tis two to one but we come off losers; for one shows a want of judgement and humility, as the other does of temper and discretion.

Not that I admire the reserved; for they are next to unnatural that are not communicable. But if reservedness be at any time a virtue, 'tis in throngs or ill company.

Beware also of affectation in speech; it often wrongs matter, and ever shows a blind side.

Speak properly, and in as few words as you can, but always plainly; for the end of speech is not ostentation, but to be understood.

They that affect words more than matter will dry up that little they have.

Sense never fails to give them that have it words enough to make them understood.

But it too often happens in some conversations, as in apothecary-shops, that those pots that are empty, or have things of small value in them, are as gaudily dressed and flourished as those that are full of precious drugs.

This labouring of slight matter with flourished turns of expression is fulsome, and worse than the modern imitation of tapestry, and East India goods, in stuffs and linens. In short, 'tis but tawdry talk, and next to very trash.

WILLIAM PENN

THERE is a false view of things which we get when we try to shut out the thought of suffering. Think of the young man and the young woman who make gaiety their home day after day and night after night, and think of Christ with the sick and maimed around Him; think of one who surrounds himself with the entertainment of this world, and think of one whose day is spent in passing from one sick chamber to another. Observe the infinite difference in the views which they respectively form of life. . . . Shut out suffering, and you see only one side of this strange and fearful thing, the life of man. Brightness and happiness and rest—that is not life. It is only one side of life. Christ saw both sides. He could be glad, He could rejoice with them that rejoice, He could bid men be merry at the marriage, He could take His part naturally in convivial conversation; and yet he has entered little into the depths of our Master's character who does not know that the settled tone of his disposition was a peculiar and subdued sadness. Take the two brightest moments of His career. When glory encircled Him on the mountain where His form was clothed in the radiance of a supernal cloud, what was His conversation with Moses and Elias—they spake to Him of His decease. When a multitude escorted Him triumphantly into Jerusalem—in the very midst of all that merriment His tears were flowing for Jerusalem. Not the splendour of a transfiguration, and not the excitement of a procession could dazzle the view which the Son of Man had formed of life. Life was too earnest for deceiving Himself; He knew that the Son of Man is 'a man of sorrows and acquainted with grief'. He had been behind the gaudy scenes. He stood in the very midst of a wretched and ruined world, and when death and retribution were so near, what had He to do with a gleam of momentary sunshine? That gave the calm depth to the character of Christ; He had got the true view of life by acquainting Himself with grief. Life is not for rest, but for seeking out misery.

F. W. ROBERTSON

WHEN the Interpreter had showed them this, he has them into the very best room in the house (a very brave room it was), so he bid them look round about and see if they could find anything profitable there. Then they looked round and round, for there was nothing there to be seen but a very great spider on the wall, and that they overlookt.

Then said Mercy, Sir, I see nothing; but Christiana held her peace.

But said the Interpreter, Look again: she therefore lookt again and said, Here is not any thing, but an ugly spider who hangs by her hands upon the wall. Then said he, Is there but one spider in all this spacious room? Then the water stood in Christiana's eyes, for she was a woman quick of apprehension: and she said, Yes, Lord, there is more than one. Yea, and spiders whose venom is far more destructive than that which is in her. The Interpreter then looked pleasantly upon her and said, Thou hast said the truth. This made Mercy blush, and the boys to cover their faces. For they all began now to understand the riddle.

Then said the Interpreter again, The spider taketh hold with her hands as you see, and is in kings' palaces. And wherefore is this recorded but to show you that how full of the venom of sin soever you be, yet you may by the hand of faith lay hold of and dwell in the best room that belongs to the King's House above.

I thought, said Christiana, of something of this; but I could not imagine it all. I thought that we were like spiders, and that we looked like ugly creatures, in what fine room soever we were. But that by this spider, this venomous and ill-favoured creature we were to learn how to act faith, that came not into my mind. And yet she hath taken hold with her hands, as I see, and dwells in the best room in the house. God has made nothing in vain.

Then they all seemed to be glad; but the water stood in their eyes.

JOHN BUNYAN

A LITTLE Boy of heavenly birth,
  But far from home today,
Comes down to find His ball, the earth,
  That sin has cast away.
O comrades, let us one and all
  Join in to get Him back His ball!

        *   *   *

The Father speaking to the Son,
In all the multitude was none
  That caught the meaning true.
And yet 'This word from heaven', said He,
'Was spoken not because of Me—
  But came because of you'.

Thus through the Son of Man alone
The mysteries of God are known;
  Thus to the chosen few.
With eye and ear attentive found
He speaks in every sense and sound,
  The old becoming new.

        *   *   *

Let my heart the cradle be
Of Thy bleak Nativity!
Tossed by wintry tempests wild,
If it rock Thee, Holy Child,
Then, as grows the outer din,
Greater peace shall reign within.

                              JOHN BANISTER TABB

THERE are souls that form great projects of doing excellent services for our Lord by eminent deeds and extraordinary sufferings, but deeds and sufferings of which there is no present opportunity, and perhaps never will be, and upon this imagine that they have done a great matter in love, in which they are very often deceived—in this way, that embracing in desire what seems to them great future crosses, they studiously avoid the burden of such as are present, which are less. Is it not a great temptation to be so valiant in imagination and so cowardly in execution? Ah, God keep us from these imaginary fervours which very often breed in the bottom of our hearts a vain and secret self-esteem! Great works do not always lie in our way, but every moment we may do little ones excellently, that is, with great love. I beg you to remark the saint who gives a cup of water for God's sake to a poor thirsty traveller; he seems to do a small thing; but the intention, the sweetness, the love with which he animates his action, is so excellent that it turns this simple water into the water of life, and of eternal life. Bees gather honey from the lily, the iris, and the rose; but they get as much booty from the little minute rosemary flowers and thyme; they not only draw more honey from these, but even better honey, because in these little vessels the honey being more closely locked up is much better preserved. Truly in small and insignificant exercises of devotion charity is practised not only more frequently, but also as a rule more humbly too, and consequently more holily and usefully. Those condescensions to the humours of others, that bearing with the troublesome actions and ways of our neighbour, those victories over our own tempers and passions; . . . all this is more profitable to our souls than we can conceive, if heavenly love only have the management of them.

ST. FRANCIS DE SALES

THERE are but two things that we can do against temptations. The first is to be faithful to the light within us, in avoiding all exposure to temptation which we are at liberty to avoid. I say, all that we are at liberty to avoid, because it does not always depend upon ourselves whether we shall escape occasions of sin. Those that belong to the situation in life in which Providence has placed us are not under our control. The other is to turn our eyes to God in the moment of temptation, to throw ourselves immediately upon the protection of heaven, as a child when in danger flies to the arms of its parent.

The habitual conviction of the presence of God is the sovereign remedy; it supports, it consoles, it calms us. We must not be surprised that we are tempted. We are placed here to be proved by temptations. Everything is temptation to us. Crosses irritate our pride and prosperity flatters it; our life is a continual warfare, but Jesus Christ combats with us. We must let temptations, like a tempest, beat upon our heads, and still move on; like a traveller surprised on the way by a storm, who wraps his cloak about him, and goes on his journey in spite of the opposing elements.

In a certain sense, there is little to do in doing the will of God. Still it is true that it is a great work, because it must be without any reserve. His Spirit enters the secret folding of our hearts, and even the most upright affections and the most necessary attachments must be regulated by His will; but it is not the multitude of hard duties, it is not the constraint and contention, that advances us on our course. On the contrary it is the yielding of our wills without restriction to tread cheerfully every day in the path in which Providence leads us; to seek nothing, to be discouraged by nothing, to see our duty in the present moment, to trust all else without reserve to the will and power of God.

FÉNELON

HOW thankful we ought to be every minute of our existence to Him who gives us all richly to enjoy! How little one has deserved this happy life, much less than many poor sufferers to whom life is a burden and a hard and bitter trial! But then, how much greater the claims on us; how much more sacred the duty never to trifle, never to waste time and power, but to live in all things, small and great, to the glory and praise of God, to have God always present with us, and to be ready to follow His voice and His voice only! Has our prosperity taught us to meet adversity when it comes? I often tremble, but then I commit all to God, and I say, 'Have mercy upon me, miserable sinner.'

     ✳   ✳   ✳

You must accustom yourself more and more to the thought that here is not our abiding city, that all that we call ours here is only lent, not given us, and that if the sorrow for those we have lost remains the same, we must yet acknowledge with gratitude to God the blessing of having enjoyed so many years with those whom He gave us as parents or children or friends. One forgets so easily the happy years one has had with those who were the nearest to us. Even these years of happiness, however short they may have been, were only given us, we had not deserved them. I know well there is no comfort for this pain of parting: the wound always remains, but one learns to bear the pain, and learns to thank God for what He gave, for the beautiful memories of the past, and the yet more beautiful hope for the future. If a man has lent us anything for several years, and at last takes it back, he expects gratitude, not anger; and if God has more patience with our weakness than men have, yet murmurs and complaints for the life He has measured out for us as is best for us, are not what He expected from us. A spirit of resignation to God's will is our only comfort, the only relief under the trials God lays upon us, and with such a spirit the heaviest as well as the lightest trials of life are not only bearable but useful, and gratitude to God and joy in life remain untroubled.

MAX MÜLLER

EACH of us is encased in an armour whose task is to ward off signs. Signs happen to us without respite, living means being addressed, we would need only to present ourselves and to perceive. But the risk is too dangerous for us, the soundless thunderings seem to threaten us with annihilation, and from generation to generation we perfect the defence apparatus. All our knowledge assures us, 'Be calm, everything happens as it must happen, but nothing is directed at you, you are not meant; it is just "the world", you can experience it as you like, but whatever you make of it in yourself proceeds from you alone, nothing is required of you, you are not addressed, all is quiet.'

Each of us is encased in an armour which we soon out of familiarity, no longer notice. There are only moments which penetrate it and stir the soul to sensibility. And when such a moment has imposed itself on us and we then take notice and ask ourselves, 'Has anything particular taken place? Was it not of the kind I meet every day?' then we may reply to ourselves, 'Nothing particular, indeed, it is like this every day, only we are not there every day.'

The signs of address are not something extraordinary, something that steps out of the order of things, they are just what goes on time and again, just what goes on in any case, nothing is added by the address. The waves of the aether roll on always, but for most of the time we have turned off our receivers.

What occurs to me addresses me. In what occurs to me the world-happening addresses me. Only by sterilizing it, removing the seed of address from it, can I take what occurs to me as a part of the world-happening which does not refer to me.

MARTIN BUBER

THE Challenge of Death is the summary challenge addressed to the universe by man. It is the spear-point of the Challenge of Life, not to be evaded on any terms, as the fashion now is with many to evade it. To find a good in life which is worth achieving in spite of the fact, consciously realized, that this visible scene on which we operate, and we, the visible agents who operate, will presently be gathered to the dark death-kingdoms and enfolded in the ever-lasting Silence—that is the spear-point of the Challenge, the acid test of philosophy, the point where philosophy must either pass into religion or retire, beaten, from the field. The philosopher may be unaware of this, often is, or will even go out of his way to repudiate all interest in the matter; but in the audience that gathers round his feet there is always a vague hope, and sometimes a poignant one, that he will come at last to the critical point where Life and Death stand confronting one another in a 'fell incensèd opposition', that he will let fall the word of wisdom which is to end that conflict and release the mind from the tension it involves —perhaps by teaching contentment with annihilation, perhaps by an argument for *carpe diem*, perhaps by proving personal immortality. Without that motive, subtly operating in all our curiosities about 'mind and matter', 'good and evil', 'reality and appearance', there would be no market for the philosopher's goods; his performance would be offered to an empty house.

L. P. JACKS

AH! wretched sin, what art thou? Thou art nought! For I saw that God is all-thing. I saw not thee. And when I saw that God has made all-thing, I saw thee not. And when I saw that God does all-thing that is done, less and more, I saw thee not. And when I saw our Lord Jesus sit in our soul so worshipfully, and love and like and rule and guard all that He has made, I saw not thee. And thus I am sure that thou art nought; and all those that love thee, and like thee, and follow thee, and wilfully end in thee, I am sure they shall be brought to nought with thee, and endlessly confounded. God shield us all from thee! Amen, for charity.

* * *

For many men and women believe that God is All-Mighty and may do all; and that He is All-Wisdom and can do all; but that He is All-Love and will do all—there they stop short.

And this lack of knowing it is that most lets God's lovers. For when they begin to hate sin, and to amend them by the ordinance of Holy Church, yet there dwells a dread that stirs them to beholding of themselves and of their sins before done. And this dread they take for a meekness; but this is a foul blindness, and a weakness if we cannot despise it. For if we knew it that, we should suddenly despise it, as we do another sin that we know; for it comes of the enemy, and it is against the truth.

For of all the properties of the blessed Trinity, it is God's will that we have most sureness in liking and love. For Love makes Might and Wisdom full meek to us. For right as by the courtesy of God He forgets our sins when we repent, right so will He that we forget our sin, and all our heaviness, and all our doubtful dreads.

LADY JULIAN OF NORWICH

AMONGST other arguments enforcing the necessity of daily prayer, this not the least, that Christ enjoins us to petition for daily bread. New bread we know is best; and in a spiritual sense our bread, though in itself as stale and mouldy as that of the Gibeonites, is every day new, because a new and hot blessing, as I might say, is daily begged, and bestowed of God upon it.

Manna must daily be gathered, and not provisionally be hoarded up. God expects that men every day address themselves unto Him, by petitioning Him for sustenance.

How contrary is this to the common practice of many. As camels in sandy countries are said to drink but once in seven days, and then in *praesens, praeteritum, et futurum*, for time past, present, and to come, so many fumble this, last, and next week's devotions all in a prayer. Yea, some defer all their praying till the last day.

Constantine had a conceit that because baptism washed away all sins, he would not be baptized till his death-bed, that so his soul might never lose the purity thereof, but immediately mount to heaven. But sudden death preventing him, he was not baptized at all, as some say, or only by an Arian bishop, as others affirm. If any erroneously, on the same supposition, put off their prayers to the last, let them take heed lest, long delayed, they prove either none at all or none in effect.

THOMAS FULLER

So was I speaking, and weeping in the most bitter contrition of my heart, when lo! I heard from a neighbouring house a voice, as of a boy or a girl, I know not, chanting and oft repeating '*Tolle, lege*; take up and read'. Instantly my countenance altered, I began to think most intently whether children were wont in any kind of play to sing such words: nor could I remember ever to have heard the like. So, checking the torrent of my tears, I arose; interpreting it to be no other than a command from God to open the book and read the first chapter I should find. For I had heard of Antony that, coming in during the reading of the Gospel, he received the admonition, as if what was being read was spoken to him: 'Go, sell all that thou hast, and give to the poor, and then shalt have treasure in heaven, and come and follow me.' And by such oracle he was forthwith converted unto Thee. Eagerly then I returned to the place where Alypius was sitting; for there had I laid the volume of the Apostle, when I arose thence. I seized, opened, and in silence read that section on which my eyes first fell: 'Not in rioting and drunkenness, not in chambering and wantonness, not in strife and envying; but put ye on the Lord Jesus Christ, and make not provision for the flesh, to fulfil the lusts thereof.' No further would I read; nor needed I: for instantly, at the end of this sentence, by a light as it were of serenity infused into my heart, all the darkness of doubt vanished away.

ST. AUGUSTINE

WITH this ambiguous earth
His dealings have been told us. These abide:
The signal to a maid, the human birth,
The lesson, and the young Man crucified.

But not a star of all
The innumerable host of stars has heard
How he administered this terrestrial ball.
Our race has kept their Lord's entrusted Word.

Of his earth-visiting feet
None knows the secret, cherished, perilous,
The terrible, shamefast, frightened, whispered, sweet,
Heart-shattering secret of His way with us.

No planet knows that this,
Our wayside planet, carrying land and wave,
Love and life multiplied, and pain and bliss,
Bears, as chief treasure, one forsaken grave.

Nor, in our little day,
May His devices with the heavens be guessed,
His pilgrimage to thread the Milky Way
Or his bestowal there be manifest.

But in the eternities,
Doubtless we shall compare together, hear
A million alien Gospels, in what guise
He trod the Pleiades, the Lyre, the Bear.

O, be prepared, my soul!
To read the inconceivable, to scan
The million forms of God those stars unroll
When, in our turn, we show to them a Man.

                                        ALICE MEYNELL

As those blessed Fathers of tender bowels enlarged themselves in this distribution and apportioning [of] the mercy of God that it consisted best with the nature of His mercy, that as His saints had suffered temporal calamities in this world, in this world they should be recompensed with temporal abundances, so did they enlarge this mercy farther, and carry it even to the Gentiles, to the pagans that had no knowledge of Christ in any established Church. You shall not find a Trismegistus, a Numa Pompilius, a Plato, a Socrates, for whose salvation you shall not find some Father, or some ancient and reverend author, an advocate. . . . St. Dionyse the Areopagite says that from the beginning of the world God hath called some men of all nations, and of all sorts, by the ministry of angels, though not by the ministry of the Church. To me, to whom God hath revealed His Son, in a Gospel, by a Church, there can be no way of salvation but by applying that Son of God, by that Gospel, in that Church. Nor is there any other foundation for any, nor other name by which any man can be saved, but the name of Jesus. But how this foundation is presented, and how this name of Jesus is notified, to them amongst whom there is no Gospel preached, no Church established, I am not curious in inquiring. I know God can be as merciful as those tender Fathers present Him to be; and I would be as charitable as they are. And therefore, humbly embracing that manifestation of His Son which He hath afforded me, I leave God to His unsearchable ways of working upon others, without further inquisition.

JOHN DONNE

Saturday, 12 January 1723, in the morning. I have this day solemnly renewed my baptismal covenant and self-dedication, which I renewed when I was received into the communion of the church. I have been before God; and have given myself, all that I am and have to God, so that I am not in any respect my own. I can claim no right in myself, no right in this understanding, this will, these affections that are in me; neither have I any right to this body or any of its members; no right to this tongue, these hands nor feet; no right to these senses, these eyes, these ears, this smell or taste. I have given myself clear away. . . . This I have done. And I pray God, for the sake of Christ, to look upon it as a self-dedication; and to receive me now as entirely His own, and deal with me in all respects as such; whether He afflicts me or prospers me, or whatever He pleases to do with me, who am His. Now henceforth I am not to act in any respect as my own. I shall act as my own, if I ever make use of any of my powers to anything that is not to the glory of God, or do not make the glorifying of Him my whole and entire business; if I murmur in the least at afflictions; if I grieve at the prosperity of others; if I am any way uncharitable; if I am angry because of injuries; if I revenge my own cause; if I do anything purely to please myself, or avoid anything for the sake of my ease, or omit anything because it is great self-denial; if I trust to myself; if I take any of the praise of any good that I do, or rather God does by me; or if I am in any way proud.

JONATHAN EDWARDS

SILENCE never shows itself to so great an advantage as when it is made the reply to calumny and defamation, provided that we give no occasion for them. We might produce an example of it in the behaviour of One in whom it appeared in all its majesty, and One whose silence, as well as His person, was altogether divine. When one considers this subject only in its sublimity, this great instance could not but occur to me; and since I only make use of it to show the highest example of it, I hope I do not offend in it. To forbear replying to an unjust reproach, and overlook it with a generous or, if possible, with an entire neglect of it, is one of the most heroic acts of a great mind; and I must confess, when I reflect upon the behaviour of some of the greatest men in antiquity, I do not so much admire them that they deserved the praise of the whole age they lived in, as because they contemned the envy and detraction of it.

All that is encumbent on a man of worth, who suffers under so ill a treatment, is to lie by for some time in silence and obscurity, till the prejudice of the times be over, and his reputation cleared. I have often read, with a great deal of pleasure, a legacy of the famous Lord Bacon, one of the greatest geniuses that our own or any country has produced. After having bequeathed his soul, body, and estate in the usual form, he adds, 'My name and memory I leave to foreign nations and to my countrymen, after some time be passed over.'

JOSEPH ADDISON

EUGENIA is a good young woman, full of pious dispositions; she is intending if ever she has a family to be the best mistress of it that ever was, her house shall be a school of religion, and her children and servants shall be brought up in the strictest practice of piety; she will spend her time and live in a very different manner from the rest of the world. It may be so, Eugenia; the piety of your mind makes me think that you intend all this with sincerity. But you are not yet at the head of a family, and perhaps never may be. But, Eugenia, you have now one maid, and you do not know what religion she is of. She dresses you for the church, you ask her for what you want, and then leave her to have as little Christianity as she pleases. You turn her away, you hire another, she comes, and goes no more instructed or edified in religion by living with you than if she had lived with anybody else. And all this comes to pass because your mind is taken up with greater things, and you reserve yourself to make a whole family religious, if ever you come to be head of it. You need not stay, Eugenia, to be so extraordinary a person; the opportunity is now in your hands, you may now spend your time and live in as different a manner from the rest of the world as ever you can in any other state. Your maid is your family at present, she is under your care; be now that religious governess that you intend to be, teach her the catechism, hear her read, exhort her to pray, take her with you to church, persuade her to love the divine service as you love it, edify her with your conversation, fill her with your own notions of piety, and spare no pains to make her as holy and devout as yourself. When you do thus much good in your present state, then you are that extraordinary person that you intend to be; and till you thus live up to your present state, there is but little hope that the altering of your state will alter your way of life.

WILLIAM LAW

'WHICH gave Himself for our sins.' These things, as touching the words, we know well enough and can talk of them. But in practice, and in the conflict, when the devil goeth about to deface Christ, and to pluck the word of grace out of our hearts, we find that we do not yet know them well, and as we should do. He that at that time could define Christ truly, and could magnify Him and behold Him as his most sweet Saviour and High Priest, and not as a strait judge, such a man hath overcome all evils and were already in the kingdom of heaven. But this to do in the conflict is of all things the most hard. I speak this by experience. . . .

And this is the cause why I do so earnestly call upon you to learn the true and proper definition of Christ out of these words of Paul, 'which gave Himself for our sins'. If He gave Himself to death for our sins, then undoubtedly He is no tyrant or judge which will condemn us for our sins. He is no caster-down of the afflicted, but a raiser-up of those that are fallen, a merciful reliever and comforter of the heavy and the broken-hearted. Else should Paul lie in saying, 'which gave Himself for our sins'. If I define Christ thus, I define Him rightly, and take hold of the true Christ, and possess Him indeed. And here I let pass all curious speculations touching the divine majesty, and stay myself in the humanity of Christ, and so I learn truly to know the will of God. Here is then no fear, but altogether sweetness, joy, peace of conscience, and suchlike. And herewithal there is a light opened, which showeth me the true knowledge of God, of myself, of all creatures, and of all the iniquity of the devil's kingdom. We teach no new thing, but we repeat and establish old things, which the apostles and all godly teachers have taught us. And would to God we could so teach and establish them that we might not only have them in our mouth, but also well grounded in the bottom of our heart, and especially that we might be able to use them in the agony and conflict of death.

MARTIN LUTHER

HOLDING a council with the wise men, he asked of every one in particular what he thought of the new doctrine and the new worship that was presented. To which the chief of his own priests, Coifi, immediately answered:

'O king, consider what this is which is now preached to us; for I verily declare to you that the religion which we have hitherto professed has, as far as I can learn, no virtue in it. For none of your people has applied himself more diligently to the worship of our gods than I; and yet there are many who receive greater favours from you, and are more preferred than I, and are more prosperous in all their undertakings. Now if the gods were good for any thing, they would rather forward me who have been more careful to serve them. It remains, therefore, that if upon examination you find those new doctrines, which are now preached among us, better and more efficacious, we receive them without any delay.'

Another of the king's chief men, approving of his words and exhortations, immediately added: 'The present life of man, O king, seems to me, in comparison with that time which is unknown to us, like to the swift flight of a sparrow through the room wherein you sit at supper in winter, with your ealdormen and thegns, while the fire blazes in the midst and the hall is warmed, but the storms of rain and snow are raging abroad without; the sparrow, flying in at one door and immediately out at another, whilst he is within is safe from the wintry tempest; but after a short space of fair weather, he immediately vanishes out of your sight, passing from winter into winter again. So this life of man appears for a short space, but of what went before and of what is to follow we know nothing at all. If, therefore, this new doctrine contains something more certain, it justly deserves to be followed.'

The other ealdormen and counsellors, by divine inspiration, spoke to the same effect.

THE VENERABLE BEDE

'THE trees of the Lord are full of sap; the cedars of Lebanon, which He hath planted.' It has happened to me—through the bounty of God, for which I shall be ever grateful—to have spent days in forests as grand as, and far stranger than, that of Lebanon and its cedars; amid trees beside which the hugest tree in Britain would be but as a sapling; gorgeous too with flowers, rich with fruits, timbers, precious gums, and all the yet unknown wealth of a tropic wilderness. And as I looked up, awe-struck and bewildered, at those minsters not made by hands, I found the words of Scripture rising again and again unawares to my lips, and said—Yes, the Bible words are the best words, the only words for such a sight as this. These too are trees of God which are full of sap. These too are trees which God, not man, has planted. Mind, I do not say that I would have said so, if I had not learnt to say so from the Bible. Without the Bible I should have been, I presume, either an idolater or an atheist. And mind, also, that I do not say that the Psalmist learnt to call the cedars trees of God by his own unassisted reason. I believe the very opposite. I believe that no man can see the truth of a thing unless God shows it him; that no man can find out God, in earth or heaven, unless God condescends to reveal Himself to that man. But I believe that God did reveal Himself to the Psalmist; did enlighten his reason by the inspiration of His Holy Spirit; did teach him, as we teach a child, what to call those cedars; and, as it were, whispered to him, though with no audible voice: 'Thou wishest to know what name is most worthy whereby to call those mighty trees: then call them trees of God. Know that there is but one God, of whom are all things; and that they are His trees; and that He planted them, to show forth His wisdom, His power, and His goodwill to man.'

CHARLES KINGSLEY

To whatever world death introduce you, the best conceivable preparation for it is to labour for the highest good of the world in which you live. Be the change which death brings what it may, he who has spent his life in trying to make this world better can never be unprepared for another. If heaven is for the pure and holy, if that which makes men good is that which best qualifies for heaven, what better discipline in goodness can we conceive for a human spirit . . . than to live and labour for a brother's welfare? To find our deepest joy, not in the delights of sense, nor in the gratification of personal ambition, nor even in the serene pursuits of culture and science—nay, not even in seeking the safety of our own souls, but in striving for the highest good of those who are dear to our Father in heaven, and the moral and spiritual redemption of that world for which the Son of God lived and died—say, can a nobler school of goodness be discovered than this? Where shall love and sympathy and beneficence find ampler training, or patience, courage, dauntless devotion, nobler opportunities of exercise, than in the war with evil? . . . Live in this, find your dearest work here, let love to God and man be the animating principle of your being; and then, let death come when it may, and carry you where it will, you will not be unprepared for it. The rending of the veil which hides the secrets of the unseen world, the summons that calls you into regions unknown, need awaken in your breast no perturbation or dismay; for you cannot in God's universe go where love and truth and self-devotion are things of naught, or where a soul, filled with undying faith in the progress and identifying its own happiness with the final triumph of goodness, shall find itself forsaken.

JOHN CAIRD

MY whole confidence rests on the certainty that neither our misdeeds nor the Devil's can change anything in the order of this
world, where chance does not exist but is only the illusion of an
impatience that obliterates our spiritual sense but can no more
prevent the activity of the Spirit than it can alter the course of the
stars.

We can destroy ourselves, indeed, but we can destroy nothing
but ourselves. We can, it is true, render ourselves insensible to
that poetic intuition that fathoms the microscopic depths of matter,
the great dynamics of the stars, and the affinities of organic life
to such a degree that a scholar, a painter, a visionary, is able to
recreate the 'real' after its pattern. But we cannot prevent all these
things from existing, gravitating, being born, dying, and carrying
their just consequences to the end of all cycles of possibility. From
the Devil's depths to the farthest edges of the cosmos a universal
resonance stirs all existence to the eternal quest of a harmony that
will be the sacred name of God. We may lie, kill, shut ourselves
out, we may commit pitiable mistakes out of pride, negligence,
or calculation, but we can do nothing, ever, to affect the eternal
miracle; which unites justice with joy, the pure speculations of
mathematics with the structure of the material world; the lover
and the object of love; prayer and the divine promise.

If I, tiny individual, insignificant error, one articulate word in
the speech of all created things, presume to isolate myself or stand
apart from the cosmos, and so bring about my own particular
catastophe, it will only be at the price of my own ruin and without knowing it that I will be contributing to the plan of Divine
Providence. But if I answer when my name is called, if I take up
the vocation that singles me out and imparts truth to my words,
if I try at least to converge towards the cosmic order and the
Divine Will, then unworthy though I may still remain, and
vulnerable in my flesh, I have conquered, I am united again with
things and with beings, with their knowledge and with their
mystery, and with my own—my kinship is restored to me.

                                        DENIS DE ROUGEMONT

HIS object was, instead of drawing up, after the example of previous legislators, a list of actions prescribed, allowed, and prohibited, to give His disciples a universal test by which they might discover what it was right and what it was wrong to do. Now as the difficulty of discovering what is right arises commonly from the prevalence of self-interest in our minds, and as we commonly behave rightly to anyone for whom we feel affection or sympathy, Christ considered that he who could feel sympathy for all would behave rightly to all. But how to give to the meagre and narrow hearts of men such enlargement? How to make them capable of a universal sympathy? Christ believed it possible to bind men to their kind, but on one condition—that they were first bound fast to Himself. He stood forth as the representative of men, He identified Himself with the cause and with the interests of all human beings, He was destined, as He began before long obscurely to intimate, to lay down His life for them. Few of us sympathize originally and directly with this devotion; few of us can perceive in human nature itself any merit sufficient to evoke it. But it is not so hard to love and venerate Him who felt it. So vast a passion of love, a devotion so comprehensive, has not elsewhere been in any degree approached, save by some of His imitators. And as love provokes love, many have found it possible to conceive for Christ an attachment the closeness of which no words can describe, a veneration so possessing and absorbing the man within them, that they have said: 'I live no more, but Christ lives in me.' Now such a feeling carries with it of necessity the feeling of love for all human beings. It matters no longer what quality men may exhibit; amiable or unamiable, as the brothers of Christ, as belonging to His sacred and consecrated kind, as the objects of His love in life and death, they must be dear to all to whom He is dear.

SIR JOHN SEELEY

NEXT morning, while we were at breakfast, Johnson gave a very earnest recommendation of what he himself practised with the utmost conscientiousness: I mean a strict attention to truth, even in the most minute particulars. 'Accustom your children (said he) constantly to this; if a thing happened at one window, and they, when relating it, say that it happened at another, do not let it pass, but instantly check them; you do not know where deviation from truth will end.' BOSWELL. 'It may come to the door: and when once an account is at all varied in one circumstance, it may by degrees be varied so as to be totally different from what really happened.' Our lively hostess, whose fancy was impatient of the rein, fidgeted at this, and ventured to say, 'Nay, this is too much. If Mr. Johnson should forbid me to drink tea, I would comply, as I should feel the restraint only once a day; but little variations in narrative must happen a thousand times a day, if one is not perpetually watching.' JOHNSON. 'Well, Madam and you *ought* to be perpetually watching. It is more from carelessness about truth than from intentional lying, that there is so much falsehood in the world.' . . .

He was indeed so much impressed with the prevalence of falsehood, voluntary or unintentional, that I never knew any person who upon hearing an extraordinary circumstance told, discovered more of the *incredulus odi*. He would say, with a significant look and decisive tone, 'It is not so. Do not tell this again.' He inculcated upon all his friends the importance of perpetual vigilance against the slightest degree of falsehood; the effect of which, as Sir Joshua Reynolds observed to me, has been that all who were of his *school* are distinguished for a love of truth and accuracy which they would not have possessed in the same degree, if they had not been acquainted with Johnson.

JAMES BOSWELL

THE first time I saw Brother Lawrence was upon the 3rd of August 1666. He told me that God had done him a singular favour in his conversion at the age of eighteen.

That in the winter, seeing a tree stripped of its leaves, and considering that within a little time the leaves would be renewed, and after that the flowers and fruit appear, he received a high view of the providence and power of God, which has never since been effaced from his soul. That this view has set him perfectly loose from the world, and kindled in him such love for God, that he could not tell whether it had increased in above forty years that he had lived since.

That he had been footman to M. Fieubert, the treasurer, and that he was a great awkward fellow who broke everything.

That he had desired to be received into a monastery, thinking that he would there be made to smart for his awkwardness and the faults he should commit: but that God had disappointed him, he having met with nothing but satisfaction in that state.

That we should establish ourselves in a sense of God's Presence, by continually conversing with Him. That it was a shameful thing to quit His conversation to think of trifles and fooleries.

That we should feed and nourish our souls with high notions of God; which would yield us great joy in being devoted to Him.

BROTHER LAWRENCE

So when they were come again into the house, because supper as yet was not ready, Christiana again desired that the Interpreter would either show or tell of some other things that are profitable. Then the Interpreter began and said:

The fatter the sow is, the more she desires the mire; the fatter the ox is, the more gamesomely he goes to the slaughter; and the more healthy the lusty man is, the more prone he is unto evil.

There is a desire in women to go neat and fine, and it is a comely thing to be adorned with that that in God's sight is of great price.

'Tis easier watching for a night or two than to sit up a whole year together: so 'tis easier for one to begin to profess well than to hold out as he should to the end.

Every ship-master, when in a storm, will willingly cast that overboard that is of the smallest value in the vessel; but who will throw the best out first? None but he that feareth not God. . . .

He that forgets his friend is ungrateful unto him: but he that forgets his Saviour is unmerciful unto himself.

He that lives in sin and looks for happiness hereafter is like him that soweth cockle and thinks to fill his barn with wheat or barley.

If a man would live well, let him fetch his last day to him, and make it always his company-keeper. . . .

Everybody will cry up the goodness of men; but who is there that is, as he should, affected with the goodness of God?

We seldom sit down to meat but we eat and leave: so there is in Jesus Christ more merit and righteousness than the whole world has need of.

JOHN BUNYAN

NOTHING in His ministry was more deeply considered than this entry into Jerusalem, and nothing required of those who saw it greater seriousness and discernment. Here He presented Himself to the assembled nation in character, bringing to the front what He counted significant. He was born to be a king, but a king whose authority rests not on compulsion but on His power to persuade the minds of men, and a king not parted from His people by the wide world of circumstance but sharing their privations and their lowliness; and He maintained that a kingdom founded thus would spread from sea to sea, and would last from age to age. That was a frank contradiction of what men have commonly believed, and thus it imposed a burden on their faith, as His deepest words are wont to do. They might very well not see the reason and the hopefulness of His plan, and they might be pardoned if they paused for information. There was nothing that, on the face of it, should have appealed to the multitude, yet it was received with the thoughtless clamour of the whole loud city. Some people would like to applaud sermons, and there are sermons which are quite adequately appraised by such a welcome. Applause is a relief to one's feelings and, like any other discharge of feeling, it helps men to remain after an appeal what they were before it. But any serious presentation of truth asks for silence that it may be considered; and Jesus could not then, and He can seldom now, enjoy that privilege of silence. Men want what stirs their blood; and thus in His Church He still rides on amongst the excited feelings of a crowd who, by their shoutings, show that they have not stopped to understand.

W. M. MACGREGOR

THIS principle underlies the ancient Carthusian conception of the Christian life as constituted by a threefold labour—of heart, mind, and hand—a conception based upon a study of the Gospel, if not actually preserved by unbroken tradition from the earliest days of Christianity. This resolving of life into three main divisions—affection, thought, and action, is practically satisfactory. In each of these realms to have some strong central interest will secure the desired equilibrium of the soul. If religion be the central preoccupation of the heart, it will gain in strength, health, and endurance, if it be balanced by some keen discipline of the mind not directly connected with religion; and both will benefit by some outward work of art, skill, or ministration, which calls mainly upon the bodily powers and the practical intelligence, and not directly upon the intellect or the spirit.

As things are, this threefold labour is largely put in commission among three classes of society, to the great detriment of each. We have those whose hands are so ceaselessly exercised that their minds are crippled and their souls stifled. And we have intellect divorced from religion and action, and degenerating into intellectualism. And we have religion neither intelligent nor practical, and out of all sympathy with intellect and labour. Some degree of such specialization is inevitable and even desirable; but when it becomes absolute and complete there is no passage from the mind of one class to that of the other, no common ground of sympathy and understanding between the men of prayer and the men of thought and the men of action; and therefore no possibility of mutual influence—of that give-and-take whereby each class can supply to the others of its superabundance, and receive of theirs.

GEORGE TYRRELL

For some time before his death all his fears were calmed and absorbed by the prevalence of his faith, and his trust in the merits and *propitiation* of Jesus Christ.

He talked to me often about the necessity of faith in the *sacrifice* of Jesus, as necessary beyond all good works whatever, for the salvation of mankind.

He pressed me to study Dr. Clarke and to read his Sermons. I asked him why he pressed Dr. Clarke, an Arian. 'Because', said he, 'he is fullest on the propitiatory sacrifice.'

Johnson having thus in his mind the true Christian scheme, at once rational and consolatory, uniting justice and mercy in the DIVINITY, with the improvement of human nature, previous to his receiving the Holy Sacrament in his apartment, composed and fervently uttered this prayer:

'Almighty and most merciful Father, I am now, as to human eyes, it seems, about to commemorate, for the last time, the death of thy Son Jesus Christ, our Saviour and Redeemer. Grant, O Lord, that my whole hope and confidence may be in His merits, and Thy mercy; enforce and accept my imperfect repentance; make this commemoration available to the confirmation of my faith, the establishment of my hope, and the enlargement of my charity; and make the death of Thy Son Jesus Christ effectual to my redemption. Have mercy upon me, and pardon the multitude of my offences. Bless my friends; have mercy upon all men. Support me, by Thy Holy Spirit, in the days of weakness, and at the hour of death; and receive me, at my death, to everlasting happiness, for the sake of Jesus Christ. Amen.'

Having, as has been already mentioned, made his will on the 8th and 9th December, and settled all his worldly affairs, he languished till Monday, the 13th of that month, when he expired, about seven o'clock in the evening, with so little apparent pain that his attendants hardly perceived when his dissolution took place.

JAMES BOSWELL

THERE are some instances of fortune and a fair condition that cannot stand with some others, but if you desire this, you must lose that, and unless you be content with one, you lose the comfort of both. If you covet learning, you must have leisure and a retired life: if to be a politician, you must go abroad and get experience, and do all businesses, and keep all company, and have no leisure at all. If you will be rich, you must be frugal: if you will be popular, you must be bountiful: if a philosopher, you must despise riches. The Greek, that designed to make the most exquisite picture that could be imagined, fancied the eye of Chione, and the hair of Paegnium, and Tarsia's lip, Philenium's chin, and the forehead of Delphia, and set all these upon Milphidippa's neck, and thought that he should outdo both art and nature. But when he came to view the proportions, he found that what was excellent in Tarsia did not agree with the other excellence of Philenium; and although singly they were rare pieces, yet in the whole they made a most ugly face. The dispersed excellences and blessings of many men, if given to one, would not make a handsome but a monstrous fortune. Use therefore that faculty which nature hath given thee, and thy education hath made actual, and thy calling hath made a duty. But if thou desirest to be a saint, refuse not his persecution: if thou wouldst be famous as Epaminondas or Fabricius, accept also of their poverty; for that added lustre to their persons, and envy to their fortune, and their virtue without it could not have been so excellent. Let Euphorion sleep quietly with his rich old wife; and let Medius drink on with Alexander: and remember thou canst not have the riches of the first, unless you have the old wife too; nor the favour which the second had with his prince, unless you buy it at his price; that is, lay thy sobriety down at first, and thy health a little after: and then their condition, though it look splendidly, yet when you handle it on all sides, it will prick your fingers.

JEREMY TAYLOR

LOVE to God is, as regards its practical efficacy, something very different from mere love to the good in and for itself. In the former case we know that our doing and suffering cause joy or sorrow to the personal good One, and that is, in many cases, the only motive which can touch the heart.

✳ ✳ ✳

He who has no consciousness, no feeling, no impression of the vastness which characterizes belief in God and Christ, should say nothing at all on the subject.

✳ ✳ ✳

He who believes in the good is for this very reason directly under subjection and responsibility to God, even although he himself may be quite unaware of the fact.

✳ ✳ ✳

That which can alone adequately counterbalance our natural egotism is a lively faith in the holy God of love.

✳ ✳ ✳

Is it possible to become free from ourselves without faith in the living God?

✳ ✳ ✳

In the case of many we may be almost glad that they do not believe in God, because in this way their habitual discontent with their situation does not appear as if directed against God.

✳ ✳ ✳

The true position of a man's heart towards God is not that to which he has given expression out of opposition to another who has been seeking in some way to force belief upon him.

✳ ✳ ✳

Truly that man knows something of religion who can only wonder, in all humility, how God is able to make such a weak and (morally) fragile vessel a creature worthy of His grace.

✳ ✳ ✳

O how man prospers, when he is obedient to God!

RICHARD ROTHE

THE sweetest wife on sweetest marriage-day,—
   Their souls at grapple in mid-way,
     Sweet to her sweet may say:

'I take you to my inmost heart, my true!'
   Ah, fool! but there is one heart you
     Shall never take him to!

The hold that falls not when the town is got,
   The heart's heart, whose immurèd plot
     Hath keys yourself keep not!

Its gates are deaf to Love, high summoner;
   Yea, Love's great warrant runs not there:
     You are your prisoner.

Yourself are with yourself the sole consortress
   In that unleaguerable fortress;
     It knows you not for portress.

Its keys are at the cincture hung of God;
   Its gates are trepidant to His nod;
     By Him its floors are trod.

And if His feet shall rock those floors in wrath,
   Or blest aspersion sleek His path,
     Is only choice it hath.

Yea, in that ultimate heart's occult abode
   To lie as in an oubliette of God;
     Or as a bower untrod,

Built by a secret Lover for His Spouse;—
   Sole choice is this your life allows,
     Sad tree whose perishing boughs
      So few birds house.

FRANCIS THOMPSON

IT is a perilous thing to separate feeling from acting; to have learnt to feel rightly without acting rightly. It is a danger to which in a refined and polished age we are peculiarly exposed. The romance, the poem, and the sermon teach us how to feel. Our feelings are delicately correct. But the danger is this: feeling is given to lead to action; if feeling be suffered to awake without passing into duty, the character becomes untrue. When the emergency for real action comes, the feeling is as usual produced: but accustomed as it is to rise in fictitious circumstances without action, neither will it lead on to action in the real ones. 'We pity wretchedness and shun the wretched.' We utter sentiments, just, honourable, refined, lofty—but somehow, when a truth presents itself in the shape of a duty, we are unable to perform it. And so such characters become by degrees like the artificial pleasure-grounds of bad taste, in which the waterfall does not fall, and the grotto offers only the refreshment of an imaginary shade, and the green hill does not strike the skies, and the tree does not grow. Their lives are a sugared crust of sweetness trembling over black depths of hollowness: more truly still, 'whited sepulchres', fair without to look upon, 'within full of all uncleanness'.

It is perilous again to separate thinking rightly from acting rightly. He is already half false who speculates on truth and does not do it. Truth is given, not to be contemplated, but to be done. Life is an action, not a thought. And the penalty paid by him who speculates on truth is that by degrees the very truth he holds becomes to him a falsehood.

F. W. ROBERTSON

THE hearts and minds of the Apostles are filled with the thought and the love of Him who had redeemed them and in whom they had found their true life, and with the work which they were to do in His service, for His glory, for the spreading of His Kingdom. This too was one of the greatest and most blessed among the truths which Luther was especially ordained to reproclaim—that we are not to spend our days in watching our own vices, in gazing at our own sins, in stirring and raking up all the mud of our past lives; but to lift our thoughts from our own corrupt nature to Him who put on that nature in order to deliver it from corruption, and to fix our contemplations and our affections on Him who came to clothe us in His perfect righteousness, and through whom and in whom, if we are united to Him by a living faith, we too become righteous. Thus, like the Apostle, we are to forget that which is behind, and to keep our eyes bent on the prize of our high calling, to which we are to press onward, and which we may attain, in Christ Jesus.

I cannot enter here into the questions how far and what kinds of self-examination are necessary as remedial, medicinal measures, in consequence of our being already in so diseased a condition. These are questions of ascetic discipline, the answers to which will vary according to the exigencies of each particular case, even as do the remedies prescribed by a wise physician for bodily ailments. I merely wish to show that, in the Christian view of man, no less than in the natural, the healthy normal state is not the subjective, but the objective, that in which, losing his own individual insulated life, he finds it again in Christ, that in which he does not make himself the object of his contemplation and action, but directs them both steadily and continually toward the will and the glory of God.

AUGUSTUS and J. C. HARE

Sero Te Amavi

WHERE then did I find Thee, that I might learn Thee? For in my memory Thou wert not, before I learned Thee. Where then did I find Thee, that I might learn Thee, but in Thyself above me? . . . Everywhere, O Truth, dost Thou give audience to all who ask counsel of Thee, and at once answerest all, though on manifold matters they ask Thy counsel. Clearly dost Thou answer, though all do not clearly hear. All consult Thee on what they will, though they hear not always what they will. He is Thy best servant who looks not so much to hear that from Thee which is conformable to his own will, as rather to conform his will to what he heareth from Thee.

Too late loved I Thee, O Thou Beauty of ancient days, yet ever new! too late I loved Thee! And behold Thou wert within, and I abroad, and there I searched for Thee; deformed as I was, running after those beauties which Thou hast made. Thou wert with me, but I was not with Thee. Things held me far from Thee —things which, unless they were in Thee, were not at all. Thou calledst and shoutedst and didst pierce my deafness. Thou flashedst and shonest and didst dispel my blindness. Thou didst send forth Thy fragrance, and I drew in breath and panted for Thee. I tasted, and still I hunger and thirst. Thou touchedst me, and I burned for Thy peace. . . .

And now my whole life is in nothing but in Thine exceeding great mercy. Give what Thou commandest, and command what Thou wilt.

ST. AUGUSTINE

BLESSED they who shall at length behold what as yet mortal eye hath not seen and faith only enjoys! Those wonderful things of the new world are even now as they shall be then. They are immortal and eternal; and the souls who shall then be made conscious of them will see them in their calmness and their majesty where they have ever been. But who can express the surprise and rapture which will come upon those who then at last apprehend them for the first time, and to whose perceptions they are new! Who can imagine by a stretch of fancy the feelings of those who, having died in faith, wake up to enjoyment! The life then begun, we know, will last for ever; yet surely if memory be to us then what it is now, that will be a day much to be observed unto the Lord through all the ages of eternity. We may increase indeed for ever in knowledge and in love; still that first waking from the dead, the day at once of our birth and our espousals, will ever be endeared and hallowed in our thoughts. When we find ourselves after long rest gifted with fresh powers, vigorous with the seed of eternal life within us, able to love God as we wish, conscious that all trouble, sorrow, pain, anxiety, bereavement is over for ever, blessed in the full affection of those earthly friends whom we loved so poorly, and could protect so feebly, while they were with us in the flesh, and above all visited by the immediate visible ineffable Presence of God Almighty, with His only-begotten Son our Lord Jesus Christ, and His co-equal, co-eternal Spirit, that great sight in which is the fullness of joy and pleasure for evermore—what deep, incommunicable, unimaginable thoughts will be then upon us! What depths will be stirred up within us! What secret harmonies awaked, of which human nature seemed incapable!

JOHN HENRY NEWMAN

I KNOW no one so good that he has not need to look ceaselessly into and test and know his heart, what is therein; and also often to find fault with all he does, which must be done with humility. God's voice taught me this because I never did anything so well that I could not have done it better. My weaknesses reproved me thus: 'Ah wretched creature! how long wilt thou hide thy useless habits in thy five senses? Our childhood was foolish, and youth troubled; how we conquered it is known only to God. Alas! now in my old age I find much to chide, for it can produce no shining works and is cold and without grace. It is powerless, now that it no longer has youth to help it to bear the fiery love of God. It is also impatient, for little ills afflict it much which in youth it hardly noticed. Yet a good old age is full of patient waiting and trusts in God alone.'

Seven years ago a troubled old soul lamented these weaknesses to our Lord. God answered thus: 'Thy childhood was a companion to My Holy Spirit; thy youth was a bride of My humanity, in thine old age thou art a humble house-wife of My Godhead.'

Alas, dear Lord! what use is it that the dog barks? While the owner sleeps the thief breaks into the house! . . . I know an enemy who, if one does not forbid him to enter, destroys God's truth in the heart. If one gives him a chance, he writes false wisdom in the heart which makes it say to itself, 'I am by nature weak and bad.' But for that reason thou canst not honourably crave forgiveness from God. Through grace thou must become strong and good. 'But I have no grace!' Then thou must call on the God of grace to grant thee grace with humble tears, steadfast prayer, and holy desire. Thus the worm of evil must die. Thou must do violence to thyself so that no suffering and no power can gain mastery over thee; thus the worm of evil is done away. If we would overcome and drive away our anger and all our imperfections, with God's help, then we must secretly stifle our sinful temptations and show ourselves outwardly full of holy joy.

MECHTHILD OF MAGDEBURG

WELL, Scholar, having taught you to paint your rod, and we having still a mile to Tottenham High Cross, I will, as we walk towards it in the cool shade of this sweet honeysuckle hedge, mention to you some of the thoughts and joys that have possessed my soul since we two met together. And these thoughts shall be told you, that you also may join with me in thankfulness to 'the Giver of every good and perfect gift' for our happiness. And that our present happiness may appear to be the greater, and we the more thankful for it, I will beg you to consider with me how many do, even at this very time, lie under the torment of the stone, the gout, and toothache; and this we are free from. And every misery that I miss is a new mercy: and therefore let us be thankful. There have been, since we met, others that have met disasters of broken limbs; some have been blasted, others thunderstrucken; and we have been freed from these: let us therefore rejoice and be thankful. Nay, which is a far greater mercy, we are free from the unsupportable burthen of an accusing tormenting conscience; a misery that none can bear: and therefore let us praise Him for His preventing grace and say, Every misery that I miss is a new mercy. Nay, let me tell you, there be many that have forty times our estates, that would give the greatest part of it to be healthful and cheerful like us; who with the expense of a little money have eat, and drunk, and laughed, and angled, and sung, and slept securely; and rose next day, and cast away care, and sung, and laughed, and angled again; which are blessings rich men cannot purchase with all their money. Let me tell you, Scholar, I have a rich neighbour that is always so busy that he has no leisure to laugh: the whole business of his life is to get money, and more money, that he may still get more and more money; he is still drudging on. . . . Let us, therefore, be thankful for health and a competence and, above all, for a quiet conscience.

IZAAK WALTON

I READ how Edward the First ingeniously surprised the Welsh into subjection, proffering them such a prince as should be,

1. The son of a king.
2. Born in their own country.
3. Whom none could tax for any fault.

The Welsh accepted the conditions, and the king tendered them his son Edward, an infant, newly born in the castle of Carnarvon.

Do not all these qualifications mystically centre themselves in my Saviour?

1. The King of heaven saith unto Him, Thou art my Son, this day have I begotten Thee.
2. Our true countryman, real flesh, whereas he took not on Him the nature of angels.
3. Without spot or blemish, like to us in all things, sin only excepted.

Away then with those wicked men who will not have this King to rule over them. May He have dominion in and over me. Thy kingdom come. Heaven and earth cannot afford a more proper prince for the purpose, exactly accomplished with all these comfortable qualifications.

THOMAS FULLER

IT must be immediately evident that every religious assurance of grace and every concomitant emotion of contrition contain certain perils to a socio-moral passion which strives to correct the imperfections of society and which must count upon impatient and, on the whole, self-righteous men to perform the task. The knowledge of the equal sinfulness of all human nature is not completely compatible with a social purpose which sets the relatively good ideal against the relative injustices of society. This incompatibility between the temper of classical religion and strenuous morality proves that the relation of religion and morality is never simple and is not exhausted in their mutual support of each other on certain levels. In certain areas the conflict is permanent; but its permanency does not justify the suppression of one in favour of the other.

All men who live with any degree of serenity live by some assurance of grace. In every life there must at least be times and seasons when the good is felt as a present possession and not as a far-off goal. The sinner must feel himself 'justified', that is, he must feel that his imperfections are understood and sympathetically appreciated as well as challenged. Whenever he finds himself in a circle of love where he is 'completely known and all forgiven', something of the mercy of God is revealed to him and he catches a glimpse of the very perfection which has eluded him. Perhaps the most sublime insight of Jewish prophets and the Christian gospel is the knowledge that since perfection is love, the apprehension of perfection is at once the means of seeing one's imperfection and the consoling assurance of grace which makes this realization bearable. This ultimate paradox of high religion is not an invention of theologians or priests. It is constantly validated by the most searching experiences of life.

REINHOLD NIEBUHR

ALL seed-sowing is a mysterious thing, whether the seed fall into the earth or into souls. Man is a husbandman; his whole work rightly understood is to develop life, to sow it everywhere. Such is the mission of humanity, and of this divine mission the great instrument is speech. We forget too often that language is both a seed-sowing and a revelation. The influence of a word in season, is it not incalculable? What a mystery is speech! But we are blind to it, because we are carnal and earthy. We see the stones and the trees by the road, the furniture of our houses, all that is palpable and material. We have no eyes for the invisible phalanxes of ideas which people the air and hover incessantly around each one of us.

Every life is a profession of faith and exercises an inevitable and silent propaganda. As far as lies in its power, it tends to transform the universe and humanity into its own image. Thus we all have a cure of souls. Every man is a centre of perpetual radiation like a luminous body; he is, as it were, a beacon which entices a ship upon the rocks if it does not guide it into port. Every man is a priest, even involuntarily; his conduct is an unspoken sermon, which is for ever preaching to others;—but there are priests of Baal, of Moloch, and of all the false gods. Such is the high importance of example. Thence comes the terrible responsibility which weighs upon us all. An evil example is a spiritual poison: it is the proclamation of a sacrilegious faith, of an impure God. Sin would be an evil only for him who commits it, were it not a crime towards the weak brethren, whom it corrupts. Therefore it has been said: 'It were better for a man not to have been born than to offend one of these little ones.'

HENRI-FRÉDÉRIC AMIEL

THEN said Christian to his fellow, Yonder is a man with his back toward Sion, and he is coming to meet us. . . . So he drew nearer and nearer, and at last came up with them. His name was Atheist, and he asked them whither they were going.

CHRISTIAN. We are going to Mount Sion.

Then fell! Atheist into very great laughter.

CHRISTIAN. What is the meaning of your laughter?

ATHEIST. I laugh to see what ignorant persons you are, to take upon you so tedious a journey; and yet ye are like to have nothing but your travel for your pains.

CHRISTIAN. Why, man? Do you think we shall not be received?

ATHEIST. Received! There is no such place as you dream of in all this world.

CHRISTIAN. But there is a world to come.

ATHEIST. When I was at home in mine own country, I heard as you now affirm, and from that hearing went out to see, and have been seeking this City this twenty years; but find no more of it than I did the first day I set out.

CHRISTIAN. We have both heard and believe that there is such a place to be found.

ATHEIST. Had not I, when at home, believed, I had not come thus far to seek. But finding none (and yet I should, had there been such a place to be found, for I have gone to seek it further than you), I am going back again, and will seek to refresh myself with the things that I then cast away, for hopes of that which I now see is not.

Then said Christian to Hopeful, his fellow, Is it true which this man hath said?

HOPEFUL. Take heed, he is one of the flatterers; remember what it hath cost us once already for our hearkening to such kind of fellows. What! No Mount Sion! Did we not see from the Delectable Mountains the Gate of the City?

JOHN BUNYAN

ONCE more the sickle had done its work, and the golden grain was garnered. For the shadow of the days had gone forward upon the dial, whose ancient graven circles, dimmed with green rust, timed the equinox and the march of the firmament. . . . The blue-stained sunbeam moved onward, the sun declined, and the weariful women came homeward from the gleaning and the labour of the field.

Do you suppose these women moved in rhythmic measures to Bacchanalian song and pastoral pipe, as the women came home from the field with corn and grape,

'In Tempé and the dales of Arcady'?

Do you suppose their brows were wreathed with the honey-suckle's second autumn bloom, with streaked convolvulus and bronzed ears of wheat?

Their backs were bowed beneath great bundles of gleanings, or faggots of dead sticks, carefully sought for fuel, and they carried weary infants, restless and fretful. Their forms had lost all semblance to the graceful curve of woman; their faces were hard, wrinkled, and angular, drawn with pain and labour. Save by their garments, none could distinguish them from men. Yet they were not penned in narrow walls, but all things green and lovely were spread around them. The fresh breezes filled their nostrils in the spring with the delicate odour of the flowering bean-field and the clover scent; the very ground was gilded with sunshine beneath their feet. But the magic of it touched them not, for their hearts were pinched with poverty. These are they to whom the old, old promise bears its full significance: 'Come unto Me, all ye that labour and are heavy laden, and I will give you rest.'

RICHARD JEFFERIES

WE must studiously avoid all those objects that not only enkindle sinful desires in us, but even these that lead towards those, though at ever so great a distance. We must not only guard against things more grossly evil, but against the least things we see sinful; for he that willingly complies with any sin, because he judges it not of the most atrocious nature, is fairly on the way to the worst sins. We must also so contradict our sinful desires as not only to abstain from that which is evil, but to incline to that which is good, by considering that virtue which is opposite to it, practising it till we have thus come to an habitual delight in that opposition to those sins which do most easily beset us. We must also study always to be well employed, and take those necessary breathings and diversions our embodied state requires with persons virtuous and pious; that even then when we slacken the strictness of our watching over our minds, there be not a hazard of our being overcome or laid open to a temptation. And there is nothing more necessary than to allow ourselves in nothing, of what kind soever it be, that our consciences do witness to us is amiss, and never to study the silencing of conscience, whether it be when it deters us from any thing or calls us to mourn for any sin we have committed; for this brings on an habitual fearing of it; and as it provokes God to withdraw His Spirit from us, so we lose that exact sense of good and evil which a spiritual man must study to preserve as much as a natural man does the organs of sense. Having our minds thus delivered from the captivity of sense, and purified to an abhorrency of that which is evil, our next work must be to delight to do the will of God, and to have a general diffused love of mankind.

HENRY SCOUGAL

YOU have now these weeks at School, and whether you take them slackly and ungenerously, or keenly and with a nobly determined heart—*there they are*. They will have to be got through. And yet I am sure that if you take them in the latter way, looking at all the best sides of the School, and throwing yourself as fully into them as ever you can—the time will not only pass quicker, but will pass *doing you good*; otherwise it will pass, yes, but will *do you harm*; I now have come to feel that there is hardly anything more radically mean and deteriorating than, as it were, *sulking through the inevitable*, and just simply counting the hours till it passes.

* * *

When we first got to Rome, she was wonderfully plucky and courageous, 'grinning and bearing', a clear Stoic. But then gradually she became, in this too, more sensitively Christian. The Cross became, not simply a fact, to bear somehow as patiently as we can, but a source and channel of help, of purification, and of humble power—of a permanent deepening, widening, sweetening of the soul.

* * *

How wonderful it is, is it not, that literally only Christianity has taught us the true peace and function of suffering. The Stoics tried the hopeless little game of denying its objective reality, or of declaring it a good in itself (which it never is), and the Pessimists attempted to revel in it, as a food to their melancholy, and as something that can no more be transformed than it can be avoided or explained. But Christ came, and He did not really explain it; He did far more, He met it, willed it, transformed it, and He taught us how to do all this, or rather He Himself does it within us, if we do not hinder the all-healing hands.

BARON FRIEDRICH VON HÜGEL

THE love of our neighbour is the only door out of the dungeon of self, where we mope and mow, striking sparks, and rubbing phosphorescence out of the walls, and blowing our own breath in our own nostrils, instead of issuing to the fair sunlight of God, the sweet winds of the universe. The man thinks his consciousness is himself; whereas his life consisteth in the inbreathing of God, and the consciousness of the universe of truth. To have himself, to know himself, to enjoy himself, he calls life; whereas, if he would forget himself, tenfold would be his life in God and his neighbours. The region of man's life is a spiritual region. God, his friends, his neighbours, his brothers all, is the wide world in which alone his spirit can find room. Himself is his dungeon. If he feels it not now, he will yet feel it one day—feel it as a living soul would feel being prisoned in a dead body, wrapped in sevenfold cerements, and buried in a stone-ribbed vault within the last ripple of the sound of chanting people in the church above. His life is not in knowing that he lives, but in loving all forms of life. He is made for the All; for God, who is the All, is his life. And the essential joy of his life lies abroad in the liberty of the All. His delights, like those of the Ideal Wisdom, are with the sons of men. His health is in the body of which the Son of Man is the head. The whole region is open to him—nay, he must live in it or perish.

GEORGE MACDONALD

WE know that in the moral, as in the physical order, nature abhors a vacancy. Consciously or unconsciously, as the years go by, all men more and more submit their lives to some allegiance; with whatever uncertainty and changefulness, some one motive, or group of motives, grows stronger and stronger in them; they tend, at least, to bring every thought into captivity to some one obedience. For better or for worse, things which seemed difficult or impossible a few years ago will come almost naturally to a man a few years hence; he will have got accustomed to take a certain course, to obey certain impulses or principles wherever they appear. We may indeed distinguish three states in which a man may be. He may be yielding his heart more and more to the love of self, in whatsoever way of pride, or avarice, or lust, or sloth. Or he may be yielding his heart more and more to the love of God, falteringly, it may be, with many struggles and failures, but still really getting to love God more, to move more readily and more loyally to do God's will wherever he sees it. Or, thirdly, he may be like the man of whom our Lord spoke. He may, by God's grace, have cast out an evil spirit from his heart; he may have broken away from the mastery of some bad passion, some tyrannous hunger or hatred; and he may be hesitating, keeping his heart swept, clear and empty; his will may be poised, as it were, between the one love and the other. Ah! but that can only be for a very little while. That balance never lasts; one way or the other the will must incline; one service or the other must be chosen, and that soon.

FRANCIS PAGET

WHEN once thy foot enters the church, be bare.
God is more there than thou; for thou art there
Only by His permission. Then beware,
And make thyself all reverence and fear.
   Kneeling ne'er spoiled silk stockings; quit thy state.
   All equal are within the church's gate. . . .

In time of service seal up both thine eyes,
And send them to thy heart; that, spying sin,
They may wash out the stains by them did rise;
Those doors being shut, all by the ear comes in.
   Who marks in church-time others' symmetry
   Makes all their beauty his deformity.

Let vain or busy thoughts have there no part,
Bring not thy plough, thy plots, thy pleasures thither.
Christ purged His temple; so must thou thy heart.
All worldly thoughts are but thieves met together
   To cozen thee. Look to thy actions well;
   For churches are either our heaven or hell.

Judge not the preacher, for he is thy judge;
If thou mislike him, thou conceiv'st him not.
God calleth preaching folly. Do not grudge
To pick out treasures from an earthen pot.
   The worst speaks something good: if all want sense,
   God takes a text, and preacheth patience.

He that gets patience, and the blessing which
Preachers conclude with, hath not lost his pains.
He that by being at church, escapes the ditch,
Which he might fall in by companions, gains.
   He that loves God's abode, and to combine
   With saints on earth, shall one day with them shine.

GEORGE HERBERT

WHERE would you expect to find the body of Christ, and what would you expect to find it doing?

For the greater part of His life, Jesus lived as a working man: He was apprenticed in a joiner's yard and, it may be inferred, became on Joseph's death the breadwinner for a household of at least eight persons. For the greater part of His life, the body of Christ was exercised in the common processes of industry. Do you think He was out to make a fortune in those years? Do you think slipshod work came out of that shop—badly mortised joints or flaws filled in with putty? Do you think that His apprentices were overworked or underpaid? Do you think that He treated them as impersonal 'hands'? The Church is called to be the Body of Christ in industry. The term 'Church worker' is apt to call up a picture of the Sunday-school teacher or the collector for Foreign Missions, and no one who knows the Church from the inside will slight their important services; but there is a kind of Church worker for whom our age even more urgently calls, and on whom the life and example of Christ set more immediately the seal of discipleship—the man who, to the glory of God and for the good of his fellows, does honest work of the everyday sort; the man who, in the context of that work, is being delivered, reach after reach, from the deep egotism of human nature . . .; the man behind the counter, or at the loom, or in the manager's office, or on the University bench or rostrum, who sees his daily life, and lives it, not as a drudgery, still less as a fight for his own advantage, but as a devotion, a thing offered, his contribution to God's plan of building a wholesome communal life upon the earth. These are the lives which all along have kept society sane and sweet, or rather— alas for human nature!—have kept it from lapsing altogether into savagery; these are Christ's Church on one great and permanent level of its manifold life; these are members of the Body of the Carpenter of Nazareth.

A. C. CRAIG

THE commandment of absolute truthfulness is really only another name for the fullness of discipleship. Only those who follow Jesus and cleave to Him are living in absolute truthfulness. Such men have nothing to hide from their Lord. He knows them and has placed them in a state where truth prevails. They cannot hide their sinfulness from Jesus; for they have not revealed themselves to Jesus, but He has revealed Himself to them by calling them to follow Him. At the moment of their call Jesus showed up their sin and made them aware of it. Absolute truthfulness is possible only where sin has been uncovered, that is to say, where it has been forgiven by Jesus. Only those who are in a state of truthfulness through the confession of their sin to Jesus are not ashamed to tell the truth wherever it must be told. The truthfulness which Jesus demands from His followers is the self-abnegation which does not hide sin. Nothing is then hidden, everything is brought forth to the light of day.

In this question of truthfulness, what matters first and last is that a man's whole condition should be exposed, his whole evil laid bare in the sight of God. But sinful men do not like this sort of truthfulness, and they resist it with all their might. That is why they persecute it and crucify it. It is only because we follow Jesus that we can be genuinely truthful, for then He reveals to us our sin upon the cross. The cross is God's truth about us, and therefore it is the only power which can make us truthful. When we know the cross we are no longer afraid of the truth.

DIETRICH BONHOEFFER

WHO that knows anything of the conditions of human knowledge, of the difficulties of the search for truth, and of the innumerable influences that affect human beliefs, can for a moment think that mental unrest and doubt may not in God's sight be free from blame, or that theological errors, even the gravest in our eyes, are sins to be punished rather than simply calamities to be pitied? No one acquainted with the theological literature of our day but must be aware how grave, thoughtful, earnest—how utterly different from the offensive levity or ribald flippancy of a former time— is the tone of many who have been led farthest aside from the path of what we deem the orthodox faith, the tone of such thinkers as Carlyle and Sterling and Clough and the brothers Newman. . . . Can we apply to such men, or think of God as applying to them, the same anathema that is pronounced on the profligate and the vile? . . . Is it not, I do not say more charitable, but more truly reverential to think that these errors and difficulties are but the discipline by which the God of Truth is leading them onwards to Himself, and that in His own time and way, here or hereafter, from the labyrinth in which they seem to be lost, His loving hand will guide them out into the light of that eternal truth for which here they have so passionately yet so vainly longed? I believe in God the Father Almighty, Maker of heaven and earth, and in Jesus Christ His only Son our Lord; all my hopes for humanity are centred in the gospel of His grace; but it would be a greater denial of that God and Saviour, it would be to ascribe to His nature an incongruity and self-contradiction more monstrous than to deny Him altogether, to conceive Him casting into irrevocable darkness souls that here in vain have been groping after the light. I do not hesitate to say that it were better to perish with the unbeliever than to be saved with the believer in such a God as this.

JOHN CAIRD

THE fear of death often proves mortal, and sets people on methods to save their lives which infallibly destroy them. This is a reflection made by some historians, upon observing that there are many more thousands killed in a flight than in a battle, and may be applied to those multitudes of imaginary sick persons that break their constitutions by physic, and throw themselves into the arms of death by endeavouring to escape it. This method is not only dangerous, but below the practice of a reasonable creature. To consult the preservation of life as the only end of it, to make our health our business, to engage in no action that is not part of a regimen or course of physic, are purposes so abject, so mean, so unworthy human nature, that a generous soul would rather die than submit to them. Besides that a continual anxiety for life vitiates all the relishes of it, and casts a gloom over the whole face of nature; as it is impossible we should take delight in anything that we are every moment afraid of losing.

I do not mean, by what I have here said, that I think anyone to blame for taking due care of their health. On the contrary, as cheerfulness of mind and capacity for business are in a great measure the effects of a well-tempered constitution, a man cannot be at too much pains to cultivate and preserve it. But this care, which we are prompted to not only by common sense but by duty and instinct, should never engage us in groundless fears, melancholy apprehensions, and imaginary distempers, which are natural to every man who is more anxious to live than how to live. In short, the preservation of life should be only a secondary concern, and the direction of it our principal. If we have this frame of mind, we shall take the best means to preserve life, without being over-solicitous about the event; and shall arrive at that point of felicity which Martial has mentioned as the perfection of happiness, of neither fearing nor wishing for death.

JOSEPH ADDISON

THEY lost all they had. Their faith? Their godliness? The possessions of the hidden man of the heart, which in the sight of God are of great price? Did they lose these? For these are the wealth of Christians, to whom the wealthy apostle said, 'Godliness with contentment is great gain. For we brought nothing into this world, and it is certain we can carry nothing out. And having food and raiment, let us be therewith content. But they that will be rich fall into temptation and a snare, and into many foolish and hurtful lusts, which drown men in destruction and perdition. For the love of money is the root of all evil; which, while some coveted after, they have erred from the faith, and pierced themselves through with many sorrows.' They, then, who lost their worldly all in the sack of Rome, if they owned their possessions as they had been taught by the apostle, who himself was poor without but rich within—that is to say, if they used the world as not using it—could say in the words of Job, heavily tried, but not overcome: 'Naked came I out of my mother's womb, and naked shall I return thither: the Lord gave, and the Lord hath taken away; as it pleased the Lord, so has it come to pass: blessed be the name of the Lord.' Like a good servant, Job counted the will of his Lord his great possession, by obedience to which his soul was enriched. But as to those feebler spirits who, though they cannot be said to prefer earthly possessions to Christ, do yet cleave to them with a somewhat immoderate attachment, they have discovered by the pain of losing these things how much they were sinning in loving them. For their grief is of their own making; in the words of the apostle quoted above, 'they have pierced themselves through with many sorrows'. For it was well that they who had so long despised these verbal admonitions should receive the teaching of experience.

ST. AUGUSTINE

No man shall ever behold the glory of Christ by sight hereafter, who doth not in some measure behold it by faith here in this world. Grace is a necessary preparation for glory, and faith for sight. Where the subject, the soul, is not previously seasoned with grace and faith, it is not capable of glory or vision. Nay, persons not disposed hereby unto it cannot desire it, whatever they pretend; they only deceive their own souls in supposing that so they do. . . .

I have seen and read somewhat of the writings of learned men concerning the state of future glory; some of them are filled with excellent notions of truth, and elegancy of speech, whereby they cannot but much affect the minds of them who duly consider what they say. But, I know not well whence it comes to pass, many complain that in reading of such discourses they are like a man who beholds his natural face in a glass and immediately forgets what manner of man he was. . . . The things spoken do not abide, nor incorporate with our minds. They please and refresh for a little while, like a shower of rain in a dry season that soaketh not into the roots of things; the power of them doth not enter unto us. Is it not all from hence, that their notions of future things are not educed out of the experience which we have of the beginnings of them in this world; without which they can make no permanent abode in our minds, nor continue any influence upon our affections? Yea, the soul is disturbed, not edified, in all contemplations of future glory when things are proposed unto it whereof in this life it hath neither foretaste, sense, experience, nor evidence. No man ought to look for anything in heaven but what one way or other he hath some experience of in this life. If men were more fully persuaded hereof, they would be, it may be, more in the exercise of faith and love about heavenly things than for the most part they are.

JOHN OWEN

ON the day of Pentecost, when the first influences of the Spirit descended on the early Church, the effects resembled intoxication. They were full of the Spirit, and mocking bystanders said, 'These men are full of new wine.' . . .

The play of imagination in the brain of the opium-eater is as free as that of genius itself, and the creations produced in that state by the pen or pencil are as wildly beautiful as those owed to nobler influences. In years gone by the oratory of the statesman in the senate has been kindled by semi-intoxication, when his noble utterances were set down by his auditors to the inspiration of patriotism.

It is this very resemblance which deceives the drunkard; he is led on by his feelings as well as by his imagination. It is not the sensual pleasure of the glutton that fascinates him. It is those fine thoughts and those quickened sensibilities which were excited in that state, which he is powerless to produce out of his own being, or by his own powers, and which he expects to reproduce by the same means. The experience of our first parent is repeated in him: at the very moment when he expects to find himself as the gods, knowing good and evil, he discovers that he is unexpectedly degraded, his health wrecked, and his heart demoralized. Hence it is almost as often the finer as the baser spirits of our race which are found the victims of such indulgence. Many will remember while I speak the names of the gifted of their species, the degraded men of genius who were the victims of these deceptive influences; the half-inspired painter, poet, musician, who began by soothing opiates to calm the over-excited nerves or stimulate the exhausted brain, who mistook the sensation for somewhat half divine, and became morally and physically wrecks of manhood, degraded even in their mental conceptions.

F. W. ROBERTSON

ZOPHAR the Naamathite mentioneth a sort of men in whose mouths wickedness is sweet, they hide it under their tongues, they spare it and forsake it not, but keep it still in their mouths. This furnisheth me with a tripartite division of men in the world.

The first and best are those who spit sin out, loathing it in their judgements, and leaving it in their practice.

The second sort, notoriously wicked, who swallow sin down, actually and openly committing it.

The third, endeavouring an expedient betwixt heaven and hell, neither do nor deny their lusts; neither spitting them out nor swallowing them down, but rolling them under their tongues, epicurizing thereon, in their filthy fancies and obscene speculations.

If God at the last day of Judgement hath three hands, a right for the sheep, a left for the goats, the middle is most proper for these third sort of men. But both these latter kinds of sinners shall be confounded together. The rather because a sin thus rolled, becomes so soft and supple, and the throat is so short and slippery a passage, that insensibly it may slide down from the mouth into the stomach; and contemplative wantonness quickly turns into practical uncleanness.

THOMAS FULLER

THE family, like the home in which they live, needs to be kept in repair, lest some little rift in the walls should appear and let in the wind and rain. The happiness of a family depends very much on attention to little things. Order, comfort, regularity, cheerfulness, good taste, pleasant conversation—these are the ornaments of daily life, deprived of which it degenerates into a wearisome routine. There must be light in the dwelling, and brightness and pure spirits and cheerful smiles. Home is not usually the place of toil, but the place to which we return and rest from our labours; in which parents and children meet together and pass a joyful and careless hour. To have nothing to say to others at such times, in any rank of life, is a very unfortunate temper of mind, and may perhaps be regarded as a serious fault; at any rate, it makes a house vacant and joyless, and persons who are afflicted by this distemper should remember seriously that if it is not cured in time it will pursue them through life. It is one of the lesser troubles of the family; and there is yet another trouble—members of a family often misunderstand one another's characters. They are sensitive or shy or retired; or they have some fanciful sorrow which they cannot communicate to others; or something which was said to them has produced too deep an impression on their minds. In their own family they are like strangers; the inexperience of youth exaggerates this trial, and they have no one to whom they can turn for advice or help. This is the time for sympathy—the sympathy of a brother or sister, or father or mother—which unlocks the hidden sorrow, and purges away the perilous stuff which was depressing the mind and injuring the character. Sympathy, too, is the noblest exercise; of it is the Spirit of God working together with our spirit; it is warmth as well as light, putting into us a new heart, and taking away the stony heart which is dead to its natural surroundings.

BENJAMIN JOWETT

'THE secret things belong unto the Lord our God: but those things that are revealed belong unto us and to our children for ever, that we may do all the works of this law.' Many people are exercised about the future of their children more than about anything else that God has kept to Himself. They would like to know how their sons will bear themselves in the battle of life, and especially how they will face its temptations. Will they pass victorious where their fathers stumbled and fell, or will their fathers be humbled and horrified to see their old sins looking out on them from the eyes of their sons? What kind of settlement will their daughters have in the days to come? Will they marry, and happily? Or will it be necessary to make them independent of any resources but their own? If only we knew what to provide against! Of all these things we neither know nor can know anything: the future is wholly in the hand of God. But we do know what is the will of God both for ourselves and for those who come after us; and it is what we know that fixes our duty. Above all other books in the Bible Deuteronomy is the book of religious education and of the promises attached to it. 'These words which I command thee this day shall be upon thine heart: and thou shalt teach them diligently unto thy children, and shalt talk of them when thou sittest in thy house, and when thou walkest by the way, and when thou liest down, and when thou risest up.' No duty could be enforced more urgently, and in our blank ignorance of the future there is none upon which so much depends. If we want to have any insurance against its painful possibilities, it is here we must find it. What God requires of parents is not a provision for the future of their children which enables them to defy Providence, but such a training of their children in the knowledge of God and in obedience to Him as will make them secure of God's friendship. It is a training 'to do all the words of this law', and where it has been effectively given the future may be safely left with God.

JAMES DENNEY

A WISE man will make haste to forgive, because he knows the true value of time, and will not suffer it to pass away in unnecessary pain. He that willingly suffers the corrosions of inveterate hatred, and gives up his days and nights to the gloom of malice and perturbation of stratagem, cannot surely be said to consult his ease. Resentment is a union of sorrow with malignity: a combination of a passion which all endeavour to avoid, with a passion which all concur to detest. The man who retires to meditate mischief and to exasperate his own rage—whose thoughts are employed only on means of distress and contrivances of ruin—whose mind never pauses from the remembrance of his own sufferings but to indulge some hope of enjoying the calamities of another—may justly be numbered among the most miserable of human beings, among those who are guilty without reward, who have neither the gladness of prosperity nor the calm of innocence.

Whoever considers the weakness both of himself and others will not long want persuasives to forgiveness. We know not to what degree of malignity any injury is to be imputed, or how much its guilt, if we were to inspect the mind of him that committed it, would be extenuated by mistake, precipitance, or negligence; we cannot be certain how much more we feel than was intended to be inflicted, or how much we increase the mischief to ourselves by voluntary aggravations. We may charge to design the effects of accident; we may think the blow violent only because we have made ourselves delicate and tender; we are on every side in danger of error and of guilt, which we are certain to avoid only by speedy forgiveness. . . .

Of him that hopes to be forgiven, it is indispensably required that he forgive. It is therefore superfluous to urge any other motive. On this great duty eternity is suspended; and to him that refuses to practise it, the throne of mercy is inaccessible, and the Saviour of the world has been born in vain.

SAMUEL JOHNSON

In meat and drink be thou scarce and wise. Whiles thou eatest or drinkest let not the memory of thy God that feeds thee pass from thy mind; but praise, bless, and glorify Him in ilka morsel, so that thy heart be more in God's praising than in thy meat, that thy soul be not parted from God at any hour. This doing, before Christ Jesu thou shalt be worthy a crown, and the temptations of the fiend that in meat and drink await most men and beguile them thou shalt eschew. Either soothly by unmannerly taking of food they are cast down from the heights of virtue, or by too mickle abstinence they break down that virtue. . . .

But truly abstinence by itself is not holiness, but if it be discreet it helps us to be holy. If it be indiscreet it lets holiness, because it destroys discipline, without which virtues are turned to vices. If a man would be singular in abstinence, he ought to eschew the sight of men and their praising, that he be not proud for nought and so lose all: for men truly ween they be holiest that they see most abstinent, when in truth ofttimes they are the worst.

He certain that has truly tasted the sweetness of endless love shall never deem himself to pass any man in abstinence, but the lower he supposes himself in abstinence anent himself, the more he shall be held marvellous among men. The best thing, and as I suppose pleasing to God, is to conform thyself in meat and drink to the time and place and estate of them with whom thou art; so that thou seem not to be wilful nor a feigner of religion. . . .

Truly the virtue of others is the more in that it is not seen of men. Who may know how much love a man has anent God, how great compassion anent his neighbour? And doubtless the virtue of charity surpasses without comparison all fasting or abstinence, and all other works that may be seen; and oft it happens that he that before men is seen least to fast, within, before Christ, is most fervent in love.

RICHARD ROLLE OF HAMPOLE

Happy those early days! when I
Shined in my angel infancy.
Before I understood this place
Appointed for my second race,
Or taught my soul to fancy ought
But a white, celestial thought,
When yet I had not walked above
A mile or two from my first love,
And looking back (at that short space,)
Could see a glimpse of his bright face;
When on some gilded cloud or flower
My gazing soul would dwell an hour,
And in those weaker glories spy
Some shadows of eternity;
Before I taught my tongue to wound
My conscience with a sinful sound,
Or had the black art to dispense
A several sin to every sense,
But felt through all this fleshly dress
Bright shoots of everlastingness.
   O how I long to travel back
And tread again that ancient track!
That I might once more reach that plain,
Where first I left my glorious train,
From whence the enlightened spirit sees
That shady City of palm trees;
But (ah!) my soul with too much stay
Is drunk and staggers in the way.
Some men a forward motion love,
But I by backward steps would move,
And when this dust falls to the urn
In that state I came return.

HENRY VAUGHAN

EVERY Jack sees in his own particular Jill charms and perfections
to the enchantment of which we stolid onlookers are stone-cold.
And which has the superior view of the absolute truth, he or we?
Which has the more vital insight into the nature of Jill's existence,
as a fact? Is he in excess, being in this matter a maniac? Or are
we in defect, being victims of a pathological anaesthesia as regards
Jill's magical importance? Surely the latter; surely to Jack are
the profounder truths revealed; surely poor Jill's palpitating little
life-throbs *are* among the wonders of creation, *are* worthy of this
sympathetic interest; and it is to our shame that the rest of us
cannot feel like Jack. For Jack realizes Jill concretely, and we do
not. He struggles towards a union with her inner life, divining
her feelings, anticipating her desires, understanding her limits
as manfully as he can, and yet inadequately too; for he also is
afflicted with some blindness, even here. Whilst we, dead clods
that we are, do not even seek after these things, but are contented
that that portion of eternal fact named Jill should be for us as if
it were not, Jill, who knows her inner life, knows that Jack's way
of taking it—so importantly—is the true and serious way; and
she responds to the truth in him by taking him seriously too.
May the ancient blindness never wrap its clouds about either of
them again! Where would any of *us* be, were there no one willing
to know us as we really are; or ready to repay us for *our* insight
by making recognizant return? We ought, all of us, to realize
each other in this intense, pathetic, and important way.

If you say that this is absurd, and that we cannot be in love
with everyone at once, I merely point out to you that, as a matter
of fact, certain persons do exist with an enormous capacity for
friendship and for taking delight in other people's lives; and that
such persons know more of truth than if their hearts were not
so big. The vice of ordinary Jack and Jill affection is not its intensity, but its exclusions and jealousies.

WILLIAM JAMES

ST. AUGUSTINE says: 'Nothing is so certain as death, and nothing is so uncertain as the hour of death.' For wherever and however it may come, of the time and the hour knoweth no man. Therefore nothing can be more necessary than that we should be ready at all times, and that we should know that we are, and not only hope so. We have been placed in this life, not only to do the works, but also that we may know, so that our works may grow out of knowledge, as fruit grows out of the tree. Therefore our work in this life is to gain more knowledge, and so to come nearer to God. He who has forced his way through and who, according to the will of God, can lift up his mind above this world, and who has ordered his life and his secret thoughts aright, will not be confused, distracted, or hindered by the things that pertain to this life, but they will serve only to drive him to God. Therefore if a man's mind and inclinations are steadfastly fixed on God with pure intention, and his ways are ordered in peace while he remains undisturbed in all good works, it is a sure sign that he is a righteous man and that all his works are pure and true. This he seems to desire earnestly at all times; for he is like a corpse buried in the ground, that his soul may be buried in the depths of the Godhead. We have been placed in this world for this reason and for none other. Whatever we neglect here will be lost to us for all eternity. To him whose superscription is on the penny will the penny be most certainly given. Therefore every man should often search out his own heart, and seek diligently till he find whose superscription is there; what it is that he most loves and thinks of, whether it is God or himself or created beings, either living or dead. That which most fills his mind, his heart, his soul, that to which he most joyfully responds, whether from without or from within, will claim the penny with the superscription and will receive it without any questioning. The man who searches out these things with real care will assuredly learn to whom he belongs; it will not only be guess-work.

JOHANN TAULER

KNOW that when unhappily thou thinkest any evil of thy brother, some root of that same evil is in thine own heart which, in proportion as it is ill disposed, readily receives any like object which it meets with.

Therefore whenever it comes into thy mind to judge others for some fault, be wroth against thyself as guilty of the same, and say in thine heart, 'How is it that I, wretched being, buried in this and far heavier faults, dare to lift up my head to see and judge the faults of others?'

And thus the weapons which, directed against others, would have wounded thee, being used against thyself, will bring healing to thy wounds. . . .

And be very sure that all good and kindly feeling towards thy neighbour is the gift of the Holy Spirit; and all contempt, rash judgement, and bitterness towards him comes from thine own evil and from the suggestions of Satan.

*   *   *

Never speak of thyself or thy doings, nor of thy kindred save in cases of absolute necessity, and then with all possible reserve and brevity. If others seem to speak overmuch of themselves, try to give a good meaning to their conduct, but do not imitate it, even though they should speak in a humble and self-accusing way.

Speak as little as may be of thy neighbour or of anything that concerns him, unless an opportunity offers to say something good of him.

LORENZO SCUPOLI

IF we are in fact strangers and pilgrims, we have certain conclusions to draw which concern our daily lives. There is a counsel which is found in most spiritual religions, and indeed also in some philosophies, that we should cultivate detachment. This has not meant, in the minds of the best spiritual guides, that we should wrap ourselves in an inhuman aloofness from the affairs of men, or that we should look on life as a spectacle in which we have no vital concern, but it does mean that we should live in this world as if we did not wholly belong to it and that we should avoid that complete absorption in its vicissitudes into which the most eager spirits easily fall. It is wise to remind ourselves that even our most cherished ambitions and interests are passing; the soul will grow out of them or at least must leave them behind.

We look backward, perhaps, at the pleasant days we have known, and we linger in the past, reluctant to let it go; or the present may be so vivid and captivating that we would hold on to it, and we resent the law which compels us to move on to unknown scenes. But to the pilgrim these passages should not be wholly sad. He may feel regret, but not desolation; they do not cause him to rebel. These phases of life are incidents of the journey, but it is the way that matters, not the accidents of the road. The time has come to move on? Then break up the camp with a good heart; it is only one more stage on the journey home!

One day we shall break camp for the last time in this world and face the final adventure of death. May we then have so passed the days of our pilgrimage, with the Lord of adventurers by our side, that we may reach, in the end, our eternal home.

W. R. MATTHEWS

THE one thing to be careful about in approaching nature is that we really come to be taught; and the same attitude is honourably due to its interpreter, science. Religion is probably only learning for the first time how to approach science. Their former intercourse, from faults on both sides, and these mainly due to juvenility, is not a thing to remember. After their first quarrel—for they began the centuries hand in hand—the question of religion to science was simply, 'How dare you speak at all?' Then, as science held to its right to speak just a little, the question became, 'What new menace to our creed does your latest discovery portend?' By and by both became wiser and the coarser conflict ceased. Then we find religion suggesting a compromise, and asking simply what particular adjustment to its last hypothesis science would demand. But we do not speak now of the right to be heard, or of menaces to our faith, or even of compromises. Our question is a much maturer one—we ask what contribution science has to bestow, what good gift the wise men are bringing now to lay at the feet of Christ. This question marks an immense advance in the relation between science and Christianity, and we should be careful to sustain it. Nothing is more easily thrown out of working order than the balance between different spheres of thought.

The result of the modern systematic study of nature has been to raise up in our midst a body of truth with almost unique claims to acceptance. The grounds of this acceptance are laid bare to all the world. There is nothing esoteric about science. It has no secrets. . . . The mere presence of this body of truth, so solid, so transparent, so verifiable, immediately affects all else that lies in the field of knowledge. Some things it scatters to the winds at once. They have been the birthright of man for ages, it may be; their venerableness matters not, they must go. And the power of the newcomer is so self-evident that they require no telling, but disappear of themselves. In this way the modern world has been rid of a hundred superstitions.

HENRY DRUMMOND

NOTHING is so paralysing and destructive to the human spirit as the thought of ultimate waste. Yet that is just the appearance which much in human life seems inevitably to take on. And the more a man loves and seeks higher things the more likely is the grim spectre of such a thought to jostle the elbow, peer grinningly into the face, and freeze the very marrow of the soul. What if things are after all exactly as they seem so often to be and there is at the heart of the universe only a great hole through which all the sacrifice, all the loving and loyalty, all the yearning of the race pours age after age and is lost. What if, whatever we do, it all comes to the same thing in the end? . . .

Well, Jesus knew that there is not a great hole at the heart of things, but GOD, and He calls His disciples to share that knowledge, calls them to have that steadiness that comes from knowing not only that there are harvests but that despite all appearances they are eternally preserved. 'He that reapeth gathereth fruit unto life eternal.'

No doubt we have here at first to commit ourselves to a faith and a vision which transcend our own. But we must do that or surrender to an ultimate despair. If Christ has grappled our hearts to Himself at all, then it were surely wise to trust His certainties and not our own doubts, however persistent. I for one have decided to take my stand by Him and to believe that howsoever or whensoever God's kingdom is consummated, it will be abundantly clear that nothing, despite all the appearances, has been lost.

H. H. FARMER

OUR songs and psalms sorely vex and grieve the devil, whereas our passions and impatiences, our complainings and cryings, our 'Alas!' and 'Woe is me!' please him well, so that he laughs in his fist. He takes delight in tormenting us, especially when we confess, praise, preach, and laud Christ. For, seeing the devil is a prince of this world and our utter enemy, we must be content to let him pass through his own country. He must needs have imposts and customs duties of us, striking our bodies with manifold plagues.

*   *   *

I am a great enemy to flies; *quia sunt imagines diaboli et haereticorum.* When I have a good book, they flock upon it and parade up and down upon it, and soil it. 'Tis just the same with the devil. When our hearts are purest, he comes and soils them.

*   *   *

When I am assailed with heavy tribulations, I rush out among my pigs rather than remain alone by myself. The human heart is like a millstone in a mill: when you put wheat under it, it turns and grinds and bruises the wheat to flour; if you put no wheat, it still grinds on, but then 'tis itself it grinds and wears away. So the human heart, unless it be occupied with some employment, leaves space for the devil, who wriggles himself in and brings with him a whole host of evil thoughts, temptations, and tribulations, which grind out the heart.

*   *   *

The devil seduces us at first by all the allurements of sin in order thereafter to plunge us into despair. He pampers up the flesh that he may by and by prostrate the spirit. We feel no pain in the act of sin, but the soul after it is sad and the conscience disturbed.

MARTIN LUTHER

IT is indeed natural to us to wish and to plan, and it is merciful in the Lord to disappoint our plans, and to cross our wishes. For we cannot be safe, much less happy, but in proportion as we are weaned from our own wills, and made simply desirous of being directed by His guidance. This truth (when we are enlightened by His Word) is sufficiently familiar to the judgement; but we seldom learn to reduce it into practice without being trained a while in the school of disappointment. The schemes we form look so plausible and convenient that when they are broken we are ready to say, What a pity! We try again, and with no better success; we are grieved, and perhaps angry, and plan another, and so on; at length, in a course of time, experience and observation begin to convince us that we are not more able than we are worthy to choose aright for ourselves. Then the Lord's invitation to cast our cares upon Him, and His promise to take care of us, appear valuable; and when *we* have done planning, His plan in our favour gradually opens, and He does more and better for us than we could either ask or think. I can hardly recollect a single plan of mine, of which I have not since seen reason to be satisfied that, had it taken place in season and circumstance just as I proposed, it would, humanly speaking, have proved my ruin; or at least it would have deprived me of the greater good the Lord had designed for me. We judge of things by their present appearance, but the Lord sees them in their consequences; if we could do so likewise, we should be perfectly of His mind; but as we cannot, it is an unspeakable mercy that He will manage for us, whether we are pleased with His management or not; and it is spoken of as one of His heaviest judgements, when He gives any person or people up to the way of their own hearts, and to walk after their own counsels.

JOHN NEWTON

PERHAPS there are comforts and compensations that one who has not suffered knows nothing of—like the lamps that nobody sees till the tunnel comes.

* * *

Noble examples are not enough to live upon: it needs the same grace which produced them to make their impress durable.

* * *

He who is near the feet of God will let any man go above him, nay, trample upon him, without offence. He is not concerned at what they say of him; he knows the subject better than anyone else.

* * *

He who has not felt what *sin* is in the Old Testament knows little what *grace* is in the New. He who has not trembled in Moses, and wept in David, and wondered in Isaiah, will rejoice little in Matthew, rest little in John. He who has not suffered under the Law will scarcely hear the glad sound of the Gospel. He who has not been awakened under the mountain will be little delighted with the cross.

* * *

God does all before He asks us to do anything; He redeems before He enjoins; and only the redeemed can truly keep His commandments.

* * *

The Lord's goodness surrounds us at every moment. I walk through it almost with difficulty, as through thick grass and flowers.

R. W. BARBOUR

IN this thy late affliction I have found a deep fellow-feeling with thee; and had a secret hope throughout that it might please the Father of Mercies to raise thee up and sanctify thy troubles to thee; that thou, being more fully acquainted with that way which the world esteems foolish, mayst feel the clothing of divine fortitude and be strengthened to resist the spirit which leads from the simplicity of the everlasting truth. . . .

And now that, on thy part, after thy sore affliction and doubts of recovery, thou art again restored, forget not Him who hath helped thee; but in humble gratitude hold fast his instructions, thereby to shun those by-paths which lead from the firm foundation. I am sensible of that variety of company to which one in thy business must be exposed; I have plentifully felt the force of conversation proceeding from men deeply rooted in an earthly mind, and can sympathize with others in such conflicts, in that much weakness still attends me.

I find that to be a fool as to worldly wisdom, and commit my cause to God, not fearing to offend men, who take offence at the simplicity of truth, is the only way to remain immoved by the sentiments of others. The fear of man brings a snare; by halting in our duty, and going back in the time of trial, our hands grow weaker, our spirits get mingled with the people, our ears grow dull as to hearing the language of the True Shepherd; that when we look at the way of the righteous, it seems as though it was not for us to follow them.

There is a love clothes my mind, while I write, which is superior to all expressions; and I find my heart open to encourage a holy emulation, to advance forward in Christian firmness. Deep humility is a strong bulwark; and as we enter into it, we find safety. The foolishness of God is wiser than man, and the weakness of God is stronger than man. Being unclothed of our own wisdom and knowing the abasement of the creature, therein we find that power to arise which gives health and vigour to us.

JOHN WOOLMAN

A HOUSE is not clean, though all the dust be swept together, if it lie still in a corner within doors. A conscience is not clean by having recollected all her sins in the memory, for they may fester there, and gangrene even to desperation, till she have emptied them in the bottomless sea of the blood of Christ Jesus, and the mercy of His Father, by this way of confession. But a house is not clean neither, though the dust be thrown out, if there hang cobwebs about the walls, in how dark corners soever. A conscience is not clean, though the sins, brought to our memory by this examination, be cast upon God's mercy and the merits of His Son by confession, if there remains in me but a cobweb, a little but a sinful delight in the memory of those sins which I had formerly committed. How many men sin over the sins of their youth again in their age, by a sinful delight in remembering those sins, and a sinful desire that their bodies were not past them? How many men sin over some sins, but imaginarily (and yet damnably) a hundred times, which they never sinned actually at all, by filling their imaginations with such thoughts as these. How would I be revenged of such an enemy, if I were in such a place of authority? How easily could I overthrow such a wasteful young man and compass his land, if I had but money to feed his humours? Those sins which we have never been able to do actually, to the harm of others, we do as hurtfully to our own souls by a sinful desire of them, and a sinful delight in them.

JOHN DONNE

JESUS hath now many lovers of the heavenly kingdom, but few bearers of His Cross. He hath many desirous of consolation, but few of tribulation. He findeth many companions of His table, but few of His abstinence. All desire to rejoice with Him, few are willing to endure anything for Him, or with Him. Many follow Jesus unto the breaking of bread, but few to the drinking of the cup of His Passion. Many reverence His miracles, few follow the ignominy of His Cross. Many love Jesus so long as no adversities befall them, many praise and bless Him so long as they receive any consolations from Him; but if Jesus hide Himself and leave them but a little while, they fall either into complaining or into too much dejection of mind.

But they who love Jesus for the sake of Jesus, and not for some special comfort of their own, bless Him in all tribulations and anguish of heart as well as in the state of highest comfort. Yea, although He should never be willing to give them comfort, they notwithstanding would ever praise Him, and wish to be always giving thanks.

O how powerful is the pure love of Jesus, which is mixed with no self-interest or self-love! Are not all those to be called mercenary who are ever seeking consolations? Do they not show themselves to be rather lovers of themselves than of Christ, who are always thinking of their own profit and advantage? Where shall one be found who is willing to serve God for nought?

. . . If thou bear the Cross cheerfully, it will bear thee, and lead thee to the desired end, namely, where there shall be an end of suffering, though here there shall not be. If thou bear it unwillingly, thou makest for thyself a burden and increasest thy load, and yet notwithstanding thou must bear it. If thou cast away one cross, without doubt thou shalt find another, and that perhaps a more heavy one.

THOMAS À KEMPIS

WHAT do I love, when I love Thee? Not beauty of bodies, nor the fair harmony of time, nor the brightness of the light so gladsome to our eyes, nor sweet melodies of varied songs, nor the fragrant smell of flowers and ointments and spices, nor manna and honey, nor limbs acceptable to embracements of flesh. None of these I love, when I love my God; and yet I love a kind of light, and melody, and fragrance, and meat, and embracement, when I love my God—the light, melody, fragrance, meat, embracement of my inner man; where there shineth unto my soul what space cannot contain, and there soundeth what time beareth not away, and there smelleth what breath dispenseth not, and there tasteth what eating diminisheth not, and there clingeth what satiety divorceth not. This is it that I love, when I love my God.

And what is this? I asked the earth, and it answered me, 'I am not He'; and whatsoever things are in it confessed the same. I asked the sea and the deeps, and the living creeping things, and they answered, 'We are not thy God; seek above us.' I asked the moving air, and the whole air with its inhabitants answered, 'Anaximenes was deceived; I am not God.' I asked the heavens, sun, moon, stars, and they say 'Nor are we the God whom thou seekest'. And I replied unto all the things which encompass the door of my flesh, 'Ye have told me of my God that ye are not He; tell me something of Him.' And they cried out with a loud voice, 'He made us.' . . . I asked the whole frame of the world about my God; and it answered me, 'I am not He, but He made me.'

ST. AUGUSTINE

How paltry and helpless, in such dark times, are all theories of mere self-education; all proud attempts, like that of Goethe's Wilhelm Meister, to hang self-poised in the centre of the abyss, and there organize for oneself a character by means of circumstances! Easy enough and graceful enough does that dream look, while all the circumstances themselves—all which stands around —are easy and graceful, obliging and commonplace, like the sphere of petty experiences with which Goethe surrounds his insipid hero. Easy enough it seems for a man to educate himself without God, so long as he lies comfortably on a sofa, with a cup of coffee and a review: but what if that 'daemonic element of the universe', which Goethe confessed, and yet in his luxuriousness tried to ignore, because he could not explain—what if that broke forth over the graceful and prosperous student, as it may at any moment? . . . What if he found himself hurled perforce amid the real experiences of humanity; and made free, in spite of himself, by doubt and fear and horror of great darkness, of the brotherhood of woe, common alike to the simplest peasant woman and to every great soul, perhaps, who has left his impress and signmanual upon the hearts of after generations? . . .

What refuge, then, in self-education; when a man feels himself powerless in the gripe of some unseen and inevitable power, and knows not whether it be chance, or necessity, or a devouring fiend? . . . There is but one escape, one chink through which we may see light, one rock on which our feet may find standing-place, even in the abyss: and that is the belief, intuitive, inspired, due neither to reasoning nor to study, that the billows are God's billows; and that though we go down to hell, He is there also; the belief that not we, but He, is educating us; that these seemingly fantastic and incoherent miseries . . . have in His mind a spiritual coherence, an organic unity and purpose (though we see it not); that sorrows do not come singly, only because He is making short work with our spirits.

CHARLES KINGSLEY

5. RESOLVED, never to lose one moment of time; but improve it in the most profitable way I possibly can.

6. Resolved, to live with all my might, when I do live.

7. Resolved, never to do anything which I should be afraid to do if it were the last hour of my life.

9. Resolved, to think much, on all occasions, of my own dying, and of the common circumstances which attend death.

17. Resolved, that I will live so as I shall wish I had done when I come to die.

34. Resolved, never to speak in narrations anything but the pure and simple verity.

46. Resolved, never to allow the least measure of any fretting or uneasiness at my father or mother. Resolved, to suffer no effects of it, so much as in the least alteration of speech, or motion of my eye; and to be especially careful of it with respect to any of our family.

47. Resolved, to endeavour to my utmost to deny whatever is not most agreeable to a good, and universally sweet and benevolent, quiet, peaceable, contented, easy, compassionate, generous, humble, meek, modest, submissive, obliging, diligent and industrious, charitable, even, patient, moderate, forgiving, sincere temper; and to do at all times what such a temper would lead me to.

65. Resolved, to exercise myself much in this all my life long, viz., with the greatest openness to declare my ways to God and lay open my soul to Him; all my sins, temptations, difficulties, sorrows, fears, hopes, desires, and everything, and every circumstance; according to Dr. Manton's 27th sermon on the 119th Psalm.

JONATHAN EDWARDS

No coward soul is mine,
No trembler in the world's storm-troubled sphere:
    I see Heaven's glories shine,
And faith shines equal, arming me from fear.

    O God within my breast,
Almighty, ever-present Deity!
    Life—that in me has rest,
As I—undying Life—have power in Thee!

    Vain are the thousand creeds
That move men's hearts: unutterably vain;
    Worthless as withered weeds,
Or idlest froth amid the boundless main,

    To waken doubt in one
Holding so fast by Thine infinity;
    So surely anchor'd on
The steadfast rock of immortality.

    With wide-embracing love
Thy Spirit animates eternal years,
    Pervades and broods above,
Changes, sustains, dissolves, creates and rears.

    Though earth and man were gone,
And suns and universes ceased to be,
    And Thou wert left alone,
Every existence would exist in Thee.

    There is not room for Death,
Nor atom that his might could render void:
    Thou—Thou art Being and Breath,
And what Thou art may never be destroy'd.

                                    EMILY BRONTË

I COULD both sigh and smile at the simplicity of a native American, sent by a Spaniard, his master, with a basket of figs, and a letter wherein the figs were mentioned, to carry them both to one of his master's friends. By the way this messenger eat up the figs, but delivered the letter, whereby his deed was discovered and he soundly punished. Being sent a second time on the like message, he first took the letter (which he conceived had eyes as well as tongue) and hid it in the ground, sitting himself on the place where he put it; and then securely fell to feed on his figs, presuming that that paper which saw nothing could tell nothing. Then, taking it again out of the ground, he delivered it to his master's friend, whereby his fault was perceived, and he worse beaten than before. Men conceive they can manage their sins with secrecy; but they carry about them a letter, or book rather, written by God's finger, their conscience bearing witness to all their actions. But sinners being often detected and accused, hereby grow wary at last and, to prevent this speaking paper from telling any tales, do smother, stifle, and suppress it, when they go about the committing of any wickedness. Yet conscience (though buried for a time in silence) hath afterwards a resurrection, and discovers all to their great shame and heavier punishment.

THOMAS FULLER

WHEN Mr. Stand-fast had thus set things in order, and the time being come for him to haste him away, he also went down to the river. Now there was a great calm at that time in the river, wherefor Mr. Stand-fast, when he was about half way in, he stood a while and talked to his companions that had waited upon him thither. And he said:

This river has been a terror to many, yea the thoughts of it also have often frightened me. But now methinks I stand easy, my foot is fixed upon that upon which the feet of the priests that bare the ark of the covenant stood while Israel went over Jordan. The waters indeed are to the palate bitter, and to the stomach cold, yet the thoughts of what I am going to, and of the conduct that waits for me on the other side, doth lie as a glowing coal at my heart.

I see myself now at the end of my journey, my toilsome days are ended. I am going now to see that Head that was crowned with thorns, and that Face that was spit upon, for me.

I have formerly lived by hear-say and faith, but now I go where I shall live by sight, and shall be with him in whose company I delight myself. I have loved to hear my Lord spoken of, and wherever I have seen the print of his shoe in the earth, there I have coveted to set my foot too.

His Name has been to me as a civet-box, yea, sweeter than all perfumes. His Voice to me has been most sweet, and his Countenance I have desired more than they that have most desired the light of the sun. His Word I did use to gather for my food, and for antidotes against my faintings. He has held me, and I have kept me from mine iniquities. Yea, my steps hath he strengthened in the way.

Now while he was thus in discourse, his countenance changed, his strong men bowed under him, and after he had said, Take me, for I come unto Thee, he ceased to be seen of them.

JOHN BUNYAN

CELIA is always telling you how provoked she is, what intolerable shocking things happen to her, what monstrous usage she suffers, and what vexations she meets with everywhere. She tells you that her patience is quite wore out, and there is no bearing the behaviour of people. Every assembly that she is at sends her home provoked; something or other has been said or done that no reasonable, well-bred person ought to bear. Poor people that want her charity are sent away with hasty answers, not because she has not a heart to part with any money, but because she is too full of some trouble of her own to attend to the complaints of others. Celia has no business upon her hands but to receive the income of a plentiful fortune; but yet by the doleful turn of her mind you would be apt to think that she had neither food nor lodging. If you see her look more pale than ordinary, if her lips tremble when she speaks to you, it is because she is just come from a visit where Lupus took no notice at all of her, but talked all the time to Lucinda, who has not half her fortune. When cross accidents have so disordered her spirits that she is forced to send for the doctor to make her able to eat, she tells him in great anger at Providence that she never was well since she was born, and that she envies every beggar that she sees in health.

This is the disquiet life of Celia, who has nothing to torment her but her own spirit. If you could inspire her with Christian humility, you need do no more to make her as happy as any person in the world. This virtue would make her thankful to God for half so much health as she has had, and help her to enjoy more for the time to come. This virtue would keep off tremblings of the spirits and loss of appetite, and her blood would need nothing else to sweeten it.

WILLIAM LAW

How, in fact, do we block His advance? Partly, of course, by
sheer resistance. We definitely desire that He should not yet take
charge of some parts of our lives; we are like St. Augustine when
he caught himself praying, 'Give me chastity, but not yet.' We
want to indulge a little longer. There is no need to dwell on this.
We know that it is wrong, and at least in our better moments set
ourselves to undermine the barriers which in our worse moments
we erect. But there is another way of blocking the divine grace.
We block it by failure of expectation. Of course this is just one
form of lack of faith. But it is so purely negative that it escapes
detection. Moreover, there is a common belief among devout
people that if we are personally devoted to Christ, His Presence
will entirely purify us and put us right in every relation of life.
Experience shows that this is simply not true. Devotion to Christ
will win from Him purification from those faults of which we are
already aware; it will also quicken our consciences and make us
aware of others besides. But it does not at all invariably do this
with completeness, especially where sins of omission are concerned. It was possible during the war to hear utterances from
unquestionably devout and even holy persons, which showed that
they had no inkling of the fact that Christ commanded them to
feel charity for the Germans. We look back now with amazement
to the attitude adopted by such saints as Wilberforce and Hannah
More towards the sufferings of the poor in the early days of the
Industrial Revolution. For saints they were; but they none the
less had their blind spots; and blind they remained despite their
saintliness.

WILLIAM TEMPLE

'No man ever saw God and lived'; and yet I shall not live till I see God; and when I have seen Him I shall never die. What have I ever seen in this world that hath been truly the same thing that it seemed to me? I have seen marble buildings, and a chip, a crust, a plaster, a face of marble hath peeled off, and I see brick-bowels within. I have seen beauty, and a strong breath from another tells me that complexion is from without, not from a sound constitution within. I have seen the state of princes, and all that is but ceremony; and I would be loath to put a master of ceremonies to define ceremony and tell me what it is, and to include so various a thing as ceremony in so constant a thing as a definition. I see a great officer, and I see a man of mine own profession, of great revenues, and I see not the interest of the money that was paid for it, I see not the pensions nor the annuities that are charged upon that office or that church. As he that fears God fears nothing else, so he that sees God sees everything else. When we shall see God *sicuti est*, as He is, we shall see all things *sicuti sunt*, as they are; for that's their essence, as they conduce to His glory. We shall be no more deluded with outward appearances: for when this sight which we intend here comes, there will be no delusory thing to be seen. All that we have made as though we saw in this world will be vanished, and I shall see nothing but God, and what is in Him.

JOHN DONNE

1. OF all the temptations that ever I met with in my life, to question the being of God and Truth of His Gospel is the worst, and the worst to be borne. When this temptation comes, it takes away my girdle from me and removeth the foundation from under me. O, I have often thought of that word, Have your loins girt about with truth; and of that, When the foundations are destroyed, what can the righteous do?

2. Sometimes when after sin committed I have looked for sore chastisement from the hand of God, the very next thing that I have had from Him hath been the discovery of His grace. Sometimes when I have been comforted, I have called myself a fool for my so sinking under trouble. And then again when I have been cast down, I thought I was not wise to give way to such comfort. With such strength and weight have both these been upon me.

3. I have wondered much at this one thing, that though God doth visit my soul with never so blessed a discovery of Himself, yet I have found again that such hours have attended me afterwards, that I have been in my spirit so filled with darkness, that I could not so much as once conceive what that God and that comfort was with which I have been refreshed.

4. I have sometimes seen more in a line of the Bible than I could well tell how to stand under; and yet at another time the whole Bible hath been to me as dry as a stick; or rather, my heart hath been so dead and dry unto it that I could not conceive the least dram of refreshment, though I have looked it all over.

5. Of all tears they are the best that are made by the blood of Christ; and of all joy that is the sweetest that is mixed with mourning over Christ. Oh! it is a goodly thing to be on our knees, with Christ in our arms, before God. I hope I know something of these things.

JOHN BUNYAN

EVERY man is represented as having a kind of court and tribunal in his own breast; where he tries himself and all his actions, and conscience, under one notion or another, sustains all parts in this trial. The *court* is called the court of a man's conscience, and the *bar* at which the sinner stands impleaded is called the bar of conscience. Conscience also is the *accuser*, and it is the *record* and the *register* of our crimes, in which the memory of them is preserved; and it is the *witness* which gives testimony for or against us; hence are those expressions of *the testimony of our consciences*, and that *a man's own conscience is to him instead of a thousand witnesses*. And it is likewise the *judge* which declares the law, and what we ought or ought not to have done, in such or such a *case*, and accordingly passes *sentence* upon us by acquitting or condemning us. Thus according to common use of speech conscience sustains all imaginable parts in this spiritual court. It is the court and the bench and the bar, the accuser and witness and register and all. . . .

Hence we should reverence our consciences and stand in awe of them, and have a great regard to their testimony and verdict. For conscience is a domestic judge, and kind of a familiar god; and therefore next to the supreme Majesty of heaven and earth, every man should be afraid to offend his own reason and conscience which, whenever we knowingly do amiss, will beat us with many stripes and handle us more severely than the greatest enemy we have in the world. . . .

The most sensual man that ever was in the world never felt his heart touched with so delicious and lasting a pleasure as that is which springs from a clear conscience and a mind fully satisfied with his own actions.

This makes all calm and serene within, when there is nothing but clouds and darkness about him.

JOHN TILLOTSON

BELIEVE it, Christians, for a certain truth that, when you come to die, your thoughts will not be: What a figure have I made in the world; how pleasantly have I passed my days; how plentifully have I lived; what pleasures have I enjoyed; what rare friends have I had; what an estate have I gotten; and what wealth do I leave behind me?

No, no. But such as these following will be your dying reflections, if you do not stifle them: How have I spent my life; how have I employed my time and my health; how have I improved the talents with which God entrusted me; what good have I done in the world; have I brought up my children in the fear of God; have I been kind and helpful to poor and needy people, according to my ability; have I been true and just in my dealings; have I lived in the fear of God and worshipped Him both in public and in private, according to my ability; and lastly, have I taken pains to be doing something good all my life, pursuant to that sentence of God, passed upon me and upon every soul of man, whether rich or poor, 'In the sweat of thy face shalt thou eat bread'?

These, I say again, will be the thoughts of such as die in their right mind. And to such whose consciences cannot answer for them that something like this has been the tenour of their past life, to such as have led an unthoughtful, fearless, useless, sinful life, and are just going into eternity, what arguments can be thought on to comfort them?

THOMAS WILSON

WE should wear our velvet within, that is to say, show ourselves most amiable to those of our own house.

*   *   *

Gentle manners and pleasant greetings are cards of invitation that circulate all the year round.

*   *   *

We should always have in our heads one free and open corner where we can give place, or lodging as they pass, to the ideas of our friends. It really becomes unbearable to converse with men whose brains are divided into well-filled pigeon-holes, where nothing can enter from outside. Let us have hospitable hearts and minds.

*   *   *

The attention of the listener serves as accompaniment to the music of the discourse. Everyone should be provided with that sort of indulgence, and that readiness to listen, which makes the thoughts of others bloom. It is a bad sort of cleverness which deprives the character of kindness, indulgence, and sympathy, which makes it difficult for us to live and talk with others, to make them pleased with us and pleased with themselves—in a word, to love and be lovable. The gentle mind is patient, gives itself without hurry to the task of understanding, is open to conviction, afraid of obstinacy, and would rather learn than take the lead.

*   *   *

There are some conversations in which neither the soul nor the body takes part. I mean those conversations in which no one speaks from the depth of his heart, nor even with the true temper of his mind; in which there is neither freedom, nor gaiety, nor flow, nor play; in which we find neither movement nor repose, neither distraction nor relief, neither concentration nor diversion; in fact, where nothing has been given and nothing received, where therefore there has been no true exchange.

*   *   *

Politeness is the blossom of our humanity. Whoever is not sufficiently polite, is not sufficiently humane.

JOSEPH JOUBERT

THE mere majesty of God's power and greatness, when offered to your notice, lays hold of one of the faculties within you. The holiness of God, with His righteous claim of legislation, lays hold of another of these faculties. The difference between them is so great that the one may be engrossed and interested to the full, while the other remains untouched and in a state of entire dormancy. Now it is no matter what it be that ministers delight to the former of these two faculties; if the latter be not arrested and put on its proper exercise, you are making no approximation whatever to the right habit and character of religion. There are a thousand ways in which we may contrive to regale our taste for that which is beauteous and majestic. It may find its gratification in the loveliness of a vale, or in the freer and bolder outlines of an upland situation, or in the terrors of a storm, or in the sublime contemplations of astronomy, or in the magnificent idea of a God who sends forth the wakefulness of his omniscient eye, and the vigour of His upholding hand, throughout all the realms of nature and of providence. The mere taste of the human mind may get its ample enjoyment in each and in all of these objects, or in a vivid representation of them; nor does it make any material difference whether this representation be addressed to you from the stanzas of a poem, or from the recitations of a theatre, or finally from the discourses and demonstrations of a pulpit. And thus it is that, still on the impulse of the one principle only, people may come in gathering multitudes to the house of God; and share with eagerness in all the glow and bustle of a crowded attendance; and have their every eye directed to the speaker; and feel a responding movement in their bosom to his many appeals and his many arguments; and carry a solemn and overpowering impression of all the services away with them; and yet, throughout the whole of this seemly exhibition, not one effectual knock may have been given at the door of conscience.

THOMAS CHALMERS

A LITTLE plan which I have found serviceable in past years is to put down every night the engagements and duties of the next day, arranging the hours well. The advantages of this are several. You get more done than if a great part of each day is spent in contriving and considering 'What next?' A healthful feeling pervades the whole of life. There is a feeling of satisfaction at the end of the day in finding that, generally, the greater part of what is planned has been accomplished. This is the secret of giving dignity to trifles. As units they are insignificant; they rise in importance when they become parts of a plan. Besides this—and I think the most important thing of all—there is gained a consciousness of will, the opposite of that which is the sense of impotency. The thought of time, to me at least, is a very overpowering and often a very annihilating one for energy: time rushing on, unbroken, irresistible, hurrying the worlds and the ages into being, and out of it, and making our 'noisy years seem moments in the *being* of the eternal Silence'. The sense of powerlessness which this gives is very painful. But I have felt that this is neutralized by such a little plan as that. You feel that you do control your own course; you are borne on, but not resistlessly. Down the rapids you go, certainly, but you are steering and trimming your own raft, and making the flood of time your vassal, and not your conqueror. . . .

'There is nothing in the drudgery of domestic duties to soften' —you quote that. No, but a great deal to strengthen with a sense of duty done, self-control, and power. Besides, you cannot calculate how much corroding rust is *kept off*—how much of disconsolate, dull despondency is hindered. Daily use is not the jeweller's mercurial polish: but it will keep your little silver pencil from tarnishing.

F. W. ROBERTSON

A RELIGION of the intellect alone makes us feel everything disputable; of the feelings, everything vague; of the conscience, everything hard. Intellect gives form to feeling, feeling gives warmth to conscience, and conscience gives basis to both.

* * *

The doubts of some are more indicative of a love of truth than the belief of others. They arise from a sense of the awful importance of the issue and an agonizing desire to be sure. But wherever this interferes with practical duty it is wrong; for duty is always incumbent, and it is God's way of leading to truth.

* * *

There is such a thing as 'unconscious faith', but those who plead it in their own behalf do not possess it. With them it is conscious unbelief.

* * *

One spiritual truth heartily believed is of far more worth than the whole of the creed received from custom or complaisance; as one artesian well piercing to the spring is of more value than a hundred tubes thrust into the surface.

* * *

We often catch a truth by a side glance when we have failed to see it by a full, direct gaze—as we perceive a star with the side of our eye sooner than with the centre.

JOHN KER

WHAT love is this of Thine, that cannot be
 In Thine infinity, O Lord, confined,
Unless it in Thy very Person see
 Infinity and finity conjoined?
 What! hath Thy Godhead, as not satisfied,
 Married our manhood, making it its bride?

Oh matchless love! Filling heaven to the brim!
 O'errunning it: all running o'er beside
This world! Nay, overflowing hell, wherein,
 For Thine elect, there rose a mighty tide!
 That there our veins might through Thy Person bleed,
 To quench the flames that else would on us feed.

Oh! that Thy love might overflow my heart!
 To fire the same with love: for love I would.
But oh! my straightened breast! my lifeless spark!
 My fireless flame! What chilly love and cold!
 In measure small! In manner chilly! See!
 Lord, blow the coal: Thy love enflame in me.

EDWARD TAYLOR

SUSPICION, however necessary it may be to our safe passage through ways beset on all sides by fraud and malice, has always been considered, when it exceeds the common measures, as a token of depravity and corruption; and a Greek writer of sentences has laid down as a standing maxim that 'He who believes not another on his oath, knows himself to be perjured'.

We can form our opinions of that which we know not, only by placing it in comparison with something that we know. Whoever therefore is over-run with suspicion, and detects artifice and stratagem in every proposal, must either have learned by experience and observation the wickedness of mankind, and been taught to avoid fraud by having often suffered or seen treachery; or he must derive his judgement from the consciousness of his own disposition, and impute to others the same inclinations which he feels predominant in himself.

To learn caution by turning our eyes upon life and observing the arts by which negligence is surprised, timidity overborne, and credulity abused, requires either great latitude of converse and long acquaintance with business, or uncommon activity of vigilance and acuteness of penetration. When therefore a young man, not distinguished by vigour of intellect, comes into the world full of scruples and diffidence; makes a bargain with many provisional limitations; hesitates in his answer to a common question, lest more should be intended than he can immediately discover; has a long reach in detecting the projects of his acquaintance; considers every caress as an act of hypocrisy, and feels neither gratitude nor affection from the tenderness of his friends, because he believes no one to have any real tenderness but himself; whatever expectations this early sagacity may raise of his future eminence or riches, I can seldom forbear to consider him as a wretch incapable of generosity or benevolence.

SAMUEL JOHNSON

THE ostrich, it will be observed, is nature's type of all unmother-
hood. She hatches her young without incubation, depositing her
eggs in the sand to be quickened by the solar heat. Her office as a
mother bird is there ended. . . .

Probably enough there may be some of you that, without being
Christians yourselves, are yet careful to teach your children all the
saving truths of religion, and who thus may take it as undue
severity to be charged with only giving your children this unnatural ostrich nurture. But how poor a teacher of Christ is anyone
who is not in the light of Christ, and does not know the inward
power of His truth, as a gospel of life to the soul. You press your
child in this manner with duties you do not practise and promises
you do not embrace; and if you do not succeed, it only means that
you cannot impose on him to that high extent. A mother teach by
words only? No! but more, a great deal more by the atmosphere of
love and patience she breathes. Besides, how easy it is for her to
make everything she teaches legal and repulsive, just because she
has no liberty or joy in it herself. What is wanted, therefore, is not
merely to give a child the law, telling him this is duty, this is right,
this God requires, this He will punish, but a much greater want
is to have the spirit of all duty lived and breathed around him; to
see, and feel, and breathe himself the living atmosphere of grace.
Therefore it is vain, let all parents so understand, to imagine that
you can really fulfil the true fatherhood and motherhood unless
you are true Christians yourselves. I am sorry to discourage you
in any good attempts. Rightly taken, what I say will not discourage you, but will only prompt you by all that is dearest to you
on earth to become truly qualified for your office. By these dear
pledges God has given you to call you to Himself, I beseech you
to turn yourselves to the true life of religion. Have it first in yourselves, then teach it as you live it; teach it by living it; for you can
do it in no other manner. Be Christians yourselves, and then it will
not be difficult for you to do your true duties to your children.
Until then it is really impossible.

HORACE BUSHNELL

OUR Lord's saying grace, and eating and drinking, and courtesy, and decorum and affability, and geniality—all that I can easily imagine and realize, with more or less clearness to myself. But how I would have watched Him as this topic of conversation and that arose all night at that table. For I feel sure there is nothing in which we are all of us more unlike Him than just in the way we carry on our conversations at table. . . .

There is no table we sit at very long that we do not more or less ruin either to ourselves or to someone else. We either talk too much, and thus weary and disgust people; or they weary and disgust us. We start ill-considered, unwise, untimeous topics. We blurt out our rude minds in rude words. We push aside our neighbour's opinion, as if both he and his opinion were worthless, and we thrust forward our own as if wisdom would die with us. We do not put ourselves into our neighbour's place. We have no imagination in conversation, and no humility, and no love. We lay down the law, and we instruct people who could buy us in one end of the market and sell us in the other if they thought us worth the trouble. It is easy to say grace; it is easy to eat and drink in moderation and with decorum and refinement; but it is our tongue that so ensnares us. For some men to command their tongue; to bridle, and guide, and moderate, and make just the right use of their tongue, is a conquest in religion, and in morals, and in good manners, that not one in a thousand of us has yet made over ourselves. But that One in a thousand sat at Simon's table that night. And, much as I would have liked to see how He acted in everything, especially would I have watched Him how He guided, and steered, and changed, and moderated, and sweetened the talk of the table.

ALEXANDER WHYTE

IT is a sure sign of mediocrity to be niggardly with praise.

* * *

We have no right to make unhappy those whom we cannot make good.

* * *

No one can be just who is without sympathy.

* * *

When we feel that we cannot gain the good opinion of another, we come very near to hating him.

* * *

We are less hurt by the contempt of fools than by the lukewarm approval of men of intelligence.

* * *

Men sometimes feel injured by praise, because it assigns a limit to their merit. Few people are humble enough to be content to be estimated at their true worth.

* * *

We detect in ourselves what others conceal from us, and recognize in others what we conceal in ourselves.

* * *

The usual excuse of those who cause others trouble is that they wish them well.

* * *

To punish unnecessarily is to interfere with the mercy of God.

* * *

We find fault with the unfortunate in order to excuse ourselves from commiserating them.

* * *

A generous heart suffers for the misfortunes of others as much as though it had caused them.

MARQUIS DE VAUVENARGUES

THE Christian faith finds the final clue to the meaning of life and history in the Christ whose goodness is at once the virtue which man ought to but does not achieve in history, and the revelation of a divine mercy which understands and resolves the perpetual contradictions in which history is involved even on the highest reaches of human achievements. From the standpoint of such a faith it is possible to deal with the ultimate social problem of human history: the creation of community in world dimensions. The insistence of the Christian faith that the love of Christ is the final norm of human existence must express itself socially in unwillingness to stop short of the whole human community in expressing our sense of moral responsibility for the life and welfare of others. The understanding of the Christian faith that the highest achievements of human life are infected with sinful corruption will help men to be prepared for new corruptions on the level of world community which will drive simpler idealists to despair. The hope of Christian faith that the divine power which bears history can complete what even the highest human striving must leave incomplete, and can purify the corruptions which appear in even the purest human aspirations, is an indispensable prerequisite for diligent fulfilment of our historic tasks. Without it we are driven to alternate moods of sentimentality and despair; trusting human powers too much in one moment and losing all faith in the meaning of life when we discover the limits of human possibilities.

REINHOLD NIEBUHR

ONE thing I *will* say, for I am most firmly persuaded of it, that a great part of your dullness and dryness about holy things, probably the whole, so far as it is accountable for by human judgement, is a symptom of your illness: and I daresay you often feel the like distressing want of interest in other matters which you would fain take an interest in: I daresay you often have to rouse yourself up, and force yourself to be or seem amused with things which in former days would have taken hold of you without any effort. If it is so in ordinary things, then its not being so in religious services and meditations would be a merciful interference, more perhaps than one could reasonably expect; and its not being granted ought not to dishearten one nor make one think oneself the subject of a special judgement. Another thing is that all religious meditation has a tendency, if it be not its direct work, to turn the mind's eye back as it were on itself; and this is necessarily a painful and wearisome effort, and causes a sort of aching which cannot well be endured when the frame or spirits are weakened by sickness of certain sorts: I suppose, then, that it is a provision of God's mercy to disqualify the mind in such cases for meditation, and keep it in a kind of dullness which, however uncomfortable, may be as good for the soul and mind as sleepiness (which is often also most uncomfortable) is for the body. . . .

In the meantime, I beg of you, do not be too severe, do not strain your inward eye by turning it too violently back upon itself: remember you are bound for others' sake, as well as your own, to be, if you can, and not only to seem, comfortable and cheerful. Do not be afraid to take, as they come, the little refreshments and amusements which His mercy provides for you, and be not too nice in comparing your interest in these with the dullness you may possibly feel in direct religious exercises.

                                                            JOHN KEBLE

REMEMBER that when with thine understanding thou goest forth to find God, in order to rest in Him, thou must place neither limit nor comparison with thy weak and narrow imagination. For He is infinite beyond all comparison; He is through all and in all, and in Him are all things. Himself thou wilt find within thy soul, wherever thou shalt seek Him in truth, that is, in order to find thyself. For His delight is to be with us, the children of men, to make us worthy of Him, though He hath no need of us. In meditation do not be so tied down to certain points that thou wilt meditate on them alone; but wherever thou shalt find rest, there stop and taste the Lord, at whatever step He shall will to communicate Himself to thee. Though thou leave what thou hadst laid down, have no scruple; for the whole end of these exercises is to taste the Lord; yet with intent not to make this the chief end; but rather to love His works the more, with purpose to imitate Him as far as we can. And having found the end, we need be no longer anxious as to the means laid down to attain it. One of the hindrances to true peace and quietness is the anxiety and thought we give to such works, binding the spirit and dragging it after one thing or another; in this way insisting that God should lead it by the path we wish, and forcing it to walk along the road of our own imagining; unconsciously caring more to do our own will in this case than the will of our Lord; and this is nothing else but to seek God by flying from Him and to wish to please Him without doing His will. If thou desire really to advance in this path, and to reach the desired end, have no other purpose, no other wish, than to find God; and wheresoever He wills to manifest Himself to thee, there quit all else and go no farther till thou have leave. Forget all other things and rest thee in the Lord.

LORENZO SCUPOLI

'WHAT does God do all day?', once asked a little boy. One could wish that more grown-up people would ask so very real a question. Unfortunately most of us are not even boys in religious intelligence, but only very unthinking babes. It no more occurs to us that God is engaged in any particular work in the world than it occurs to a little child that its father does anything except be its father. Its father may be a cabinet minister absorbed in the nation's work or an inventor deep in schemes for the world's good; but to this master-egoist he is father and nothing more. Childhood, whether in the physical or in the moral world, is the great self-centred period of life; and a personal God who satisfies personal ends is all that for a long time many a Christian understands.

But as clearly as there comes to the growing child a knowledge of his father's part in the world, and a sense of what real life means, there must come to every Christian, whose growth is true, some richer sense of the meaning of Christianity and a larger view of Christ's purpose for mankind. To miss this is to miss the whole splendour and glory of Christ's religion. Next to losing the sense of a personal Christ, the worst evil that can befall a Christian is to have no sense of anything else. To grow up in complacent belief that God has no business in this great groaning world of human beings except to attend to a few saved souls is the negation of all religion. The first great epoch in a Christian's life, after the awe and wonder of its dawn, is when there breaks into his mind some sense that Christ has a purpose for mankind, a purpose beyond him and his needs, beyond the churches and their creeds, beyond heaven and its saints—a purpose which embraces every man and woman born, every kindred and nation formed, which regards not their spiritual good alone, but their welfare in every part, their progress, their health, their work, their wages, their happiness in this present world.

HENRY DRUMMOND

ILL fortune néver crushed that man whom good fortune deceived not. I therefore have counselled my friends never to trust to her fairer side, though she seemed to make peace with them; but to place all things she gave them so, as she might ask them again without their trouble; she might take them from them, not pull them: to keep always a distance between her and themselves. He knows not his own strength that hath not met adversity. Heaven prepares good men with crosses; but no ill can happen to a good man. Contraries are not mixed. Yet that which happens to any man, may to every man. But it is in his reason what he accounts it, and will make it.

*   *   *

Wisdom without honesty is mere craft and cozenage. And therefore the reputation of honesty must first be gotten; which cannot be but by living well. A good life is a main argument.

*   *   *

Truth is man's proper good and the only immortal thing was given to our mortality to use. No good Christian or ethnic, if he be honest, can miss it; no statesman or patriot should. For without truth all the actions of mankind are craft, malice, or what you will rather than wisdom. Homer says he hates him worse than hell-mouth that utters one thing with his tongue and keeps another in his breast. Which high expression was grounded on divine reason; for a lying mouth is a stinking pit, and murders with the contagion it venteth. Beside, nothing is lasting that is feigned; it will have another face than it had, ere long. As Euripides said, 'No lie ever grows old.'

BEN JONSON

In all our spiritual drynesses and barrennesses let us never lose courage but, waiting with patience for the return of consolation, earnestly pursue our course. Let us not omit any of our exercises of devotion, but if possible let us multiply our good works; and not being able to present liquid sweetmeats to our dear Spouse, let us offer Him dry ones; for it is all one to Him, if only the heart which offers them is perfectly fixed in the resolution of loving Him. When the spring is fair, the bees produce more honey and fewer young ones; for, the fine weather favouring them, they are so occupied in their harvest among the flowers that they forget the production of their young; but when the spring is cold and dull, they produce more young ones and less honey; since, not being able to go abroad, they employ themselves at home to increase and multiply their race. Thus it happens frequently that the soul, finding herself in the fair spring of spiritual consolations, amuses herself so much in gathering and sucking them that, in the abundance of these sweet delights, she produces fewer good works; whilst on the contrary, in the midst of spiritual dryness, the more destitute she finds herself of the consolations of devotion, the more she multiplies her good works and abounds in the interior generation of the true virtues of patience, humility, self-contempt, resignation, and renunciation of self-love. . . .

It is no such great matter to serve a prince in the quietness of a time of peace and amongst the delights of the court; but to serve him amidst the hardships of war, in troubles and persecutions, is a true mark of constancy and fidelity. The Blessed Angela de Foligno says that the prayer which is most acceptable to God is that which we make by force and constraint, the prayer to which we apply ourselves not for any relish we find in it, nor by inclination, but purely to please God; to which our will carries us against our inclinations, violently forcing its way through the midst of the dryness and repugnance which oppose it. I say the same of all sorts of good works, whether interior or exterior; for the more contradictions we find in doing them, whether exterior or interior, the higher they are esteemed in the sight of God. ST. FRANCIS DE SALES

WHILE it is of the heart of true morality that it is aware of an objective moral order to which we ought to conform, yet to attempt to achieve that conformity by our own effort corrupts morality. Let us try to make that clear by a simple everyday example. When we have done wrong or failed in respect of some duty, our ordinary natural reaction is to say 'I will make up for it by being better, kinder, more conscientious next time'. . . . I think this is a fair description of the way our minds work when we are 'trying to be good'. 'I have done badly today, but I will do better tomorrow'; and the second clause is intended to compensate for the first. In other words, we find compensation for a past fault in a future merit. We have put ourselves in debt, as it were, to the moral order, but tomorrow by an extra effort of goodness we hope to make up the deficit. . . .

But now let us see what we have done. In the first place we have corrupted moral motives. We are going to do better tomorrow to make up for today; we are going to do good deeds, not because they are good, but to justify ourselves. A fundamental selfishness has got into the very heart of our motives. We have introduced just that seed of egocentricity which turns free spontaneous self-forgetting goodness into 'good works' done with an ulterior motive—between which two things there is the difference of light and darkness. . . .

But we have not only corrupted moral motives. We have also lowered moral standards. For if we suppose, as a legalistic morality constantly does, that we can make up for past failure by extra effort in the future, we are acting on the assumption that it is possible to have a sort of credit balance in goodness—in other words, that it is possible to do more than our duty. If I suppose that my goodness today is going to compensate for my failure yesterday, I am really supposing, as far as today is concerned, that I can be better than necessary.

LESSLIE NEWBIGIN

HIM first to love great right and reason is,
Who first to us our life and being gave,
And after, when we farèd had amiss,
Us wretches from the second death did save;
And last the food of life, which now we have,
Even He Himself, in His dear sacrament,
To feed our hungry souls, unto us lent.

Then next, to love our brethren that were made
Of that self mould, and that self Maker's hand,
That we, and to the same again shall fade,
Where they shall have like heritage of land,
However here on higher steps we stand;
Which also were with self-same price redeemed
That we, however of us light esteemed.

And were they not, yet since that loving Lord
Commanded us to love them for His sake,
Even for His sake, and for His sacred word,
Which in His last bequest He to us spake,
We should them love, and with their needs partake;
Knowing that whatso'er to them we give,
We give to Him by whom we all do live.

Such mercy He by His most holy rede
Unto us taught, and to approve it true,
Ensampled it by His most righteous deed,
Showing us mercy (miserable crew!)
That we the like should to the wretches show,
And love our brethren; thereby to approve
How much Himself that loved us we love.

EDMUND SPENSER

IF persons are religious only by fits and starts; if they now and then seem to be raised up to the clouds in their affections and then suddenly fall down again, lose all, and become quite careless and carnal, and this is their manner of carrying on religion; if they appear greatly moved and mightily engaged in religion only in extraordinary seasons, in the time of a remarkable out-pouring of the Spirit or other uncommon dispensation of providence, or upon the real or supposed receipt of some great mercy, but quickly return to such a frame that their hearts are chiefly upon other things—I say, when it is thus with persons, it is a sign of the un-soundness of affections. They are like the waters in the time of a shower of rain, which during the shower and a little after run like a brook and flow abundantly, but are presently quite dry; and when another shower comes, then they will flow again. Whereas a true saint is like a stream from a living spring which, though it may be greatly increased by a shower of rain and diminished in time of drought, yet constantly runs; or like a tree planted by such a stream, that has a supply at the root and is always green, even in time of the greatest drought. Many hypocrites are like comets, that appear for a while with a mighty blaze, but are very unsteady and irregular in their motion, and their blaze soon disappears, and they appear but once in a great while. But the true saints are like the fixed stars which, though they rise and set, and are often clouded, yet are steadfast in their orb, and may truly be said to shine with a constant light.

*   *   *

It is the nature of true grace that, however it loves Christian society in its place, yet in a peculiar manner it delights in retire-ment and secret converse with God. So that, if persons appear greatly engaged in social religion, and but little with the religion of the closet, and are often highly affected when with others, and but little moved when they have none but God and Christ to converse with, it looks very darkly upon their religion.

JONATHAN EDWARDS

HUMILITY, that is lowliness or self-abasement, is an inward bowing down or prostrating of the heart and of the conscience before God's transcendent worth. Righteousness demands and orders this, and through charity a loving heart cannot leave it undone. When a lowly and loving man considers that God has served him so humbly, so lovingly, and so faithfully; and sees God so high, so mighty, and so noble, and man so poor, and so little, and so low; then there springs up within the humble heart a great awe and a great veneration for God. For to pay homage to God by every outward and inward act, this is the first and dearest work of humility, the most savoury among those of charity, and the most meet among those of righteousness. The loving and humble heart cannot pay homage enough either to God or to His noble manhood, nor can it abase itself as much as it would. And that is why a humble man thinks that his worship of God and his lowly service are always falling short. And he is meek, reverencing Holy Church and the sacraments. And he is discreet in food and drink, in speech, in the answers which he makes to everybody; and in his behaviour, dress, and lowly service he is without hypocrisy and without pretence. And he is humble in his devotions, both outwardly and inwardly, before God and before all men, so that none is offended because of him. And so he overcomes and casts out pride, which is the source and origin of all other sins. By humility the snares of the devil, and of sin, and of the world are broken, and man is set in order and established in the very condition of virtue. And heaven is opened to him, and God stoops to hear his prayers, and he is fulfilled with grace. And Christ, that strong rock, is his foundation. Whosoever therefore grounds his virtue in humility, he shall never err.

JOHN OF RUYSBROECK

AWAKE now, O my soul, shake thyself from the dust, and with deeper attention contemplate this wondrous Man whom, in the glass of the gospel story, thou, as it were, gazest upon, present before thee. Consider, O my soul, who He is, who walketh with the fashion as it were of a king; and nevertheless is filled with the confusion of a most despised slave. He goeth crowned: but His very crown is a torture to Him and woundeth with a thousand punctures His most glorious head. He is clothed in royal purple: yet more is He despised than honoured in it. He beareth a sceptre in His hand: but with it His reverend head is beaten. They worship before Him with bowed knee; they hail Him king: but forthwith they leap up to spit upon His cheeks lovely to look upon, they smite His jaws with the palms of their hands and dishonour His honourable neck. See further how in all things He is constrained, spit upon, despised. He is bid to bend His neck beneath the burden of His Cross, and He Himself to bear His own ignominy. Brought to the place of punishment, He is given to drink myrrh and gall. He is lifted up upon the Cross and He saith, 'Father, forgive them, they know not what they do.' What manner of man is this, who in all His afflictions never once opened His mouth to utter a word of complaint or pleading, or of threatening or cursing against those accursed dogs, and last of all poured forth over His enemies a word of blessing such as hath not been heard from the beginning? What more gentle than this man, what more kind, O my soul, hast thou seen? Gaze on Him, however, yet more intently, for He seemeth worthy both of great admiration and of most tender compassion. See Him stripped naked, and torn with stripes, between thieves ignominiously fixed with nails of iron to the Cross, given vinegar to drink upon the Cross, and after death pierced in His side with the spear, and pouring forth plentiful streams of blood from the five wounds of His hands and feet and side. Pour down your tears, mine eyes; melt, O my soul, with the fire of compassion at the sufferings of that Man of love, whom in the midst of such gentleness thou seest afflicted with so bitter griefs.

ST. ANSELM

WHERE men are enlightened with the true light, they perceive that all which they might desire or choose is nothing to that which all creatures, as creatures, ever desired or chose or knew. Therefore they renounce all desire and choice, and commit and commend themselves and all things to the Eternal Goodness. Nevertheless there remaineth in them a desire to go forward and get nearer to the Eternal Goodness; that is to come to a clearer knowledge, and warmer love, and more comfortable assurance, and perfect obedience and subjection, so that every enlightened man could say: 'I would fain be to the Eternal Goodness what his own hand is to a man.' And he feareth always that he is not enough so, and longeth for the salvation of all men. And such men do not call this longing their own, nor take it unto themselves, for they know well that this desire is not of man, but of the Eternal Goodness; for whatsoever is good shall no one take unto himself as his own, seeing that it belongeth to the Eternal Goodness only.

Moreover, these men are in a state of freedom, because they have lost the fear of pain or hell, and the hope of reward or heaven, but are living in pure submission to the Eternal Goodness, in the perfect freedom of fervent love. This mind was in Christ in perfection, and is also in His followers, in some more, in some less. But it is a sorrow and shame to think that the Eternal Goodness is ever most graciously guiding and drawing us, and we will not yield to it. What is better and nobler than true poorness in spirit? Yet when that is held up before us, we will have none of it, but are always seeking ourselves and our own things, that we may have in ourselves a lively taste of pleasure and sweetness. When this is so, we are well pleased, and think it standeth not amiss with us. This is a great error and a bad sign.

THEOLOGIA GERMANICA

ONCE it was the Apostles' turn. It was St. Paul's turn once. He had all cares upon him all at once; covered from head to foot with cares, as Job with sores. And, as if all this were not enough, he had a thorn in the flesh added—some personal discomfort ever with him. Yet he did his part well—he was as a strong and bold wrestler in his day, and at the close of it was able to say, 'I have fought a good fight, I have finished my course, I have kept the faith.' And after him, the excellent of the earth, the white-robed army of martyrs, and the cheerful company of confessors, each in his turn, each in his day, have likewise played the man. And so down to this very time, when faith has well-nigh failed, first one and then another have been called out to exhibit before the Great King. It is as though all of us were allowed to stand round his throne at once, and He called on first this man, and then that, to take up the chant by himself, each in his turn having to repeat the melody which his brethren have before gone through. Or as if we held a solemn dance to His honour in the courts of heaven, and each had by himself to perform some one and the same solemn and graceful movement at a signal given. Or as if it were some trial of strength or of agility, and, while the ring of bystanders beheld and applauded, we in succession, one by one, were actors in the pageant. Such is our state; angels are looking on, Christ has gone before—Christ has given us an example, that we may follow in His steps. He went through far more, infinitely more, than we can be called to suffer. Our brethren have gone through much more; and they seem to encourage us by their success, and to sympathize in our essay. Now it is our turn; and all ministering spirits keep silence and look on. O let not your foot slip, or your eye be false, or your ear dull, or your attention flagging!

JOHN HENRY NEWMAN

To walk in the light means that we confess our sins without reserve. Sometimes we do not really confess our sins when we think we are doing so: we rather admit our sins than confess them, and we seek in all possible ways to explain, to extenuate, and to excuse them. . . . We think of the evil nature we have inherited, of the bias in our constitution to this or that attractive vice, of the defects of our education, of the violence of temptation, of the compulsion of circumstances; we do not deny what we have done —we cannot—but we mitigate it by every possible plea. This is not walking in the light. In all such self-excusing there is a large element of voluntary self-deception which keeps the life in the dark. To walk in the light requires us to accept our responsibilities without reserve, to own our sin that we may be able to disown it, and not to own it with such qualifications and reserves as amount to saying in the long run, It was indeed I who did it, but after all it is not I who should bear the blame. A man who makes it his business not to confess his sin, but to understand it and explain it, no matter how philosophical he may seem, is walking in darkness, and the truth is not in him. . . .

Finally, to walk in the light means that when we confess our sins to God we do not keep a secret hold of them in our hearts. Where there is something hidden in the heart, hidden from God and from man, the darkness is as deep and dreadful as it can be. The desire to keep such a secret hold of sin is itself a sin to be confessed, to be declared in its exceeding sinfulness, to be unreservedly renounced. . . . The man who has a guilty secret in his life is a lonely man. There can be no cordial Christian overflow from his heart to the hearts of others, nor from theirs to his. And he is a man doomed to bear in his loneliness the uneffaced stain of his sin. The cleansing virtue of the atonement cannot reach him where he dwells by himself in the dark.

JAMES DENNEY

'HE maketh me to lie down in green pastures, he leadeth me beside the still waters'—the very beauty of this picture may serve only to hide from us the depths of its meaning. We seem to see the shepherd walking before his flock through fields decked out with green and gold and all the glory of a generous God, coming at last to the silent pool with the reflection of the sky sleeping in its heart, and it seems as though it were for the glory of the summer and the sleeping beauty of the pool that the sheep followed the shepherd. And indeed it is for that reason that many do seek the Good Shepherd. They think of religion not as a necessity but as a luxury, not as life but as a kind of addition to life which it is very nice to have but which we could quite well do without. But it is not for the green and gold of summer fields that the sheep seeks to find them, but because they are good to eat. It is not for the sleeping beauty in the heart of silent waters that the flock follows on to find them, but because they are good to drink. It is not luxury that they ask of the shepherd, it is the bare necessities. And we cannot make too sure of this: that religion, communion with God, is not luxury, but a necessity for the soul. We must have God.

*   *   *

The Good Shepherd intensifies to the point of torture the hunger of the soul until it becomes a passion in man to make the world in which he lives as beautiful and as good as he perceives that it is meant to be; He intensifies the hunger to the point of torture that He may satisfy it by the gift of communion with Himself and the moral power that springs from that communion.

G. A. STUDDERT KENNEDY

KNOW of a truth that if thine own honour is of more importance to thee and dearer than that of another man, thou doest wrongfully. Know this, that if thou seekest something that is thine own, thou seekest not God only; and thou wilt never find Him. Thou art acting as though thou madest of God a candle to seek for something and, when thou hast found it, thou castest the candle away. Therefore, when thou doest this, that which thou seekest with God, whatever it may be, it is nothing; gain, reward, favour, or whatever it may be, thou seekest nothing, therefore thou wilt find nothing. There is no other cause for finding nothing but that thou seekest nothing. All creatures are absolutely nothing. I do not say that they are small or anything else, but that they are absolutely nothing. That which has no being is nothing. And creatures have no being, because they have their being in God; if God turned away for a moment, they would cease to exist. He who desired to have all the world with God would have nothing more than if he had God alone. . . .

Know that of ourselves we have nothing; for this and all other gifts are from above. Therefore he who would receive from above must of necessity place himself beneath, in true humility. And know of a truth that if he leave anything out, so that all is not beneath, he will have nothing and receive nothing. Dost thou trust to thyself, or to anything else or anybody else, thou art not beneath and wilt receive nothing; but if thou hast placed thyself beneath, then thou wilt receive all things fully. It is God's nature to give; and He lives and moves that He may give unto us when we are humble. If we are not lowly, and yet desire to receive, we do Him violence, and kill Him, so to speak; and though we may not wish to do this, yet we do it as far as in us lies. That thou mayest truly give Him all things, see to it that thou castest thyself in deep humility at the feet of God, and beneath all created things.

JOHANN TAULER

ALL Science . . . is essentially the ceaseless seeking, the ceaseless restating, the ceaseless discovering of error, and the substituting of something nearer to the truth. I do not see how Science can be asked to start with a definite God, with a definite Future Life, with anything like a Church; I think it cannot even end with anything more than a vague reverence and sense of a deep background —a very elementary Theism will, at best, and can hardly, be reached by it; such Theism will be, I believe, its maximum. Now Religion, on the other hand, begins with a full affirmation of a Reality, of a Reality other and more than all mankind. It is certain of God, certain of Christ, certain of the Church. It is a gift from above downwards, not a groping from below upwards. It is not like Science a coral-reef, it is more like a golden shower from above. Assimilate Religion to Science, and you have levelled down to something which, though excellent for Science, has taken from Religion its entire force and good; you have shorn Samson of his locks with a vengeance. On the other hand, force Science up to the level of Religion, or think that you have done so, and Science affirms far more than, as such, it can affirm, and you, on your part, are in a world of unreality. . . .

For myself, I must have both movements: the palace of my soul must have somehow two lifts—a lift which is always going up from below, and a lift which is always going down from above. I must both be seeking and be having. I must both move and repose.

BARON FRIEDRICH VON HÜGEL

WE mislead ourselves by thinking of the supreme crises in the moral and spiritual life as though they were always choices between things good and things obviously and definitely evil. But they are not always, they are not even usually, that. The associations of the word temptation lead us astray. The temptations of life!—ah! yes, insincerity, impurity, intemperance, callousness, cowardice, and so on, through the whole catalogue of man's obvious and miserable sins. Such things are real enough, and important enough, and the man who could put up a good fight against them all would do very well indeed. But we should still have to ask of such a man how far he had really got in the achievement of a character fit for the Kingdom; we should still have to ask, indeed, whether he had yet met and overcome his major temptations. And the answer, if he were in a position to give it, might very well be that he had not got so very far after all, and that the most searching tests, as well as those most truly creative of character and insight, if rightly met, were still to come. For to get rid of the intrinsically and obviously nasty things from life is but to clear the ground for building a rich and Christ-like positivity of character, and that takes place very largely through temptations of a different order. In the one case a man has to find strength to curb the animal in himself, to give up dirt, even if it be for the moment very attractive dirt, for pearls; in the other case he is often called upon to do something far more difficult, namely, to have the austerity and the insight to give up pearls for pearls, things really good for things better.

H. H. FARMER

WHERE then shall Hope and Fear their objects find?
Must dull suspense corrupt the stagnant mind?
Must helpless man, in ignorance sedate,
Roll darkling down the torrent of his fate?
Must no dislike alarm, no wishes rise,
No cries attempt the mercies of the skies?
Enquirer, cease, petitions yet remain,
Which heav'n may hear, nor deem religion vain.
Still raise for good the supplicating voice,·
But leave to heav'n the measure and the choice,
Safe in His power, whose eyes discern afar
The secret ambush of a specious pray'r.
Implore His aid, in His decisions rest,
Secure whate'er He gives, He gives the best.
Yet when the sense of sacred presence fires,
And strong devotion to the skies aspires,
Pour forth thy fervours for a healthful mind,
Obedient passions, and a will resign'd:
For love, which scarce collective man can fill;
For patience sov'reign o'er transmuted ill;
For faith, that panting for a happier seat,
Counts death kind Nature's signal of retreat:
These goods for man the laws of heav'n ordain,
These goods He grants, who grants the pow'r to gain;
With these celestial wisdom calms the mind,
And makes the happiness she does not find.

SAMUEL JOHNSON

AFTER this the saint goes out of the granary and, returning to the monastery, sits down half-way at the place where afterwards a cross, fixed in a mill-stone, and standing to this day, is to be seen at the roadside. And while the saint, weary with age as I have said, rested there, sitting for a little while, behold the white horse, a faithful servant, runs up to him, the one which used to carry the milk-pails to and fro between the byre and the monastery. He, coming up to the saint, wonderful to tell, lays his head against his breast—inspired, as I believe, by God, by whose dispensation every animal has sense to perceive things according as its Creator Himself has ordained—knowing that his master was soon about to leave him, and that he would see him no more, began to whinny and to shed copious tears into the lap of the saint as though he had been a man, and weeping and foaming at the mouth. And the attendant, seeing this, began to drive away the weeping mourner, but the saint forbade him, saying, 'Let him alone, let him alone, for he loves me. Let him pour out the tears of his bitter lamentation into this my bosom. Lo! now, thou, man as thou art, and possessing a rational soul, couldst in no wise know anything about my departure save what I myself have just now told thee: but to this brute beast, devoid of reason, the Creator Himself has clearly in some way revealed that his master is about to go away from him.' And so saying, he blessed his servant the horse as it sadly turned to go away from him. And then, going on and ascending the hill that overlooks the monastery, he stood for a little while on its top, and there standing and raising both hands he blessed his monastery, saying, 'Upon this place, small though it be and mean, not only the kings of the Scotic people with their peoples, but also the rulers of barbarous and foreign races with the people subject to them, shall confer great and no common honour: by the saints also even of other churches shall no common reverence be accorded to it.'

ST. ADAMNAN

THOSE who are united by religion should be united by charity.

*   *   *

Our fallibility and the shortness of our knowledge should make us peaceable and gentle. Because I may be mistaken, I must not be dogmatical and confident, peremptory and imperious. I will not break the certain laws of charity for a doubtful doctrine or of uncertain truth.

*   *   *

Whoever is bound to obey in the first instance, if he fails is bound to repent in the second.

*   *   *

Religion begins in knowledge, proceeds in practice, and ends in happiness.

*   *   *

We never better enjoy ourselves than when we most enjoy God.

*   *   *

Nothing should alienate us from one another but that which alienates us from God.

*   *   *

It is impossible for a man to be made happy by putting him into a happy place, unless he be first in a happy state.

*   *   *

He that hath no government of himself hath no enjoyment of himself.

*   *   *

He that commands others is not so much as free, if he doth not govern himself. The greatest performance in the life of man is the government of his spirit.

*   *   *

We ought to be such as we intend to appear.

BENJAMIN WHICHCOTE

THERE is hardly a man or woman in the world who has not got some corner of self into which he or she fears to venture with a light. The reasons for this may be various, as various as the individual souls. Nevertheless, in spite of the variety of reasons, the fact is universal. For the most part we hardly know our own reasons. It is an instinct, one of the quick instincts of corrupt nature. We prophesy to ourselves that, if we penetrate into that corner of self, something will have to be done which either our laziness or our immortification would shrink from doing. If we enter that sanctuary, some charm of easy devotion or smooth living will be broken. We shall find ourselves face to face with something unpleasant, something which will perhaps constrain us to all the trouble and annoyance of a complete interior revolution, or else leave us very uncomfortable in conscience. We may perhaps be committed to something higher than our present way of life, and that is out of the question. Religion is yoke enough as it is. So we leave this corner of self curtained off, locked up like a room in a house with disagreeable associations attached to it, unvisited like a lumber closet where we are conscious that disorder and dirt are accumulating, which we have not just now the vigour to grapple with. But do we think that God cannot enter there except by our unlocking the door? Or see anything when He is there, unless we hold Him a light? . . .

We know how His eye rests upon us incessantly, and takes us all in, and searches us out, and as it were burns us up with His holy gaze. His perfections environ us with the most awful nearness, flooding us with insupportable light. To His eye there is not only no concealment, there is not even a softening shade, or a distance to subdue the harshness and veil the unworthiness. Yet, for all this, to be straightforward with God is neither an easy nor a common grace. O with what unutterable faith must we believe in our own falsehood, when we can feel it to be anything like a shelter in the presence of the all-seeing God!

FREDERICK WILLIAM FABER

IF I build my felicity upon my estate or reputation, I am happy so long as the tyrant or the railer will give me leave to be so. But when my concernment takes up no more room or compass than myself, then so long as I know where to breathe and to exist, I know also where to be happy: for I know I may be so in my own breast, in the court of my own conscience; where, if I can but prevail with myself *to be* innocent, I need bribe neither judge nor officer to *be pronounced* so. The pleasure of the religious man is an easy and a portable pleasure, such a one as he carries about in his bosom without alarming either the eye or envy of the world. A man putting all his pleasures into this one is like a traveller's putting all his goods into one jewel; the value is the same, and the convenience greater.

There is nothing that can raise a man to that generous absoluteness of condition as neither to cringe, to fawn, or to defend meanly, but that which gives him that happiness within himself for which men depend upon others. For surely I need salute no great man's threshold, sneak to none of his friends or servants, to speak a good word for me to my conscience. It is a noble and a sure defiance of a great malice, backed with a great interest; which yet can have no advantage of a man but from his own expectations of something that is without himself. But if I can make my duty my delight; if I can feast and please and caress my mind with the pleasures of worthy speculations or virtuous practices; let greatness and malice vex and abridge me if they can: my pleasures are as free as my will; no more to be controlled than my choice or the unlimited range of my thoughts and my desires.

ROBERT SOUTH

'I WILL sing of thy mercy and judgement', says David. When we fix ourselves upon the meditation and the modulation of the mercy of God, even His judgements cannot put us out of tune, but we shall sing and be cheerful even in them. As God made grass for beasts before He made beasts, and beasts for man before He made man; as in that first generation, the creation, so in the regeneration, our re-creating, He begins with that which was necessary for that which follows, mercy before judgement. Nay, even to say that mercy was first is to post-date mercy; to prefer mercy but so, is to diminish mercy. The names of first or last derogate from it, for first and last are but rags of time, and His mercy has no relation to time, no limitation in time; it is not first nor last, but eternal, ever-lasting. Let the devil make me so far desperate as to conceive a time when there was no mercy, and he hath made me so far an atheist as to conceive a time when there was no God. If I despoil Him of His mercy any one minute and say, Now God hath no mercy, for that minute I discontinue His very Godhead, and His being. . . . Mercy considered externally, and in the practice and in the effect, began not at the helping of man, when man was fallen and became miserable, but at the making of man, when man was nothing. . . . Particular mercies are feathers of His wings, and that prayer 'Lord, let Thy mercy lighten upon us, as our trust is in Thee', is our birdlime. Particular mercies are that cloud of quails which hovered over the host of Israel, and that prayer, 'Lord, let Thy mercy lighten upon us' is our net to catch, our garner to fill of, those quails.

JOHN DONNE

HOLY purity of heart sees God, and true devotion enjoys Him.

If thou lovest, thou shalt be loved.

If thou servest, thou shalt be served.

If thou fearest, thou shalt be feared.

If thou dost good to others, fitting it is that others should do good to thee.

But blessed is he who truly loves and desires not to be loved again.

Blessed is he who serves and desires not to be served.

Blessed is he who fears and desires not to be feared.

Blessed is he who does good to others and desires not that others should do good to him.

But because these things are very sublime and of high perfection, therefore they that are foolish can neither understand them nor attain unto them.

There are three things that are very sublime and very profitable, which he who has once acquired shall never fall.

The first is that thou bear willingly and gladly, for the love of Christ, every affliction that shall befall thee.

The second is that thou daily humble thyself in everything thou doest, and in everything thou seest.

The third is that thou love faithfully with all thy heart that invisible and supreme Good which thou canst not behold with thy bodily eyes.

BROTHER GILES

THE golden apple of selfhood, thrown among the false gods, became an apple of discord because they scrambled for it. They did not know the first rule of the holy game, which is that every player must by all means touch the ball and then immediately pass it on. To be found with it in your hands is a fault: to cling to it, death. But when it flies to and fro among the players too swift for eye to follow, and the great Master Himself leads the revelry, giving Himself eternally to His creatures in the generation, and back to Himself in the sacrifice, of the Word, then indeed the eternal dance 'makes heaven drowsy with the harmony'. All pains and pleasures we have known on earth are early initiations in the movements of that dance: but the dance itself is strictly incomparable with the sufferings of this present time. As we draw nearer to its uncreated rhythm, pain and pleasure sink almost out of sight. There is joy in the dance, but it does not exist for the sake of joy. It does not even exist for the sake of good, or of love. It is Love Himself, and Good Himself, and therefore happy. It does not exist for us, but we for it. . . . As our earth is to all the stars, so doubtless are we men and our concerns to all creation; as all the stars are to space itself, so are all creatures, all thrones and powers and mightiest of the created gods, to the abyss of the self-existing Being, who is to us Father and Redeemer and indwelling Comforter, but of whom no man nor angel can say nor conceive what He is in and for Himself, or what is the work that He 'maketh from the beginning to the end'. For they are all derived and unsubstantial things. Their vision fails them and they cover their eyes from the intolerable light of utter actuality, which was and is and shall be, which never could have been otherwise, which has no opposite.

C. S. LEWIS

THE decisive test of character occurs, not in any abstract realm whatever, but in those concrete situations of life where, person confronting person, the demand arises for fully personal deed and dealing. Chesterton says somewhere that a man can make only one great discovery, namely, that there are other persons in the world besides himself; other beings, that is to say, who, because they are persons, obstruct the free and lordly passage of thought, refusing to be mastered as the mind can master and make its own a theorem of thought, and opposing to the will a different kind of barrier from that which inert matter offers. Persons have their private and peculiar ideas, feelings and needs organized in an inaccessible citadel of independence, and therefore create a situation of problem and responsibility. Once made or even glimpsed, the discovery of the other person is deeply disturbing to the egotism of human nature, so disturbing that we are all adepts at evading the responsibilities which it imposes. The crudest way of evasion is to ride rough-shod over the other person, thus denying the reality of his personal being by seeking to exploit, enslave, or crush him. . . . The subtlest way of evading the discovery of the other person is the way of abstraction. Humanitarianism is a grand-sounding word, but it can sometimes mean something very much thinner than human kindness. It can mean a gush of sentiment which leaves selfishness unbroken at its centre; it can mean a bleak theory advocated by thin-lipped intellectualists who love their theories better than their fellows; it can be a policy of State or a scheme of charity organization which raises the standard of living and leaves untouched the quality of life.

A. C. CRAIG

IT is infinitely easier to suffer in obedience to a human command than to accept suffering as free, responsible men. It is infinitely easier to suffer with others than to suffer alone. It is infinitely easier to suffer as public heroes than to suffer apart and in ignominy. It is infinitely easier to suffer physical death than to endure spiritual suffering. Christ suffered as a free man alone, apart and in ignominy, in body and in spirit, and since that day many Christians have suffered with Him.

*   *   *

We always used to think it was one of the elementary rights of man that he should be able to plan his life in advance, both private life and professional. That is a thing of the past. The pressure of events is forcing us to give up 'being anxious for the morrow'. But it makes all the difference in the world whether we accept this willingly and in faith (which is what the Sermon on the Mount means) or under compulsion. For most people not to plan for the future means to live irresponsibly and frivolously, to live just for the moment, while some few continue to dream of better times to come. But we cannot take either of these courses. We are still left with only the narrow way, a way often hardly to be found, of living every day as if it were our last, yet in faith and responsibility living as though a splendid future still lay before us. 'Houses and fields and vineyards shall yet again be bought in this land', cries Jeremiah as the Holy City is about to be destroyed, a striking contrast to his previous prophecies of woe. It is a divine sign and pledge of better things to come, just when all seems blackest. Thinking and acting for the sake of the coming generation, but taking each day as it comes without fear and anxiety— that is the spirit in which we are being forced to live in practice. It is not easy to be brave and hold out, but it is imperative.

DIETRICH BONHOEFFER

SAY, what saw you, Man?
　And say, what heard?
I saw while Angels sang,
　Jesus the Word.

Saw you aught else, Man?
　Aught else heard you?
I saw the Son of Man,
　And the wind blew.

Saw you beside, Man?
　Or heard beside?
I saw, while murderers mocked,
　The Crucified.

Nay! what is this, Man?
　And who is He?
The Holy Child must die
　For you and me.

Oh! say, Brother! Oh! say, Brother!
　What then shall be?
Home in His Sacred Heart
　For you and me.

Oh! what can we give, Brother!
　For such a thing?
Body and soul, Brother!
　To Christ the King.

LIONEL JOHNSON

MY common conversation I do acknowledge austere, my behaviour full of rigour, sometimes not without morosity; yet at my
Devotion I love to use the civility of my knee, my hat, my hand,
with all those outward and sensible motions which may express or
promote my invisible Devotion. I should violate my own arm
rather than a Church; nor willingly deface the name of saint or
martyr. At the sight of a Cross or Crucifix I can dispense with
my hat, but scarce with the thought or memory of my Saviour. I
cannot laugh at, but rather pity, the fruitless journeys of Pilgrims, or contemn the miserable condition of Fryars; for, though
misplaced in Circumstances, there is something in it of Devotion.
I could never hear the Ave-Mary Bell without an elevation; or
think it a sufficient warrant, because *they* erred in one circumstance, for me to err in all, that is in silence and dumb contempt.
Whilst, therefore, they directed their Devotions to *Her*, I offered
mine to God, and rectified the Errors of their Prayers by rightly
ordering my own. At a solemn Procession I have wept abundantly,
while my consorts, blind with opposition and prejudice, have
fallen into an excess of scorn and laughter. There are, questionless,
both in Greek, Roman, and African Churches, Solemnities and
Ceremonies, whereof the wiser zeals do not make Christian use,
and stand condemned by us, not as evil in themselves, but as
allurements and baits of superstition to those vulgar heads that
look asquint on the face of Truth, and those unstable Judgements
that cannot consist in the narrow point and centre of virtue without a reel or stagger to the Circumference.

SIR THOMAS BROWNE

THE Renaissance began with the affirmation of man's creative individuality; it has ended with its denial. Man without God is no longer man: that is the religious meaning of the internal dialectic of modern history, the history of the grandeur and of the dissipation of humanist illusions. Interiorly divided and drained of his spiritual strength, man becomes the slave of base and unhuman influences; his soul is darkened and alien spirits take possession of it. The elaboration of the humanist religion and the divinization of man and of humanity properly forbode the end of humanism. The flowering of the idea of humanity was possible only so long as man had a deep belief in and consciousness of principles above himself, and was not altogether cut off from his divine roots. During the Renaissance he still had this belief and consciousness and was therefore not yet completely separated; throughout modern history the European has not totally repudiated his religious basis. It is thanks to that alone that the idea of humanity remained consistent with the spread of individualism and of creative activity. The humanism of Goethe had a religious foundation, he kept his faith in God. The man who has lost God gives himself up to something formless and inhuman, prostrates himself before material necessity. Nowadays there is none of that 'Renaissential' play and inter-play of human powers which gave us Italian painting and Shakespeare and Goethe; instead inhuman forces, spirits unchained from the deep, crush man and becloud his image, beating upon him like waves from every side. It is they, not man, who have been set free. Man found his form and his identity under the action of religious principles and energies; the confusion in which he is losing them cannot be re-ordered by purely human efforts.

NICHOLAS BERDYAEV

WE begin, I think, when we set out to lie and deceive, by having an increased sense of power. When I am lying, if I am at all good at the art, I am conscious of occupying a superior position. I know the truth, but to get my own way I impose delusions on others, thus triumphing over them doubly—by having a monopoly of truth on the matter in question and by altering the world in accordance with my will. . . .

I suppose the successful liar may continue to enjoy this feeling of triumph and superiority, so that he does not notice what is happening to him. But something very terrible is happening. The lie does not stay outside his soul; it does not remain the mere instrument used so cleverly by the self; it invades the self and becomes part of it. I have heard that actors who have played one part for a long time sometimes become temporarily deranged and cannot distinguish their real selves from the person whom they were representing in the drama. Something of the same kind happens to the man who has cultivated insincerity, but his is not a temporary derangement. He has played a part before the world so long, he has adapted his opinions and his conduct so often to match the circumstances, he has projected so many different versions of himself, that he does not know what he is really like in himself; or worse still, he may have played the part of the disinterested and noble character so long that he has come to believe that he is really disinterested and noble. . . .

What has happened to him? He has lost the power to know himself, and with it the power to repent, unless the grace of God should, in some flash of revelation, dissolve the blinding veil he has bound upon his own eyes. One who cannot know himself cannot repent—that is why the Heavenly City includes none 'that loveth or maketh a lie'.

W. R. MATTHEWS

BOTH the spiritual and the bodily powers of a man increase and become perfected and strengthened by their exercise. By exercising your hand in writing, sewing, or knitting you will accustom it to such work; by frequently exercising yourself in composition you will learn to write easily and well; by exercising yourself in doing good works or in conquering your passions and temptations you will in time learn to do good works easily and with delight and with the help of God's all-active grace you will easily learn to conquer your passions. But if you cease writing, sewing, knitting or if you only do so seldom, you will write, sew, and knit badly. If you do not exercise yourself in composition, or do so very seldom, if you live in the material cares of life only, it will probably become difficult for you to connect a few words together, especially upon spiritual subjects; the work set you will seem to you like an Egyptian labour. If you cease praying, or pray seldom, prayer will be oppressive to you. If you do not fight against your passions, or only do so seldom and feebly, you will find it very difficult to fight against them; they will give you no rest, and your life will be poisoned by them, if you do not learn how to conquer these evil inward enemies that settle in your heart. Therefore labour and activity are indispensable for all. Life without activity is not life, but something monstrous—a sort of phantom of life. This is why it is the duty of every man to fight continually and persistently against the slothfulness of the flesh. God preserve every Christian from indulging it! 'They that are Christ's have crucified the flesh with the affections and lusts.' 'Unto every one that hath shall be given, and he shall have abundance; but from him that hath not shall be taken away even that which he hath.'

FATHER JOHN SERGIEFF

HOW much care is necessary to preserve the life of some flowers! They must be boxed up in the winter, others must be covered with glasses in their springing up, the finest and richest mould must be sifted about their roots, and assiduously watered, and all this is little enough, and sometimes too little to preserve them, whilst other common and worthless flowers grow without any help of ours; yet we have no less to do to rid our gardens of them than we have to make the former grow there.

Thus stands the case with our hearts in reference to the motions of grace and sin. Holy thoughts of God must be assiduously watered by prayer, earthed up by meditation, and defended by watchfulness; and yet all this is sometimes too little to preserve them alive in our souls. Alas! the heart is a soil that agrees not with them; they are tender things, and a small matter will nip and kill them. To this purpose is the complaint of the divine poet (Herbert):

> Who would have thought a joy
>   so coy?
> To be offended so,
>   and go
> So suddenly away?
> Hereafter I had need
>   take heed,
> Joys among other things
>   have wings
> And watch their opportunities of flight,
> Converting in a moment day to night.

But vain thoughts and unholy suggestions, these spread themselves, and root deep in the heart, they naturally agree with the soil; so that it is almost impossible at any time to be rid of them. It is hard to forget what it is our sin to remember.

JOHN FLAVEL

ALL beneficent and creative power gathers itself together in silence, ere it issues out in might. Force itself indeed is naturally silent and only makes itself heard, if at all, when it strikes upon obstructions to bear them away as it returns to equilibrium again. The very hurricane that roars over land and ocean flits noiselessly through spaces where nothing meets it. The blessed sunshine says nothing as it warms the vernal earth, tempts out the tender grass, and decks the field and forest in their glory. Silence came before creation, and the heavens were spread without a word. Christ was born at dead of night; and though there has been no power like His, 'He did not strive nor cry, neither was His voice heard in the streets.' Nowhere can you find any beautiful work, any noble design, any durable endeavour, that was not matured in long and patient silence ere it spake out in its accomplishment. *There* it is that we accumulate the inward power which we distribute and spend in action, put the smallest duty before us in dignified and holy aspects, and reduce the severest hardships beneath the foot of our self-denial. There it is that the soul, enlarging all its dimensions at once, acquires a greater and more vigorous being, and gathers up its collective forces to bear down upon the piecemeal difficulties of life and scatter them to dust. There alone can we enter into that spirit of self-abandonment by which we take up the cross of duty, however heavy, with feet however worn and bleeding they may be. And thither shall we return again, only into higher peace and more triumphant power, when the labour is over and the victory won, and we are called by death into God's loftiest watch-tower of contemplation.

JAMES MARTINEAU

BETTER it is to be heavy-laden and near one that is strong than relieved of one's load and near one that is weak. When thou art heavy-laden, thou art near to God, who is thy strength and is with them that are in trouble. When thou art relieved, thou art near but to thyself, who art thine own weakness. For the virtue and strength of the soul grows and is confirmed by trials of patience.

He that desires to be alone without the support of a master and guide will be like the tree that is alone in the field and has no owner. However much fruit it bears, passers-by will pluck it all, and it will not mature.

The tree that is cultivated and kept with the favour of its owner gives in due season the fruit that is expected of it.

The soul that is alone and without a master, and has virtue, is like the burning coal that is alone. It will grow colder rather than hotter.

He that falls alone remains on the ground alone and holds his soul of small account, since he trusts it to himself alone.

If thou fearest not to fall alone, how dost thou presume to rise alone? See how much more can be done by two together than by one alone!

He that falls heavy laden will have difficulty in rising with his load.

And he that falls and is blind will not, in his blindness, rise up alone; and if he rise up alone he will journey whither it is not fitting.

ST. JOHN OF THE CROSS

I OFTEN think how heavy a responsibility we should feel it, how careful we should be, if we realized how great an influence casual words may have. When one is young, one's whole life is waiting to be swayed, without as a rule any very definite bias on one's own part: and the most important things are often settled by the chance remark of someone we love or admire. I often think of this when I am with young people, who always seem to take to me and trust me very quickly: I suppose because they know that I do love youth not grudgingly as elders are apt to do. Their trust is so magnificently generous: one would like to deserve it by saying now and then something which in moments of doubt or difficulty may be of use to them: at least one would wish to avoid anything which might hinder instead of helping their sense of the proportion of things. If one's words have been ever a help and never a hindrance, that surely is a useful life and no other justification needed for it, even if it has accomplished nothing more tangible.

*   *   *

So far as my personal object in life goes, I should wish to attain two things: first the confidence of more time, not to be confined within the narrow limits of one life; secondly the sense of death as a new and wonderful adventure. If these two can attain to a real sense of certainty, my own inner life will have succeeded—and I hope to succeed. It will mean the absolute liberation from fear, which is a form of slavery.

It is for this reason that I am willing to risk my life, not from any natural fearlessness or recklessness. I am careful of the things that I need to enjoy life: careful of money, health as far as may be, and time as far as I can: these are necessary. But to be careful of life itself is to assume that it is more important than what is beyond life. To risk one's life seems to me the only way in which one can attain to a real (as distinct from a merely theoretic) sense of immortality unless one happens to be among the lucky people in whom faith is born perfect.

FREYA STARK

HE is wise to Godward, however it be with him in the world; and, well knowing that he cannot serve two masters, he cleaves to the better, making choice of that good part which cannot be taken from him, not so much regarding to get that which he cannot keep, as to possess himself of that good which he cannot lose.

He is just in all his dealings with men, hating to thrive by injury and oppression, and will rather leave behind something of his own than filch from another's heap.

He is not closefisted, where is just occasion of his distribution, willingly parting with those metals which he regards only for use, not caring for either their colour or substance; earth is to him no other than itself, in what hue soever it appeareth.

In every good cause he is bold as a lion, and can neither fear faces nor shrink at dangers, and is rather heartened with opposition; pressing so much the more, where he finds a large door open and many adversaries, and when he must suffer, doth as resolutely stoop as he did before valiantly resist.

He is holily temperate in the use of all God's blessings, as knowing by whom they are given, and to what end; neither dares either to mislay them or to mis-spend them lavishly, as duly weighing upon what terms he receives them, and fore-expecting an account.

Such a hand doth he carry upon his pleasures and delights, that they turn not away with him; he knows how to slacken the reins without a debauched kind of dissoluteness, and how to straiten them without a sullen rigour.

                                        JOSEPH HALL

I THINK that self-consciousness, a terrible malady, is one's misfortune as well as one's fault. But the want of any earnest effort at correcting a fault is worse, perhaps, than the fault itself. And I feel such great, such very great, need for amendment here. This great fault brings its punishment in part even now. I mean there is a want of brightness, cheerfulness, elasticity of mind about the conscious man or woman. He is prone to have gloomy, narrow, sullen thoughts, to brood over fancied troubles and difficulties; because, making everything refer to and depend on self, he naturally can get none of that comfort which they enjoy whose minds naturally turn upwards for help and light. In this way I do suffer a great deal. My chariot wheels often drag very heavily. And yet I know that I am writing now under the influence of a depressing disorder, and that I may misinterpret my real state of mind. No one ought to be happier, as far as advantages of employment in a good service, and kindness of friends, can contribute to make me happy. And on the whole, I know my life is a happy one. I am sure that I have a far larger share of happiness than falls to the lot of most people. . . . Well, one does not often say these things to another person. But it is a relief to say them. I know the remedy quite well. It is a very simple case for the doctor to deal with, but it costs the patient just everything short of life, when you have to dig right down, and cut out by the roots an evil of a whole life's standing. I assure you it is hard work, because these feelings of ours are such intangible, intractable things. It is hard to lay hold of and mould and direct them. But I pray God that I may not willingly yield to these gloomy, unloving feelings. As often as I look out of myself upon Him, His love and goodness, then I catch a bright gleam. I have much need of your prayers, indeed, for grace and strength to correct faults of which I am conscious, to say nothing of unknown sin.

JOHN COLERIDGE PATTESON

IT is at once delicate and dangerous to speak of one's own spiritual condition, or of the emotional sentiments on which one's conclusions regarding it are often so doubtfully founded. Egotism in the religious form is perhaps more tolerated than in any other; but it is not on that account less perilous to the egotist himself. There need be, however, less delicacy in speaking of one's beliefs than of one's feelings; and I trust I need not hesitate to say that I was led to see at this time, through the instrumentality of my friend, that my theologic system had previously wanted a central object to which the heart, as certainly as the intellect, could attach itself; and that the true centre of an efficient Christianity is, as the name ought of itself to indicate, 'the Word made flesh'. Around this central sun of the Christian system—appreciated, however, not as a *doctrine* which is a mere abstraction, but as a Divine Person—so truly Man, that the affections of the human heart can lay hold upon Him, and so truly God, that the mind, through faith, can at all times and in all places be brought into direct contact with Him—all that is really religious takes its place in a subsidiary and subordinate relation. I say subsidiary and subordinate. The Divine Man is the great attractive centre, the sole gravitating point of a system which owes to Him all its coherency, and which would be but a chaos were He away. It seems to be the existence of the human nature in this central and paramount object that imparts to Christianity, in its subjective character, its peculiar power of influencing and controlling the human mind. There may be men who, through a peculiar idiosyncrasy of constitution, are capable of loving, after a sort, a mere abstract God, unseen and inconceivable; though as shown by the air of sickly sentimentality borne by almost all that has been said and written on the subject, the feeling in its true form must be a very rare and exceptional one. In all my experience of men I never knew a genuine instance of it.

HUGH MILLER

THEY are all gone into the world of light!
  And I alone sit lingering here;
Their very memory is fair and bright,
  And my sad thoughts doth clear.

It glows and glitters in my cloudy breast
  Like stars upon some gloomy grove,
Or those faint beams in which this hill is drest,
  After the sun's remove.

I see them walking in an air of glory,
  Whose light doth trample on my days:
My days, which are at best but dull and hoary,
  Mere glimmering and decays.

O holy hope! and high humility,
  High as the heavens above!
These are your walks, and you have show'd them me
  To kindle my cold love.

Dear, beauteous death! the Jewel of the Just,
  Shining no where but in the dark;
What mysteries do lie beyond thy dust;
  Could man outlook that mark!

He that hath found some fledg'd bird's nest may know
  At first sight if the bird be flown;
But what fair well or grove he sings in now,
  That is to him unknown.

And yet, as angels in some brighter dreams
  Call to the soul when man doth sleep:
So some strange thoughts transcend our wonted themes,
  And into glory peep.

                                        HENRY VAUGHAN

THUS time passed on: my heart was replenished with mirth and wantonness, and pleasing scenes of vanity were presented to my imagination, till I attained the age of eighteen years; near which time I felt the judgements of God in my soul like a consuming fire; and looking over my past life, the prospect was moving. I was often sad and longed to be delivered from these vanities; then again my heart was strongly inclined to them and there was in me a sore conflict; at times I turned to folly, and then again sorrow and confusion took hold of me. In a while, I resolved totally to leave off some of my vanities; but there was a secret reserve in my heart of the more refined part of them, and I was not low enough to find true peace. Thus for some months I had great troubles; there remaining in me an unsubjected will, which rendered my labours fruitless, till at length through the merciful continuance of heavenly visitations, I was made to bow down in spirit before the Lord. I remember one evening I had spent some time in reading a pious author; and, walking out alone, I humbly prayed to the Lord for His help, that I might be delivered from all those vanities which so ensnared me. Thus, being brought low, He helped me; and as I learned to bear the Cross, I felt refreshment to come from His presence; but, not keeping in that strength which gave victory, I lost ground again; the sense of which greatly affected me; and I sought deserts and lonely places, and there with tears did confess my sins to God and humbly craved help of Him. And I may say with reverence, He was near to me in my troubles, and in those times of humiliation opened my ear to discipline. I was now led to look seriously at the means by which I was drawn from pure truth, and learned this—that if I would live in the life which the faithful servants of God lived in, I must not go into company as heretofore in my own will; but all the cravings of sense must be governed by a divine principle.

JOHN WOOLMAN

THE only really vital thing in religion is to become acquainted with God. Solomon says, 'Acquaint thyself with God, and be at peace'; and I believe every one of us would find that a peace that passes all understanding must necessarily be the result of this acquaintance. . . .

It is difficult to explain just what I mean by this acquaintance with God. We are so accustomed to think that knowing things *about* Him is sufficient—what He has done, what He has said, what His plans are, and what are the doctrines concerning Him—that we stop short of that knowledge of what He really is in nature and character, which is the only satisfactory knowledge.

In human relations we may know a great deal about a person without at all necessarily coming into any actual acquaintance with that person; and it is the same in our relations with God. We may blunder on for years thinking we know a great deal about Him, but never quite sure of what sort of a Being He actually is, and consequently never finding any permanent rest or satisfaction. And then, perhaps suddenly, we catch a sight of Him as He is revealed in the face of Jesus Christ, and we discover the real God, as He is, behind, beneath, and within all the other conceptions of Him which may have heretofore puzzled us, and from that moment our peace flows like a river; and in everything and through everything, when perhaps we can rejoice in nothing else, we can always and everywhere 'rejoice in God, and joy in the God of our salvation'. We no longer need His promises; we have found Himself, and He is enough for every need.

MRS. PEARSALL SMITH

To read an account of Christ as written by an indifferent person is to read an unchristian account of Him. Because no one who acknowledges Him can be indifferent to Him, but stands in such relations to Him that the highest reverence must ever be predominant in his mind when thinking or writing of Him. And again, what is the impartiality required? Is it that a man shall neither be a Christian, nor yet not a Christian? The fact is that religious veneration is inconsistent with what is called impartiality, which means that as you see some good and some evil on both sides, you identify yourself with neither, and are able to judge of both. And this holds good with all human parties and characters, but not with what is divine and consequently perfect; for then we should identify ourselves with it, and are perfectly incapable of passing judgement upon it. If I think that Christ was no more than Socrates (I do not mean in degree, but in kind), I can, of course, speak of him impartially—that is, I assume at once that there are faults and imperfections in His character, and on these I pass my judgement; but if I believe in Him, I am not His judge, but His servant and creature, and He claims the devotion of my whole nature, because He is identical with goodness, wisdom, and holiness. Nor can I, for the sake of strangers, assume another feeling and another language, because this is compromising the highest duty—it is like denying Him instead of confessing Him. This all passed through my mind when I heard that the article was written in a purely historical tone, and yet stated the resurrection as a matter of fact. Now, if the resurrection be true, Christianity surely is true; and then how can any one think of Christ except religiously?

THOMAS ARNOLD OF RUGBY

THAT God should deal familiarly with man, or, which is the same thing, that He should permit man to deal familiarly with Him, seems not very difficult to conceive, or presumptuous to suppose, when some things are taken into consideration. Woe to the sinner that shall dare to take a liberty with Him that is not warranted by His word, or to which He Himself has not encouraged him! When he assumed man's nature He revealed Himself as the Friend of man, as the Brother of every soul that loves Him. He conversed freely with man while He was upon the earth, and as freely with him after His resurrection. I doubt not, therefore, that it is possible, even now, to enjoy an access to Him unaccompanied by ceremonious awe, easy, delightful, and without constraint. This, however, can only be the lot of those who make it the business of their lives to please Him and to cultivate communion with Him. And then, I presume, there can be no danger of offence, because such a habit of soul is of His own creation and, near as we come, we come no nearer to Him than He is pleased to draw us. If we address Him as children, it is because He tells us He is our Father. If we unbosom ourselves to Him as a Friend, it is because He calls us friends; and if we speak to Him in the language of love, it is because He first used it, thereby teaching us that it is the language He delights to hear from His people. But I confess that through the weakness, the folly and corruption of human nature, this privilege, like all other Christian privileges, is liable to abuse. There is a mixture of evil in everything we do; indulgence encourages us to encroach, and while we exercise the rights of children, we become childish.

WILLIAM COWPER

IN regard to some of the most important things in life it is remarkable how little human beings know their liberty—how little they realize that the grand discoveries of the various inductive sciences still leave us free to range with the upper parts of our minds. In these days also when people are so much the prisoners of systems —especially the prisoners of those general ideas which mark the spirit of the age—it is not always realized that belief in God gives us greater elasticity of mind, rescuing us from too great subservience to intermediate principles, whether these are related to rationality or ideology or science. It even enables us to leave more play in our minds for the things that nature or history may still have to reveal to us in the near future. Similarly Christianity is not tied to régimes—not compelled to regard the existing order as the very end of life and the embodiment of all our values. Christians have too often tried to put the brake on things in the past, but at the critical turning-points in history they have less reason than others to be afraid that a new kind of society or civilization will leave them with nothing to live for. We are told by many people that a new age needs a new mentality, but so often when one reads these writers further all that they really say is that if we don't do now the things they have been continually telling us to do since 1919 we shall have the atomic bomb and probably deserve it. I have nothing to say at the finish except that if one wants a permanent rock in life and goes deep enough for it, it is difficult for historical events to shake it. There are times when we can never meet the future with sufficient elasticity of mind, especially if we are locked in the contemporary systems of thought. We can do worse than remember a principle which both gives us a firm Rock and leaves us the maximum elasticity for our minds— the principle: Hold to Christ, and for the rest be totally uncommitted.

HERBERT BUTTERFIELD

I HAVE no knowledge to take up the Lord in all His strange ways, and passages of deep and unsearchable providences. For the Lord is before me, and I am so bemisted that I cannot follow Him; He is behind me and following at my heels, and I am not aware of Him; He is above me, but His glory so dazzleth my twilight of short knowledge that I cannot look up to Him. He is upon my right hand, and I see Him not; He is upon my left hand, and within me, and goeth and cometh, and His going and coming are a dream to me; He is round about me, and compasseth all my goings, and still I have Him to seek. He is every way higher and deeper and broader than the shallow and ebb hand-breadth of my short and dim light can take up; and therefore I would that my heart could be silent and sit down in the learnedly-ignorant wondering at the Lord whom men and angels cannot comprehend. I know that the noon-day light of the highest angels, who see Him face to face, seeth not the borders of His infiniteness. They apprehend God near at hand; but they cannot comprehend Him. And therefore it is my happiness to look afar off, and to come near to the Lord's back parts, and to light my candle at His brightness, and to have leave to sit and content myself with a traveller's light, without the clear vision of an enjoyer. I would seek no more till I were in my country than a little watering and sprinkling of a withered soul, with some half out-breakings and half out-lookings of the beams, and small ravishing smiles, of a revealed and believed-in Godhead. A little of God would make my soul bank-full.

SAMUEL RUTHERFORD

THE first thing to be said is that whatever religious faith, feelings and hopes we have, we are bound to shape them into form in life, not only at home, but in the work we do in the world. Whatever we feel justly, we ought to shape; whatever we think, to give it clear form; whatever we have inside of us, our duty is to mould it outside of ourselves into clear speech or act, which, if it be loving, will be luminous. 'If ye know these things, happy are ye if ye do them.' The true successes of life are contained in that principle. It is a first law. It is, for example, the beginning, middle, and end of education. The knowledge poured into the young nowadays is worth little or nothing unless we also make them gain the habit first of shaping it clearly in their mind, and then putting it into form in word or act outside of their mind. . . . The secret of education and of self-education is to learn to embody our thoughts in words, luminously; to realize our knowledge in experiment; to shape our feelings into action; to represent without us all we are within; and to do this steadily all our life long.

It is the secret also of religion in life. As God shapes His love in the universe, as the Master of Love lived His love into action and speech, so our religion is to be done, not dreamed; lived, not contemplated. We must bring it into the open air, let it go in and out among men, test it in daily life, shape it in our manners, our voice, our decisions, in all our doings. Every effort thus made, and not given up till the shaping is completed, is at once education and aspiration. For the shaping of one religious act is the impulse to, and the foundation of, another and higher act. But if we keep our religious faiths, feelings, and hopes within, unshaped in life, we shall never realize them; least of all in these days of trial and temptation when we need them most; and in the end they will die of starvation. The proper food of all inward religion is the forms we give it outwardly.

STOPFORD BROOKE

WE want an assurance that the soul in reaching out to the unseen world is not following an illusion. We want security that faith and worship, and above all love, directed towards the environment of the spirit are not spent in vain. It is not sufficient to be told that it is good for us to believe this, that it will make better men and women of us. We do not want a religion that deceives us for our own good. There is a crucial question here; but before we can answer it, we must frame it.

The heart of the question is commonly put in the form, 'Does God really *exist*? It is difficult to set aside this question without being suspected of quibbling. But I venture to put it aside because it raises so many unprofitable side issues, and at the end it scarcely reaches deep enough into religious experience. . . . Theological or anti-theological argument to prove or disprove the existence of a deity seems to me to occupy itself largely with skating among the difficulties caused by our making a fetish of this word. It is all so irrelevant to the assurance for which we hunger. In the case of our human friends we take their existence for granted, not caring whether it is proven or not. Our relationship is such that we could read philosophical arguments designed to prove the non-existence of each other, and perhaps even be convinced by them—and then laugh together over so odd a conclusion. I think that it is something of the same sort of security we should seek in our relationship with God. The most flawless proof of the existence of God is no substitute for it; and if we have that relationship, the most convincing disproof is turned harmlessly aside. If I may say it with reverence, the soul and God laugh together over so odd a conclusion.

SIR ARTHUR EDDINGTON

I SAY to all those who complain of the want of the precious out-pourings of the Spirit:

1. Bless God if you want nothing essential for the making out of a saving interest in Christ. God hath given unto you Christ Jesus, the greatest gift He had; and since your heart is laid out for Him, He will with Him give you all things that are good for you in their season.

2. I do believe, upon a strict search and trial, after you have understood the communications of the Spirit, you are not so great a stranger to many things as you suspected yourself to be. But,

3. Remember the promises of life and of peace with God are nowhere in Scripture made unto those special things of which you allege the want: the promises are made unto faith followed with holiness; and it may be presumed that many heirs of glory do not in this life partake of some of these things, but 'are in bondage all their days through fear of death': we may seek after them, but God is free to give or withhold them.

4. Many do seek after such manifestations before they give credit by faith to God's word. He hath borne record that there is life enough for men in Christ Jesus; and if men would, by believing, set to their seal that God is true, they should partake of more of these excellent things.

5. I may say, many have not honourable thoughts of the Spirit of God, whose proper work is to put forth the foresaid noble operations. They do not adore Him as God, but vex and resist Him; and many, complaining of the want of these things, are not at the pains to seek the Spirit in His outgoings, and few do set themselves apart for such precious receptions. Therefore be at more pains in religion, give more credit to His word, and esteem more highly of the Spirit of God, and so you may find more of these excellent things.

WILLIAM GUTHRIE

IF you take my advice you will try to get a certain amount of time alone with yourself. I think when we are alone we sometimes see things a little bit more simply, more as they are. Sometimes when we are with others, especially when we are talking to others on religious subjects, we persuade ourselves that we believe more than we do. We talk a great deal, we grow enthusiastic, we speak of religious emotions and experiences. This is, perhaps, sometimes good. But when we are alone we see just how much we really believe, how much is mere enthusiasm excited at the moment. We get face to face with Him, and our heat and passion go, and what is really permanent remains. We begin to recognize how very little love we have, how very little real pleasure in that which is alone of lasting importance. Then we see how poor and hollow and unloving we are; then, I think, we also begin to see that this poverty, this hollowness, this unloving void, can be filled only by Him who fills all in all. To get alone—to dare to be alone—with God, this, I am persuaded, is one of the best ways of doing anything in the world. ... . If we are ever to be or to do anything, if we are ever to be full of deep, permanent, rational enthusiasm, we must know God. If we are ever to know each other, we must know Him first. . . . I believe that we do most for those whom God has begun to teach us to love, not by constantly thinking of their goodness, their grace, their simplicity, but by never thinking of them apart from God, by always connecting their beauty and purity with a higher Beauty and a higher Purity, by seeing God in them. Let us learn to make every thought of admiration and love a kind of prayer of intercession and thanksgiving. Thus human love will correct itself with, and find its root in, divine love. But this we can do only if we are willing to be alone with Him.

FORBES ROBINSON

THE glories of our blood and state
   Are shadows, not substantial things;
There is no armour against fate;
   Death lays his icy hand on kings:
     Sceptre and crown
     Must tumble down
And in the dust be equal made
With the poor crooked scythe and spade.

Some men with swords may reap the field,
   And plant fresh laurels where they kill;
But their strong nerves at last must yield;
   They tame but one another still:
     Early or late
     They stoop to fate,
And must give up their murmuring breath,
When they, pale captives, creep to death.

The garlands wither on your brow,
   Then boast no more your mighty deeds!
Upon Death's purple altar now,
   See, where the victor-victim bleeds.
     Your heads must come
     To the cold tomb:
Only the actions of the just
Smell sweet and blossom in their dust.

                             JAMES SHIRLEY

No spot of sin or sorrow there; all pollution wiped away, and all tears with it; no envy or strife; not as here among men, one supplanting another, one pleading and fighting against another, dividing this point of earth with fire and sword:—no, this inheritance is not the less by division, by being parted among so many brethren; everyone hath it all, each his crown, and all agreeing on casting them down before His throne from whom they have received them, and in the harmony of His praises.

This inheritance is often called a kingdom, and a crown of glory. This last word may allude to those garlands of the ancients, and this is its property, that the flowers in it are all amaranths (as a certain plant is named) and so it is called a crown of glory that fadeth not away.

No change at all there, no winter and summer: not like the poor comforts here, but a bliss always flourishing. The grief of the saints here is not so much for the changes of outward things as of their inward comforts. *Suavis hora, sed brevis mora.* Sweet presences of God they sometimes have, but they are short, and often interrupted; but there no cloud shall come betwixt them and their sun; they shall behold Him in His full brightness for ever. As there shall be no change in their beholding, so no weariness nor abatement of their delight in beholding. They sing a new song, always the same, and yet always new. The sweetest of our music, if it were to be heard but for one whole day, would weary them who are most delighted with it. What we have here cloys, but satisfies not; the joys above never cloy, and yet always satisfy.

ROBERT LEIGHTON

MAKE not the consequences of virtue the ends thereof. Be not beneficent for a name or cymbal of applause; nor exact and just in commerce for the advantages of trust and credit, which attend the reputation of true and punctual dealing: for these rewards, though unsought for, plain virtue will bring with her. To have other by-ends in good actions sours laudable performances, which must have deeper roots, motives and instigations, to give them the stamp of virtues.

*　　　　*　　　　*

Let not the law of thy country be the non-ultra of thy honesty; nor think that always good enough which the law will make good. Narrow not the law of charity, equity, mercy. Join gospel righteousness with legal right. Be not a mere Gamaliel in the faith, but let the sermon in the mount be thy targum unto the law of Sinai.

*　　　　*　　　　*

Let not the sun in Capricorn go down upon thy wrath, but write thy wrongs in ashes. Draw the curtain of night upon injuries, and shut them up in the tower of oblivion, and let them be as though they had not been. To forgive our enemies, yet hope that God will punish them, is not to forgive enough. To forgive them ourselves, and not to pray God to forgive them, is a partial piece of charity. Forgive thine enemies totally, and without any reserve that however God will revenge thee.

SIR THOMAS BROWNE

THE feast which Levi gave to our Lord on his conversion is such a cheerful type to me of the Christian life. It is a festival of joy and gratitude for a conversion. We are sinners forgiven; *there* is a reason for perpetual praise. A feast represents a forgiven sinner's whole course; he is welcomed home, and he has brought more joy to heaven than there was before. His sorrow for sin is not a mortified, humiliated, angry disgust with himself. It is a humble, hopeful sorrow, always 'turning into joy'. So if his very sorrows are the material of joy, his life may be represented by the feast which Levi the Publican gave to our Lord, who had forgiven and called him. 'But I am unworthy of joy; I am willing to work and suffer if need be as a sinner. I don't look for joy.' That is a sentiment true for a pagan, but it contradicts the whole Creed of the Catholic Church. 'I believe in the Holy Catholic Church, the communion of saints, the forgiveness of sins.' So our life ought to be full of the joy of grateful love; the remembrance of sin means the remembrance of the love that called us out of our sins and forgave us the whole debt. And besides, Levi made Him a great feast. It is not that we are to be cheerful for our own gratification, but our life is to be full of praise and thanksgiving, singing and making melody in our hearts to the Lord, for the honour of Jesus. Levi made *Him* a feast. Our habitual joy is due to God, and honours God; and our joy means not a reflection of the joy of God, but is the very joy of God. . . . If we are sinners forgiven, we ought to behave as forgiven, welcomed home, crowned with wonderful love in Christ, and so cheer and encourage all about us, who often go heavily because we reflect our gloom upon them instead of our grateful love, hope, confidence.

FATHER CONGREVE

THERE are two deep principles in Nature in apparent contradiction—one, the aspiration after perfection; the other, the longing after repose. In the harmony of these lies the rest of the soul of man. There have been times when we have experienced this. Then the winds have been hushed, and the throb and tumult of the passions have been blotted out of our bosoms. That was a moment when we were in harmony with all around, reconciled to ourselves and to our God; when we sympathized with all that was pure, all that was beautiful, all that was lovely.

This was not stagnation, it was fulness of life—life in its most expanded form, such as nature witnessed in her first hour. This is life in that form of benevolence which expands into the mind of Christ. And when this is working in the soul, it is marvellous how it distils into a man's words and countenance. Strange and magical is the power of that collect wherein we pray to God, 'Who alone can order the wills and affections of sinful men, to grant unto His people that they may love the thing which He commands, and desire that which He promises; that so among the sundry and manifold changes of the world, our hearts may surely there be fixed where true joys are to be found.' There is a wondrous melody in that rhythm; the words are the echoes of the thought. The mind of the man who wrote them was in repose—all is ringing of rest. We do not wonder when Moses came down from the mount on which he had been bowing in adoration before the harmony of God that his face was shining with a brightness too dazzling to look upon.

F. W. ROBERTSON

Thinking of God

GOD thinks continuously of each one of us as if He had no one but ourselves: it is therefore no more than just if we think continuously of Him, as if we had no one but Himself. Oh, the blindness of men who, not having yet understood that they were created only for God, dare to think it strange that we should always think of God, and that we have no more familiar object than God. There is a time to speak and a time to be silent, says the Sage; a time to laugh and a time to weep; a time to sow and a time to reap. There are fixed times for all things, and it would manifestly be out of order to do at one moment what we ought to do at another. But there is no time in which we ought not to love God and think of Him. We ought to think of Him by day and by night, when we are busy and when we are at rest, in company and in solitude, at all times and in every place. The holy companionship of God never wearies us, never embarrasses us; it is not troublesome nor bitter nor inconvenient, and when we take it with us in our familiar thoughts, it has the blessed property of mingling with whatever we are doing; it never separates itself from our affairs, not even from our most trifling conversations.

But in what way, they ask, are we always to think of God, so that this continual application shall not greatly interfere with our worldly life? Think of Him often, and such thoughts will not disturb or deflect you; they will rather accompany you, go before you, follow you, and generally awaken you. If someone ordered you to make twenty-five or thirty respirations every minute, you would repulse such a suggestion; you would think it would impede all your actions. Yet you breathe every moment without noticing it, and you do not cease to act with as much liberty as if nothing were going on in you.

FRANCOIS MALAVAL

My friends, learn from this story of Joseph and the prominent place in the Bible which it occupies—learn, I say, how hateful to God are family quarrels; how pleasant to God are family unity and peace, and mutual trust, and duty, and helpfulness. And if you think that I speak too strongly on this point, recollect that I do no more than St. Paul does, when he sums up the most lofty and mystical of all his Epistles, the Epistle to the Ephesians, by simple commands to husbands and wives, parents and children, masters and servants, as if he should say—You wish to be holy? you wish to be spiritual? Then fulfil these plain family duties, for they too are sacred and divine, and he who despises them despises the ordinances of God. And if you despise the laws of God, they will surely avenge themselves on you. If you are bad husbands or bad wives, bad masters or servants, you will smart for it, according to the eternal laws of God, which are at work around you all day long, making the sinner punish himself whether he likes it or not.

Examine yourselves—ask yourselves, each of you, Have I been a good brother? . . . son? . . . husband? . . . father? . . . servant? If not, all professions of religion will avail me nothing. If not, let me confess my sins to God, and repent and amend at once, whatever it may cost me. The fulfilling these plain duties is the true test of my faith, the true sign and test whether I really believe in God and in Jesus Christ our Lord. Do I believe that the world is Christ's making? and that Christ is governing it? Do I believe that these plain family relationships are Christ's sacred appointments? Do I believe that our Lord Jesus was made very man of the substance of His mother, to sanctify these family relationships, and claim them as the ordinances of God His Father?

CHARLES KINGSLEY

IT cannot be thought that God sends events to a living soul in order that the soul may be simply passive under the events. If God sends you an event, it must have a meaning; it must be a sign to you that you are to do something, to brace yourself up to some action or to some state of feeling. All that God sends to a human spirit must be significant. God has sent us His Word. We know that He designs us not simply to hear it, but to embrace it with a living faith and a loving obedience. We are to meditate upon it, to apply it to our consciences, mould our character and conduct in conformity to it. Now the same God who has sent us His Word equally sends us the daily occurrences of life, the chief difference being that, whereas the Word has a general voice for all, in which each is to find his own case represented, the occurrences are charged with a more specific message to individuals. Now there is many a man who says, 'I will conform myself to the general indication of God's will made to me by His Word'; comparatively few who say, 'I will conform myself to the special indications of God's will made to me by His Providence.' But why so few? Does not God come home to us more closely, more searchingly, more personally by His Providence than even by His Word? Does not His finger rest upon each of us more particularly in the government of affairs than even in revelation? And why are we to imagine, as many seem to imagine, that no other events but such as are afflictive and calamitous have a voice for us? Why not every event? Why is not the ordinary intercourse of life to be regarded as furnishing in God's design and intention opportunities of either doing or receiving good? I say of doing *or* receiving good. Surely either one or the other is a thing greatly to be coveted. In nine cases out of ten we may fail of *doing good*; but if in those cases we have received good, and received it too in the course of His plan for us, and in the way of His Providence, surely the occurrence which has called us off from our ordinary pursuit is not to be regretted.

EDWARD MEYRICK GOULBURN

It is this that constitutes the link between religion and art—that both point to an ideal perfection beyond all that is ever realized in the present and actual experience of man; and further, may we not add, that the highest end and use of material and outward beauty, and the secret of its power over us, is mainly in this, that it is the symbol and type, the unconscious expression of a deeper beauty than meets the eye, the beauty of love and purity and truth and goodness. If we try to conceive why it is that this strange, indefinable thing we call beauty exists, or why the hand of God has scattered it with infinite prodigality over the face of the visible world,—why it is that beyond mere material form, and ordered sequence of material phenomena, and adaptation to the uses of man, far and wide over heaven and earth, over mountain and forest and stream and sea, suffusing, insinuating itself into all the processes of nature, the dawn and the sunset, the spring, the summer glory, the fading splendour of autumn woods and fields, the softened play of light and shadow, the infinitely varied wealth and harmony of colour and form, into all fair scenes and sweet sounds—if we ask why God has so made the world that this strange element of beauty is everywhere added to use, and what is the secret of its power over us—its power not merely to awaken admiration, to charm and thrill us, but, at least in some minds, to stir in them inexpressible longings and aspirations that transcend the range of experience—if we ask such questions as these, I think the answer must be that the highest end and use of all this material glory of God's world lies in its power to carry us beyond itself, to be the suggestive type and symbol of a beauty which eye hath not seen, nor ear heard, not imagination conceived.

JOHN CAIRD

CHRIST has been misunderstood by those who think of Him as offering a consolation prize. He told them how to keep the fire living in the grate; told them that the fire itself was of the same nature with the stars. He promised them a passion freed from its cage; seeing in it not a danger to the soul but the soul itself, passionate for that which is not itself, the soul become all a lover and finding everywhere the scent and beauty, the allurement, of that which it loves. He knew the error of those philosophers who see nothing between their own lonely selves and God in an infinite distance; for Him man was not a lonely spirit on the earth, lonely in his private search for a far distant God. God is to be found and seen, not through an illimitable vacancy between Himself and the spirit of man, but in and through all things that stir men to love. He is to be seen in the light of a cottage window as well as in the sun or the stars.

Only those who know this escape from the dullness and routine of life. Blake has told us that Satan is the god of things that are not, 'the lost traveller's dream under the hill'. He is the god of the rainbow in the next field but one, in seeking whom men miss the true God in the meadow where they stand. . . . Christ tells us to value men and things for their own sake; we must have a passion for men if we are to have one for God. 'Inasmuch as ye have done it unto one of these little ones, ye have done it unto me.' It is not only of conduct that these words are true. If we are to understand Christianity, we must extend them and say—Inasmuch as ye have seen one of these little ones, ye have seen me; and—Inasmuch as ye have understood one of these little ones, ye have understood me. God is revealed to us in the known, not hidden in the unknown; and we have to find Him where we are.

ARTHUR CLUTTON-BROCK

I WONDER if I can venture to tell you what is in my mind about intercessory prayer at this moment. I wonder if I dare tell you, I wonder if it would be wise to speak, as I feel compelled to speak, to such a mixed multitude as you are. Yes, I will venture and will risk. For I am a debtor to all the devout and serious-minded people among you with a debt I can never fully discharge. And then, who knows but it may be the same with some of you some day as it was with me. Well, a dear friend of mine was sick and was seemingly nigh unto death. And I was much in prayer for him that he might be spared to his family and to his friends and to his great work. And one night as I was in that intercessory prayer a Voice suddenly spake and said to me—'Are you in real earnest in what you ask? Or are you uttering, as usual, so many of your idle words in this solemn matter? Now to prove the sincerity and the integrity of your love for your friend, and to seal the truth of what you say about the value of his life, will you give Me and yourself a solid proof that you are in real earnest in what you say?' 'What is the proof?' I asked, all trembling, and without looking up. And the Voice said, 'Will you consent to transfer to your sick friend the half of your remaining years? Suppose you have two more years to live and work yourself, will you give over one of them to your friend? Or if you have ten years yet before you, will you let your friend have five of them?' I sprang to my feet in a torrent of sweat. It was a kind of Garden of Gethsemane to me. But, like Gethsemane, I got strength to say, 'Let it be as Thou hast said. Thy will be done. Not my will but Thine be done.' Till I lay down that never-to-be-forgotten night with a clean heart and a good conscience as never before both toward God and toward my much-talented friend. How the matter is to end I know not. How the case is to work out I cannot tell. Enough for me and enough for you that my story is true and is no idle tale.

ALEXANDER WHYTE

ONCE when St. Francis was about to eat with Brother Leo, he was greatly delighted to hear a nightingale singing. So he suggested to his companion that they also should sing praise to God alternately with the bird. While Leo was pleading that he was no singer, Francis lifted up his voice and, phrase by phrase, sang his duet with the nightingale. Thus they continued from vespers to lauds, until the saint had to admit himself beaten by the bird. Thereupon the nightingale flew on to his hand, where he praised it to the skies and fed it. Then he gave it his blessing and it flew away.

*   *   *

Brother Tebaldo once told us something that he himself had seen. When St. Francis was preaching one day to the people of Trevi, a noisy and ungovernable ass went careering about the square, frightening people out of their wits. And when it became clear that no one could catch it or restrain it, St. Francis said to it, 'Brother ass, please be quiet and allow me to preach to the people.' When the donkey heard this it immediately bowed its head and, to everyone's astonishment, stood perfectly quiet. And the Blessed Francis, fearing that the people might take too much notice of this astonishing miracle, began saying funny things to make them laugh.

*   *   *

Brother Masseo has said that he was present with the Blessed Francis when he preached to the birds. Rapt in devotion, Francis once found by the roadside a large flock of birds, to whom he turned aside to preach, as he had done before to another lot. But when the birds saw him approaching, they all flew away at the very sight of him. Then he came back and began to accuse himself most bitterly, saying, 'What effrontery you have, you impudent son of Peter Bernardone!'—and this because he had expected irrational creatures to obey him as if he, not God, were their Creator.

JOHN R. H. MOORMAN

WHAT do I mean by saying that Christianity is unthinkable apart from the Church? In the first place, if Christianity is the revelation of the depths of the personal and of love as the ultimate meaning of the universe, it can find expression only in a community. Love can exist only between persons. It demands community. Christ is not Christ without the community of love which He founded. . . .

The Church is indispensable, secondly, as the society which has to do with men's ultimate concern. Our ultimate concern is about our fundamental being and the meaning of our life and destiny. Other associations have to do with men's immediate concerns in their temporal existence. If one admits that men have an ultimate concern, distinct from the endless variety of their immediate interests, and if one believes or hopes that the universe is not indifferent to that ultimate concern, then there must be an association in which that ultimate concern finds expression in religious worship.

Thirdly, the Church is necessary because Christianity is essentially the proclamation, not of a demand, but of fulfilment. It is not the insistence on love as an ideal to be striven after, but the joyful news that *God is* love and that we know this because His love has been manifested in history. Grace and truth *came* by Jesus Christ. The Church is the witness to that revelation and the continuing embodiment of that new life. Take away the Church and Christianity itself disappears. It is a delusion to suppose that we can cut out twenty centuries of lived experience and establish a direct relation between ourselves and the historic Jesus. . . . If we relate ourselves to Him, it is as those who stand in the living stream of tradition and are caught up and borne forward by it.

J. H. OLDHAM

To wisest moralists 'tis but given
To work rough border-law of Heaven,
Within this narrow life of ours,
These marches 'twixt delimitless Powers.
Is it, if Heaven the future showed,
Is it the all-severest mode
To see ourselves with the eyes of God?
God rather grant, at His assize,
He sees us not with our own eyes!

Heaven, which man's generations draws,
Nor deviates into replicas,
Must of as deep diversity
In judgement as creation be.
There is no expeditious road
To pack and label men for God,
And save them by the barrel-load.
Some may perchance, with strange surprise,
Have blundered into Paradise.
In vasty dusk of life abroad,
They fondly thought to err from God,
Nor knew the circle that they trod;
And wandering all the night about,
Found them at morn where they set out.
Death dawned; Heaven lay in prospect wide:—
Lo! they were standing at His side!

FRANCIS THOMPSON

Passion and Affection

THE problem life sets us is that of a steady progress in the conversion of passion ennobled by affection into affection intensified by its connexion with passion, but the element of passion steadily tends to recede into the background of a mellow and golden past. It is good, in season, to have been the romantic lover, but it is permanently good only on condition that one reaches out to what is beyond, that the actual experience of ardent youth is made a stage on the way to the different experiences of a perfect middle age and later life. And the task of so living in the present while it lasts that one is helped, not hindered, in the advance to the future is so easily spoiled by the natural human reluctance to meet the new and untried that it demands unremitting vigilance and unrelaxing effort to escape the danger of moral sloth.

This is but one example of the problem which is raised by all the relations and situations of the personal moral life. To evade any of them is detrimental; to rest in any of them as final equally spoils them. All have to be used, as good in their measure, and all have to be transformed. It is because, with advancing years, we all tend to grow weary of the progressive transformation, and try to put off our harness, that middle age is attended, for all of us, with grave danger of moral stagnation. We all want to say to ourselves, 'I have now come to the point when I may stand still; I want to be no better, no wiser, no more responsive to the call of moral adventure, than I am now. Henceforth let my life be a placid backwater.' But to yield to the suggestion is moral death. Here is the special witness of the moral life to man's position in the universe as a creature whose being is rooted at once in time and in eternity.

A. E. TAYLOR

THE SERVANT. Eternal Wisdom, if anyone were to give me the whole earth for my own, it would not be so agreeable to me as the truth and the advantage which I have found in Thy sweet doctrines. Therefore do I desire from the very bottom of my heart that Thou, the Eternal Wisdom, wouldst teach me still more. Lord, what is that which belongs, above all things, to a servant of Eternal Wisdom who is desirous to live for Thee alone? Lord, I should like to hear about the union of Pure Reason with the Holy Trinity when, in the true reflection of the eternal birth of the Word, and in the regeneration of her own Spirit, Reason is ravished from herself and stands face to face with God.

ETERNAL WISDOM. Let not him ask about what is highest in doctrine, who still stands on what is lowest in a good life. I will teach thee what will profit thee more.

THE SERVANT. Lord, what wilt Thou teach me?

ETERNAL WISDOM. I will teach thee to die and will teach thee to live. I will teach thee to receive Me lovingly, and will teach thee to praise Me lovingly. Behold, this is what properly belongs to thee.

THE SERVANT. Eternal Wisdom, if I had the power to fulfil my wishes, I know not whether, in this temporal state, I ought to wish anything else, as to doctrine, than how to die to myself and all the world, how to live wholly for Thee. But Lord, dost Thou mean a spititual dying or a bodily dying?

ETERNAL WISDOM. I mean both one and the other.

THE SERVANT. What need have I, Lord, of being taught how to die bodily? Surely it teaches itself when it comes.

ETERNAL WISDOM. He who puts his teaching off till then, will find it too late.

THE BLESSED HENRY SUSO

THERE are wonders in true affection: it is a body of enigmas, mysteries and riddles; wherein two so become one as they both become two. I love my friend before my self, and yet methinks I do not love him enough: some few months hence my multiplied affection will make me believe I have not loved him at all. When I am from him, I am dead till I be with him; when I am with him, I am not satisfied, but would still be nearer him. United souls are not satisfied with imbraces, but desire to be truly each other; which being impossible, their desires are infinite, and must proceed without a possibility of satisfaction. Another misery there is in affection, that whom we truly love like our own selves, we forget their looks, nor can our memory retain the idea of their faces; and it is no wonder, for they are our selves, and our affection makes their looks our own. . . . Now, if we can bring out affections to look beyond the body, and cast an eye upon the soul, we have found out the true object, not only of friendship, but charity; and the greatest happiness that we can bequeath the soul is that wherein we all do place our last felicity—salvation; which though it be not in our power to bestow, it is in our charity and pious invocations to desire, if not procure and further. I cannot contentedly frame a prayer for my self in particular, without a catalogue for my friends; nor request a happiness wherein my sociable disposition doth not desire the fellowship of my neighbour. I never hear the toll of a passing bell, though in my mirth, without my prayers and best wishes for the departing spirit; I cannot go to cure the body of my patient, but I forget my profession, and call unto God for his soul; I cannot see one say his prayers but, in stead of imitating him, I fall into a supplication for him, who perhaps is no more to me than a common nature: and if God hath vouchsafed an ear to my supplication, there are surely many that never saw me, and enjoy the blessing of mine unknown devotions.

SIR THOMAS BROWNE

THE commands of God are all designed to make us more happy than we can possibly be without them.

* * *

Begin the day with God, and 'tis probable 'twill end with Him and goodness.

* * *

We are accountable to God for our time as for His other favours; and to squander it is a sin.

* * *

The greatest of all disorders is to think we are whole, and need no help.

* * *

God evermore gives power answerable to what He requires of us.

* * *

Forgiveness of sins is the first thing we ought to pray for, because sin is the occasion of all other evils that ever befall us.

* * *

There is no man but knows more evil of himself than of any other.

* * *

If you feel the need of a Saviour, as the sick do the want of ease and help, you are in the way of salvation. It is but to ask, and God will give you what you desire.

* * *

Never do anything which you are sure you must repent of before you die.

* * *

Nothing promotes atheism and impiety more than the great disagreement between the faith and practice of men professing to be Christians.

* * *

You call yourself a Christian. Pray how are you distinguished from an heathen?

THOMAS WILSON

THE mind is a fire, of which thought is a flame. Like flame it tends upwards. Men do their best to smother it by turning the point downwards.

*   *   *

Our mind has more thoughts than our memory can store; it delivers many judgements of which it could not give the reasons; it sees further than it can reach, it knows more truths than it can explain. A large part of itself could be very usefully employed in searching out the arguments which have determined it, in defining the perceptions which have touched and then escaped it. There is for the soul many a lightning-flash with which she has little to do; they pass over and illuminate her so rapidly that she loses the recollection of them. We should be astonished at the number of things she would be found to have seen if, in returning upon all that has passed within her, record could be made of it, if only from memory, and by a careful searching out of all the circumstances. We do not *hunt* enough in ourselves; and like children we neglect what we have in our pockets, and think only of what is in our hands, or before our eyes.

*   *   *

Those who have denied themselves grave thoughts are apt to fall into sombre thoughts.

*   *   *

Do not let your intellect be more exacting than your taste, nor your judgement more severe than your conscience.

*   *   *

Let us have an uplifted heart; and a humble mind.

*   *   *

A mind has still some strength, so long as it has strength to bewail its feebleness.

JOSEPH JOUBERT

EVERMORE bestow the greatest part of thy goods in works of mercy, and the less part in voluntary works. . . . If men be so foolish that they will bestow the most part of their goods in voluntary works which they be not bound to keep but willingly and by their devotion, and leave the necessary works undone which they are bound to do, they and all their voluntary works are like to go unto everlasting damnation. And I promise you, if you build a hundred churches, give as much as you can make to the gilding of saints and honouring of the church; and if thou go as many pilgrimages as thy body can well suffer and offer as great candles as oaks; if thou leave the works of mercy and the commandments undone, these works shall nothing avail thee. No doubt the voluntary works be good and ought to be done, but yet they must be so done that by their occasion the necessary works and the works of mercy be not delayed and forgotten. If you will build a glorious church unto God, see first yourselves to be in charity with your neighbours, and suffer not them to be offended by your works. . . . Again, if you list to gild and paint Christ in your churches, and honour him in vestments, see that before your eyes the poor people die not for lack of meat, drink, and clothing. Then do you deck the very true temple of God, and honour Him in rich vestures that will never be worn, and so forth use yourselves according unto the commandments; and then, finally, set up your candles and they will report what a glorious light remaineth in your hearts; for it is not fitting to see a dead man light candles. Then, I say, go your pilgrimages, build your material churches, do all your voluntary works; and they will then represent you unto God, and testify with you that you have provided Him a glorious place in your hearts.

HUGH LATIMER

CERTAIN things verily be of such manner filthy that they cannot be honest, as to avenge wrong or to wish evil of another. Those things ought to be had in hate, yea though thou shouldst have never so great advantage to commit them, or never so great punishment if thou didst them not; for nothing can hurt a good man but filthiness only. Certain things on the other side be in such manner honest that they cannot be filthy, of which kind be to will or wish all men good, to help thy friends with honest means, to hate vices, to rejoice with virtuous communication. Certain things verily be indifferent or between both, of their own nature neither good nor bad, honest nor filthy; as health, beauty, strength, fecundity, cunning, and such other. Of this last kind of things therefore nothing ought to be desired for itself, neither ought to be usurped more or less, but so far forth as they make and be necessary to the chief mark, I mean to follow Christ's living. The very philosophers have certain marks also imperfect and indifferent, in which a man ought not to stand still nor tarry, which also a man may conveniently use, referring them to a better purpose, and not to enjoy them and tarry upon them, putting his whole felicity in them: notwithstanding those intermediate and indifferent things do not all, after one manner and equally, either further or hinder them that be going unto Christ; therefore they must be received or refused, after as each of them is more or less of value unto thy purpose. Knowledge helpeth more unto piety than beauty or strength of body or riches, and though all learning may be applied to Christ, yet some helpeth more compendiously than other. Of this end and purpose see thou measure the profitableness or unprofitableness of all intermediate things.

ERASMUS

OUR first step is the sociableness, the communicableness of God; He loves holy meetings, He loves the communion of saints, the household of the faithful: *deliciae eius*, says Solomon, 'His delight is to be with the sons of men', and that the sons of men should be with Him. Religion is not a melancholy: the Spirit of God is not a damp: the Church is not a grave: it is a fold, it is an ark, it is a net, it is a city, it is a kingdom, not only a house but a house that hath many mansions in it. Always it is a plural thing, consisting of many. And very good grammarians amongst the Hebrews have thought and said that that name by which God notifies Himself to the world in the very beginning of Genesis, which is *Elohim*, as it is a plural word there, so it hath no singular. They say we cannot name God but plurally; so sociable, so communicable, so extensive, so derivative of Himself, is God, and so manifold are the beams and the emanations that flow from Him.

*   *   *

One of the most convenient hieroglyphics of God is a circle; and a circle is endless. Whom God loves He loves to the end; and not only to their own end, to their death, but to His end, and His end is that He might love them still. His hailstones and His thunderbolts and His showers of blood (emblems and instruments of His judgements) fall down in a direct line, and affect and strike some one person or place. His sun and moon and stars (emblems and instruments of His blessings) move circularly and communicate themselves to all. His Church is His chariot; in that He moves more gloriously than in the sun; as much more as His begotten Son exceeds His created Sun, and His Son of glory and of His right hand, the Sun of the firmament; and this Church, His chariot, moves in that communicable motion circularly; it began in the East, it came to us, and is passing now, shining out now, in the farthest West.

JOHN DONNE

TOUCHING musical harmony whether by instrument or by voice, it being but of high and low in sounds a due proportionable disposition, such notwithstanding is the force thereof, and so pleasing effects it hath in that very part of man which is most divine, that some have been thereby induced to think that the soul itself by nature is or hath in it harmony. A thing which delighteth all ages and beseemeth all states; a thing as seasonable in grief as in joy; as decent being added unto actions of greatest weight and solemnity, as being used when men most sequester themselves from action. . . .

In church music curiosity and ostentation of art, wanton or light or unsuitable harmony, such as only pleaseth the ear, and doth not naturally serve to the very kind and degree of those impressions which the matter that goeth with it leaveth or is apt to leave in men's minds, doth rather blemish and disgrace that we do than add either beauty or furtherance unto it. On the other side, these faults prevented, the force and equity of the thing itself, when it drowneth not utterly but fitly suiteth with matter altogether sounding to the praise of God, is in truth most admirable, and doth much edify, if not the understanding because it teacheth not, yet surely the affection, because therein it worketh much. They must have hearts very dry and tough, from whom the melody of psalms doth not sometime draw that wherein a mind religiously affected delighteth. Be it as Rabanus Maurus observeth, that at first the Church in this exercise was more simple and plain than we are, that their singing was little more than only a melodious kind of pronunciation; that the custom which we now use was not instituted so much for their cause which are spiritual, as to the end that into grosser and heavier minds, whom bare words do not easily move, the sweetness of melody might make some entrance for good things. St. Basil himself, acknowledging as much, did not think that from such inventions the least jot of estimation and credit thereby should be derogated.

RICHARD HOOKER

THERE is a class of philanthropists who act from a sense of abstract duty—they live and labour for man, self-devoted even to pain, but they have no tie to individuals and are ready to sacrifice the one and his rights in their zeal for the many. We can admire, but we cannot love them. There are others who have a strong tie to persons and give warm, loving help to what they see of want and suffering, but what they do not see scarcely exists to them, and they have not the comprehensive mind to act on high, far-reaching principle. We love, but cannot venerate them. The first belongs more to man, the second to woman. The first forgets the individual in the cause, the second sees no cause, only the individual.

Jesus Christ combined both, and how perfectly! There was a great ideal before Him, for which He lived and died—'the joy set before Him', to glorify God, and save the lost. But on His way He entered the house of Bethany. He knit bonds of personal sympathy, stopped to do many an act of tender compassion—to the widow's son, the poor blind beggar, the leper. Nay, in doing this He was doing the other. The personal benefits were types of the universal, and steps to it. Weeping before the grave of Lazarus, He was weeping over poor dead humanity, and His tears were dropping down into spiritual death to touch torpid hearts and quicken them—divine dew that became in a deeper agony drops of blood. It is this which gives all His life such power—that brings it so close to us, and yet makes it so grand, so tender, and so sublime, all that can still and satisfy the heart, and yet fill us with adoring awe, when we think of the end of the sacrifice of the Cross. It is like the sun that has a ray for the smallest chink in a prison but a flood of light for a world,—or the sea with little creek and rippling wave to touch the foot, but which spreads out into measureless breadths and sinks into fathomless depths. He is all for every one, and He is One for all.

JOHN KER

THEN he took him by the hand, and led him into a very large parlour that was full of dust, because never swept; the which, after he had reviewed a little while, the Interpreter called for a man to sweep. Now when he began to sweep, the dust began so abundantly to fly about that Christian had almost therewith been choked. Then said the Interpreter to a damsel that stood by, Bring hither the water and sprinkle the room; which when she had done, it was swept and cleansed with pleasure.

Then said Christian, What means this?

The Interpreter answered: This parlour is the heart of a man that was never sanctified by the sweet grace of the Gospel: the dust is his original sin and inward corruptions that have defiled the whole man. He that began to sweep at first is the Law; but she that brought water and did sprinkle it is the Gospel. Now, whereas thou sawest that so soon as the first began to sweep, the dust did so fly about that the room by him could not be cleansed, but that thou wast almost choked therewith: this is to shew thee that the Law, instead of cleansing the heart (by its working) from sin, doth revive, put strength into, and increase it in the soul, even as it doth discover and forbid it, but doth not give power to subdue.

Again, as thou sawest the damsel sprinkle the room with water, upon which it was cleansed with pleasure; this is to shew thee that when the Gospel comes in the sweet and precious influences thereof to the heart, then, I say, even as thou sawest the damsel lay the dust by sprinkling the floor with water, so is sin vanquished and subdued, and the soul made clean, through the faith of it, and consequently fit for the King of Glory to inhabit.

JOHN BUNYAN

ALTHOUGH I must indeed confess that very often, even through my bodily sensibilities, God has made my life uncommonly hard, I must also at once acknowledge that He has, on the other hand, been near me with quite uncommon aids of grace, so that I have been able to get through so many decades of this painful life already. Here, then, surely, there is room only for humble and adoring thankfulness.

*　　　*　　　*

A retrospect of my whole life, from the earliest period of my recollection down to the present hour, leaves me with this impression, that I have been, and am being, guided by a gracious and a mighty Hand, which has made, and is making, that possible to me which otherwise to me had been impossible. Oh that I had at all times unhesitatingly trusted and yielded myself to its guidance!

*　　　*　　　*

Of myself I can only say that I am an unprofitable servant; but I serve a good Master, who loves me with unwearied faithfulness.

*　　　*　　　*

I shall never be perfectly happy until I have reached my own fitting place in the lowest room, as *homo gregarius*—which will certainly be given me, at least in the world to come.

*　　　*　　　*

I have an insatiable longing for a condition in which, surrounded by realities, I should myself be real.

*　　　*　　　*

Oh what blessedness it will be for a man, when he has reached his destination and rest, when he has become a being perfectly balanced, completely in harmony with himself and with the external conditions of his existence!

RICHARD ROTHE

IF we would judge ourselves, we should not be judged. Be not deceived; for sin doth not end as it begins. When the terrors of Judas come upon the soul, the tongue cannot hide his sins; for despair and horror cannot be smothered; but he which hath Saul's spirit haunting him will rage as Saul did. There is a warning conscience, and a gnawing conscience. The warning conscience cometh before sin; the gnawing conscience followeth after sin. The warning conscience is often lulled asleep; but the gnawing conscience wakeneth her again. If there be any hell in this world, they which feel the worm of conscience gnaw upon their hearts may truly say that they have felt the torments of hell. Who can express that man's horror but himself? Nay, what horrors are there which he cannot express himself? Sorrows are met in his soul at a feast; and fear, thought, and anguish divide his soul between them. All the furies of hell leap upon his heart like a stage. Thought calleth to fear, fear whistleth to horror, horror beckoneth to despair and saith, Come and help me to torment this sinner. One saith that she cometh from this sin, and another saith that she cometh from that sin; so he goeth through a thousand deaths and cannot die. Irons are laid upon his body like a prisoner: all his lights are put out at once: he hath no soul fit to be comforted. Thus he lies as it were upon the rack, and saith that he bears the world upon his shoulders; and that no man suffereth that which he suffereth. So let him lie (saith God) without ease, until he confess and repent, and call for mercy. This is the goodly way which the serpent said would make you gods, and made him a devil. Therefore at the last learn the sleight of Satan in this wretched traitor. His subtilties are well called the depths of Satan; for he is so deep that few can sound him.

HENRY SMITH THE SILVER-TONGUED

LOOK in thy soul, and thou shalt beauties find
Like those which drowned Narcissus in the flood.
Honour and pleasure both are in thy mind,
And all that in the world is counted good.

Think of her worth, and think that God did mean
This worthy mind should worthy things embrace;
Blot not her beauties with thy thoughts unclean,
Nor her dishonour with thy passions base.

Kill not her quickening power with surfeitings;
Mar not her sense with sensuality;
Cast not her serious wit on idle things;
Make not her free will slave to vanity.

*   *   *

And thou my soul, Which turn'st thy curious eye
To view the beams of thine own form divine,
Know that thou can'st know nothing perfectly
While thou art clouded with this flesh of mine.

Take heed of overweening, and compare
Thy peacock's feet with thy gay peacock's train;
Study the best and highest things that are,
But of thyself an humble thought retain.

Cast down thyself, and only strive to raise
The glory of thy Maker's sacred Name;
Use all thy powers that blessed Power to praise
Which gives thee power to be, and use the same.

SIR JOHN DAVIES

SINCE life itself is uncertain, nothing which has life for its basis can boast much stability. Yet this is but a small part of our perplexity. We set out on a tempestuous sea, in quest of some port, where we expect to find rest but where we are not sure of admission; we are not only in danger of sinking in the way, but of being misled by meteors mistaken for stars, of being driven from our course by the changes of the wind, and of losing it by unskilful steerage; yet it sometimes happens that cross winds blow us to a safer coast, that meteors draw us aside from whirlpools, and that negligence or error contributes to our escape from mischiefs to which a direct course would have exposed us. Of those that by precipitate conclusions involve themselves in calamities without guilt, very few, however they may reproach themselves, can be certain that other measures would have been more successful.

In this state of universal uncertainty, where a thousand dangers hover about us, and none can tell whether the good that he pursues is not evil in disguise, or whether the next step will lead him to safety or destruction, nothing can afford any rational tranquillity but the conviction that, however we amuse ourselves with unideal sounds, nothing in reality is governed by chance, but that the universe is under the perpetual superintendence of Him who created it; that our being is in the hands of omnipotent Goodness, by whom what appears casual to us is directed for ends ultimately kind and merciful; and that nothing can finally hurt him who debars not himself from the divine favour.

SAMUEL JOHNSON

To the person that begins to understand spiritual and divine things, and that begins to know them, I understand that befalls which befalls those persons who, having by some accident lost the sight of their eyes, begin to recover it. I would say that, as those persons go knowing the being of things, according as they go recovering the sight of their eyes, first confusedly, as it befell to the blind man in the Gospel who, beginning to open his eyes, saw men and it seemed to him that they were trees; and afterwards less confusedly, until such time as little by little they come to see and know things in their own proper being; in the selfsame manner these persons go on knowing spiritual and divine things accordingly as they go purifying their minds with faith and with love and with union with God.

First they know them confusedly, and afterwards less confusedly, and so by little and little they go advancing in the knowledge of them, until such time as they arrive unto such pass, as they come to know God and the things that are God's in that manner which may be in this present life. And hence, so I understand, it proceeds that that thing which a person without the Spirit holds for holy and just and good in the things of God, another person who hath the Spirit condemns and reputes defective and evil. . . . Going on thus from one step to another, the clearness of that judgement increases which spiritual persons have of divine matters. Whereby I understand that the error of pious persons when, in those divine and spiritual matters which they know, they form conceptions according to that which they come to know by the first knowledge, not expecting other knowledges more clear and more evident, is no less than that of the blind man who begins to recover the sight of his eyes, when in the things which he begins to see he forms his conceptions according to that which they appeared unto him at the first, not expecting to see them better and more clearly.

JUAN DE VALDES

IT is the desire or, what is perhaps stronger still, the unconscious tendency to live as the rich man lived that defeats the claims of the poor. One of the inevitable results of civilization is the multiplication of artificial necessities, and of those who are eager to meet the demand for them. We need or think we need a thousand things we could very well do without, and there are a thousand people importuning us to spend our money on them—thrusting them into our very hands on the most tempting terms. Plainly there are many people who find the temptation to spend so strong that they simply cannot keep their money in their pockets. It is drawn from them as by an irresistible attraction. They have no bad conscience about it, but they just do not know where it goes. It goes on dress, on travelling, on trinkets, on personal adornments, and indulgence of every kind; and the result is that when the call of charity comes there is nothing to meet it. All works of love, from Christian missions down, are carried on under the pressure of a perpetual deficit. When people say they have not anything to give for such causes, they are as a rule telling the truth. They have nothing to give because they have already spent everything. But the true moral of this is that the call for charity is often also a call for self-denial and thrift. No one will ever have anything to give who has not learned to save, and no one learns to save without checking the impulse to spend his money for things which it would no doubt be pleasant enough to have, but which he can quite well do without. The rising generation is credited rightly or wrongly with excessive lack of restraint here. Everything goes. They live up to their means and beyond them, and have nothing to give away. This is not the way to become rich on earth, but what the parable teaches is the more serious lesson that it is not the way to become rich toward God. The man who has spent nothing on charity has no treasure in heaven. He is as poor as Lazarus there. He is on the way to a world in which he will not have a single friend.

JAMES DENNEY

THOUGH we are to treat all mankind as neighbours and brethren as any occasion offers, yet, as we can only live in the actual society of a few, and are by our state and condition more particularly related to some than others, so when our intercession is made an exercise of love and care for those amongst whom our lot is fallen, or who belong to us in a nearer relation, it then becomes the greatest benefit to ourselves and produces its best effects in our own hearts. If, therefore, you should always change and alter your intercessions according as the needs and necessities of your neighbours and acquaintances seem to require, beseeching God to deliver them from such and such particular evils, or to grant them this or that particular gift or blessing, such intercessions, besides the great charity of them, would have a mighty effect upon your own heart, as disposing you to every other good office, and to the exercise of every other virtue towards such persons as have so often a place in your prayers. This would make it pleasant to you to be courteous, civil, and condescending to all about you, and make you unable to say or do a rude or hard thing to those for whom you had used yourself to be so kind and compassionate in your prayers. For there is nothing that makes us love a man so much as praying for him; and when you can once do this sincerely for any man, you have fitted your soul for the performance of everything that is kind and civil towards him. . . . By considering yourself as an advocate with God for your neighbours or acquaintance you would never find it hard to be at peace with them yourself. It would be easy to you to bear with and forgive those for whom you particularly implored the divine mercy and forgiveness.

WILLIAM LAW

LET us then view God's providences towards us more religiously than we have hitherto done. Let us try to gain a truer view of what we are, and where we are, in His kingdom. Let us humbly and reverently attempt to trace His guiding hand in the years we have hitherto lived. Let us thankfully commemorate the many mercies He has vouchsafed to us in time past, the many sins He has not remembered, the many dangers He has averted, the many prayers He has answered, the many mistakes He has corrected, the many warnings, the many lessons, the much light, the abounding comfort which He has from time to time given. Let us dwell upon times and seasons, times of trouble, times of joy, times of trial, times of refreshment. How did He cherish us as children! How did He guide us in that dangerous time when the mind began to think for itself, and the heart to open to the world! How did He with His sweet discipline restrain our passions, mortify our hopes, calm our fears, enliven our heavinesses, sweeten our desolateness, and strengthen our infirmities! How did He gently guide us towards the strait gate! How did He allure us along His everlasting way, in spite of its strictness, in spite of its loneliness, in spite of the dim twilight in which it lay! He has been all things to us, He has been, as He was to Abraham, Isaac and Jacob, our God, our shield, and great reward, promising and performing, day by day. 'Hitherto hath He helped us'. 'He hath been mindful of us, and He will bless us'. He has not made us for naught; He has brought us thus far, in order to bring us further, in order to bring us to the end.

JOHN HENRY NEWMAN

I⊤ has been said by some that there is no religion in Shakespeare or, what is the same thing, no element of the divine in his view of the world. To this it may be said, there is the same element of the divine which is to be seen in the world itself. Shakespeare's purpose is to give a section of the real world that we may read the whole world by it. He does not himself moralise, but lets the picture speak.

But a poet may do much without moralizing. He may indicate the presence of two elements, destiny or what Christians call providence, and free-will, not always harmonizing—for this would not be true—but always present and therefore urging a wish for some solution which can only be found finally in a right view of God and man. Next, he may indicate how moral faults and weaknesses bring catastrophes in good characters—irresolution in Hamlet, jealousy in Othello, parental partiality in Lear, &c. Further, he may make us prefer, like Cato, to share the lot of the good man in adversity rather than that of the bad man in success, to love the right and hate the wrong, whatever circumstances surround them. And lastly, he may give such views of man's nature as exalt our conceptions of it, admiring without deifying it in some of its aspects, condemning without despising it in others. Besides, there may be the introduction of touches of Christian truth which make us feel that the heart of the author was with the speaker:

> Those holy fields
> Over whose acres walk'd those blessed feet
> Which, fourteen hundred years ago, were nail'd
> For our advantage on the bitter cross.

JOHN KER

IN the discharge of thy place set before thee the best examples; for imitation is a globe of precepts. And after a time set before thee thine own example; and examine thyself strictly, whether thou didst not best at first. Neglect not also the examples of those that have carried themselves ill in the same place; not to set off thyself by taxing their memory, but to direct thyself what to avoid. Reform, therefore, without bravery or scandal of former times and persons; but yet set it down to thyself as well to create good precedents as to follow them. Reduce things to the first institution, and observe wherein and how they have degenerate; but yet ask counsel of both times; of the ancient time, what is best; and of the latter time, what is fittest. Seek to make thy course regular, that men may know beforehand what they may expect; but be not too positive and peremptory; and express thyself well when thou digressest from thy rule. Preserve the right of thy place; but stir not questions of jurisdiction: and rather assume thy right in silence and *de facto*, than voice it with claims and challenges. Preserve likewise the rights of inferior places; and think it more honour to direct in chief than to be busy in all. Embrace and invite helps and advices touching the execution of thy place; and do not drive away such as bring thee information, as meddlers; but accept of them in good part.

FRANCIS BACON

HOW much soever men may differ in the course of life they prefer, and in their ways of palliating and excusing their vices to themselves; yet all agree in one thing, desiring to die the death of the righteous. This is surely remarkable. The observation may be extended further and put thus: Even without determining what that is which we call guilt or innocence, there is no man but would choose, after having had the pleasure or advantage of a vicious action, to be free of the guilt of it, to be in the state of an innocent man. This shows at least the disturbance and implicit dissatisfaction in vice. If we inquire into the grounds of it, we shall find it proceeds partly from an immediate sense of having done evil, and partly from an apprehension that this inward sense shall one time or another be seconded by an higher judgement, upon which our whole being depends. Now to suspend and drown this sense, and these apprehensions, be it by the hurry of business or of pleasure, or by superstition, or moral equivocations, this is in a manner one and the same, and makes no alteration at all in the nature of our case. Things and actions are what they are, and the consequences of them will be what they will be: why then should we desire to be deceived? As we are reasonable creatures, and have any regard to ourselves, we ought to lay these things plainly and honestly before our mind, and upon this, act as you please, as you think most fit; make that choice, and prefer that course of life, which you can justify to yourselves, and which sits most easy upon your mind. It will immediately appear that vice cannot be the happiness, but must upon the whole be the misery, of such a creature as man; a moral, an accountable agent. Superstitious observances, self-deceit though of a more refined sort, will not in reality at all mend matters with us. And the result of the whole can be nothing else but that with simplicity and fairness we keep innocency, and take heed unto the thing that is right; for this alone shall bring a man peace at the last.

JOSEPH BUTLER

IT is the excellency of friendship to rectify, or at least to qualify, the malignity of those surmises that would misrepresent a friend and traduce him in our thoughts. Am I told that my friend has done me an injury, or that he has committed an indecent action? Why, the first debt that I both owe to his friendship, and that he may challenge from mine, is rather to question the truth of the report than presently to believe my friend unworthy. Or if matter of fact breaks out and blazes with too great an evidence to be denied or so much as doubted of; why, still there are other lenitives that friendship will apply before it will be brought to the decretory rigours of a condemning sentence. A friend will be sure to act the part of an advocate before he will assume that of a judge. And there are few actions so ill, unless they are of a very deep and black tincture indeed, but will admit of some extenuation, at least from those common topics of human frailty; such as are ignorance or inadvertency, passion or surprise, company or solicitation, with many other such things, which may go a great way towards an excusing of the agent, though they cannot absolutely justify the action. All which apologies for and alleviations of faults, though they are the heights of humanity, yet they are not the favours but the duties of friendship. Charity itself commands us, where we know no ill, to think well of all. But friendship, that always goes a pitch higher, gives a man a peculiar right and claim to the good opinion of his friend. . . .

We have seen here the demeanour of friendship between man and man: but how is it, think we now, between Christ and the soul that depends upon Him? Is He any ways short in these offices of tenderness and mitigation? No, assuredly: but by infinite degrees superior. For where our heart does but relent, His melts; where our eye pities, His bowels yearn. How many frowardnesses of ours does He smother, how many indignities does He pass by, with how many affronts does He put up at our hands, because His love is invincible, and His friendship unchangeable!

ROBERT SOUTH

'HE went about doing good.' So we might say in our own age of two or three who have been personally known to us, 'He or she went about doing good.' They are the living witnesses to us of His work. If we observe them we shall see that they did good because they were good—because they lived for others and not for themselves, because they had a higher standard of truth and therefore men could trust them, because their love was deeper and therefore they drew others after them. These are they of whom we read in Scripture that they bear the image of Christ until His coming again, and of a few of them that they have borne the image of His sufferings, and to us they are the best interpreters of His life. They too have a hidden strength which is derived from communion with the Unseen; they pass their lives in the service of God, and yet only desire to be thought unprofitable servants. The honours or praises which men sometimes shower upon them are not much to their taste. Their only joy is to do the will of God and to relieve the wants of their brethren. Their only or greatest sorrow is to think of the things which, from inadvertence or necessity, they have been compelled to leave undone. Their way of life has been simple; they have not had much to do with the world; they have not had time to accumulate stores of learning. Sometimes they have seen with superhuman clearness one or two truths of which the world was especially in need. They may have had their trials too—failing health, declining years, the ingratitude of men—but they have endured as seeing Him who is invisible.

BENJAMIN JOWETT

CHRISTIAN life means a walking; it goes by steps. There is a straight fence run for us between right and wrong. There is no *sitting on* that fence. No; only walking, one side or other. You can hardly look *across* without stepping *through*.

*   *   *

Did you ever hear his whisper who offered you the pleasant bread of temptation when God had bidden you tread the lonely wilderness of self-denial with its hard stones and heart-emptying hunger? Why forbid yourself one harmless indulgence? What harm will it do? Be a little kinder to yourself. You need not give up the spirit in order to mind the flesh a little. The bread will help you over the stones. Stop cutting off that right hand; at least leave three fingers on it; do not maim yourself; you can have the hand and the Kingdom. Cease plucking out that right eye; you can close it at times, and at times use it. Do not cut off that right foot; tread lightly on it; that is all.

Did you ever heed that voice of the Tempter? Did you ever take the matter into consideration instead of felling him with a pebble from the brook of God, the divine Word? Ah me, for the saints of God who are pinioned and powerless, because of some secret compact with the adversary of souls; the redeemed of the Lord who are bondsmen because they allow themselves some little gratification about which they are not sure, about which they cannot be happy!

R. W. BARBOUR

THOSE whose spirits are stirred by the breath of the Holy Spirit go forward even in sleep.

*   *   *

You need not cry very loud: He is nearer to us than we think.

*   *   *

I hope that when I have done what I can, He will do with me what He pleases.

*   *   *

There is need neither of art nor of science for going to God, but only a heart resolutely determined to apply itself to nothing but Him, or for His sake, and to love Him only.

*   *   *

A little lifting up of the heart suffices; a little remembrance of God, one act of inward worship, though upon a march and sword in hand, are prayers which, however short, are nevertheless very acceptable to God; and far from lessening a soldier's courage, they best serve to fortify it.

*   *   *

One way to recall easily the mind in time of prayer, and to preserve it more in rest, is not to let it wander too far at other times. You should keep it strictly in the Presence of God, and being accustomed to think of Him often from time to time, you will find it easy to keep your mind calm in the time of prayer, or at least to recall it from its wanderings.

*   *   *

I wish you could convince yourself that God is often nearer to us, and more effectually present with us, in sickness than in health.

BROTHER LAWRENCE

IT is evident that in the mind of God the good of all is the good of each, and no less particularly the good of each because also the good of all. In other words, the final good for which I am told to look as the issue of all the pain and incoherence of my life is not the good of some remote entity called 'the whole' or 'the race' in which I have only the share that a drop of water has in the ocean —or, more insubstantial still, the share that present existence has in posterity—it is my own individual good as wholly and truly and singly as it is the good of every other 'I', and of all of us together.

When an individual for the sake of some desired good denies himself a present pleasure or faces pain and effort because he knows that that is the price which he must pay for it, he is doing for himself, but with infinitely less knowledge and certainty, what God, from whom nothing is hid, ceaselessly does for him (and none the less entirely for him because also entirely for everyone else) in all the labour and suffering of which he so bitterly complains. What is lacking to him, however, is the ability to see how the individual can be identified with the whole and with all the interests of the whole without confusion or sacrifice of the least thing that is his own. We say that we must subordinate our aims and gains to those of collective humanity, and this is perfectly true. But we do not understand how this subordination involves no forfeiture or frustration or loss of any kind to ourselves. Our daily experience misleads us, from which we seem to learn that successful combination can be achieved only by the sacrifice of the best in the interests of the average, for in God's plans there can be no incompatibility or collision of ends.

R. H. J. STEUART

The Poplar Field

THE poplars are felled; farewell to the shade,
And the whispering sound of the cool colonnade!
The winds play no longer and sing in the leaves,
Nor Ouse on his bosom their image receives.

Twelve years have elapsed since I first took a view
Of my favourite field, and the bank where they grew;
And now in the grass behold they are laid,
And the tree is my seat that once lent me a shade!

The blackbird has fled to another retreat,
Where the hazels afford him a screen from the heat,
And the scene where his melody charmed me before
Resounds with his sweet flowing ditty no more.

My fugitive years are all hasting away,
And I must ere long lie as lowly as they,
With a turf on my breast, and a stone at my head,
Ere another such grove shall arise in its stead.

'Tis a sight to engage me, if anything can,
To muse on the perishing pleasures of man;
Though his life be a dream, his enjoyments, I see,
Have a being less durable even than he.

                                        WILLIAM COWPER

'IT is written, Man shall not live by bread alone.' What a man finds in his own consciousness, he is strengthened by being able to recognize in the whole history of his race. 'It is written' long ago, this which he is doing now. He is only tracing over with his blood the unfaded characters which other men have written in theirs. It is not a mere whim of his, this conviction that it is better to serve God than to eat bread. It is the corporate conviction of mankind. That is a very mysterious support, but it is a very real one. It plants the weak tree of your will or mine into the rich soil of humanity. Do not lose that strength. Do not so misread history that it shall seem to you when you try to do right as if you were the first man that ever tried it. Put yourself with your weak little struggle into the company of all the strugglers in all time. Recognize in your little fight against your avarice, or your untruthfulness, or your laziness, only one skirmish in that battle whose field covers the earth, and whose clamour rises and falls from age to age, but never wholly dies. See in the perpetual struggle of good and evil that the impulse after good is eternal, and the higher needs are always asserting their necessity. In their persistent assertion read the prophecy of their final success and take courage.

PHILLIPS BROOKS

WE must preach the law for the sake of the evil and wicked, but for the most part it lights upon the good and godly who, although they need it not, except so far as may concern the old Adam, yet accept it. The preaching of the gospel we must have for the sake of the good and godly, yet it falls among the wicked and ungodly, who take it to themselves, whereas it profits them not; for they abuse it, and are thereby made confident. It is even as when it rains in the water or on a desert wilderness, while meantime the good pastures and grounds are parched and dried up. The ungodly suck only a fleshly liberty out of the gospel, and become worse thereby; therefore not the gospel but the law belongs to them. Even as when my little son John offends, if then I should not whip him but call him to the table to me and give him sugarplums, I should thereby make him worse, yea, quite spoil him.

The gospel is like a fresh, mild, and cool air in the extreme heat of summer, a solace and comfort in the anguish of the conscience. But as this heat proceeds from the rays of the sun, so likewise the terrifying of the conscience must proceed from the preaching of the law, to the end that we may know we have offended against the laws of God.

Now, when the mind is refreshed and quickened again by the cool air of the gospel, we must not then be idle, or lie down and sleep. That is, when our consciences are settled in peace, quieted and comforted through God's Spirit, we must prove our faith by such good works as God has commanded. But so long as we live in this vale of misery, we shall be plagued and vexed with flies, with beetles, and with vermin, that is, with the devil, the world, and our own flesh. Yet we must press through, and not suffer ourselves to recoil.

MARTIN LUTHER

1. EVERY child should find itself a member of a family housed with decency and dignity, so that it may grow up as a member of that basic community in a happy fellowship unspoilt by under-feeding or overcrowding, by dirty and drab surroundings or by mechanical monotony of employment.

2. Every child should have the opportunity of an education till years of maturity, so planned as to allow for his peculiar aptitudes and make possible their full development. This education should throughout be inspired by faith in God and find its focus in worship.

3. Every citizen should be secure in possession of such income as will enable him to maintain a home and bring up children in such conditions as are described in paragraph 1 above.

4. Every citizen should have a voice in the conduct of the business or industry which is carried on by means of his labour, and the satisfaction of knowing that his labour is directed to the well-being of the community.

5. Every citizen should have sufficient daily leisure, with two days of rest in seven, and, if an employee, an annual holiday with pay, to enable him to enjoy a full personal life with such interests and activities as his tasks and talents may direct.

6. Every citizen should have assured liberty in the forms of freedom of worship, of speech, of assembly, and of association for special purposes.

WILLIAM TEMPLE

I HAVE a much greater sense of my universal, exceeding dependence on God's grace and strength and mere good pleasure, of late, than I used formerly to have; and have experienced more of an abhorrence of my own righteousness. The very thought of any joy arising in me on any consideration of my own amiableness, performances or experiences or any goodness of heart and life, is nauseous and detestable to me. And yet I am greatly afflicted with a proud and self-righteous spirit, much more sensibly than I used to be formerly. I see that serpent rising and putting forth its head continually everywhere, all around me.

Though it seems to me that in some respects I was a far better Christian for two or three years after my first conversion than I am now, and lived in a more constant delight and pleasure, yet of late years I have had a more full and constant sense of the absolute sovereignty of God . . . and of the glory of Christ. On one Saturday night in particular, I had such a discovery of the excellency of the Gospel above all other doctrines that I could not but say to myself, 'This is my chosen light, my chosen doctrine'; and of Christ, 'This is my chosen Prophet.' It appeared sweet beyond all expression to follow Christ; to learn of Him, and to live to Him. Another Saturday night (January 1739) I had such a sense how sweet and blessed a thing it was to walk in the way of duty; to do that which was right and meet to be done and agreeable to the holy mind of God; that it caused me to break forth into a kind of loud weeping, which held me some time, so that I was forced to shut myself up and to fasten doors. I could not but, as it were, cry out, 'How happy are they which do right in the sight of God!' I had at the same time a very affecting sense how meet and suitable it was that God should govern the world, and order all things according to His own pleasure; and I rejoiced in it that God reigned, and that His will was done.

JONATHAN EDWARDS

WHAT meaneth this restlessness of our nature? What meaneth this unceasing activity which longs for exercise and employment, even after every object is gained which first roused it to enterprise? What mean those unmeasurable longings which no gratification can extinguish, and which still continue to agitate the heart of man, even in the fullness of plenty and of enjoyment? If they mean anything at all, they mean that all which this world can offer is not enough to fill up his capacity for happiness—that time is too small for him and he is born for something beyond it—that the scene of his earthly existence is too limited and he is formed to expatiate in a wider and a grander theatre—that a nobler destiny is reserved for him—and that to accomplish the purpose of his being he must soar above the littleness of the world and aim at a loftier prize.

It forms the peculiar honour and excellence of religion that it accommodates to this property of our nature—that it holds out a prize suited to our high calling—that there is a grandeur in its objects which can fill and surpass the imagination—that it reveals to the eye of faith the glories of an imperishable world—and how from the high eminencies of heaven a great cloud of witnesses are looking down upon earth, not as a scene for the petty anxieties of time, but as a splendid theatre for the ambition of immortal spirits.

THOMAS CHALMERS

IT is but right that our hearts should be on God, when the heart of God is so much on us. If the Lord of glory can stoop so low as to set His heart on sinful dust, methinks we should easily be persuaded to set our hearts on Christ and glory, and ascend to Him, in our daily affections, who so much condescends to us. Christian, dost thou not perceive that the heart of God is set upon thee, and that He is still minding thee with tender love, even when thou forgettest both thyself and Him? Is He not following thee with daily mercies, moving upon thy soul, providing for thy body, preserving both? Doth He not bear thee continually in the arms of His love, and promise that all things shall work together for thy good, and suit all His dealings to thy greatest advantage, and give His angels charge over thee? And canst thou be taken up with the joys below and forget thy Lord who forgets not thee? Unkind ingratitude! When He speaks of His own kindness for us, hear what He says: 'Zion said, The Lord hath forsaken me, and my Lord hath forgotten me. Can a woman forget her sucking child, that she should not have compassion on the son of her womb? Yea, they may forget, yet will I not forget thee. Behold, I have graven thee upon the palms of my hands; thy walls are continually before me.' But when He speaks of our regards to Him, the case is otherwise: 'Can a maid forget her ornaments, or a bride her attire? Yet my people have forgotten me days without number.' As if He should say, 'You will not rise one morning and forget your vanity of dress; and are these of more worth than your God, of more importance than your eternal life? And yet you can forget these day after day.' Let us not give God cause thus to expostulate with us. Rather let our souls get up to God, and visit Him every morning, and our hearts be towards Him every moment.

RICHARD BAXTER

THE Wise Man observes that there is a time to speak and a time to keep silence. One meets with people in the world who seem never to have made the last of these observations. And yet these great talkers do not at all speak from their having anything to say, as every sentence shows, but only from their inclination to be talking. Their conversation is merely an exercise of the tongue: no other human faculty has any share in it. It is strange these persons can help reflecting that unless they have in truth a superior capacity, and are in an extraordinary manner furnished for conversation, if they are entertaining, they are entertaining at their own expense. Is it possible that it should never come into people's thoughts to suspect whether or no it be to their advantage to show so very much of themselves? Oh that you would altogether hold your peace, and it should be your wisdom! Remember likewise that there are persons who love fewer words, an inoffensive sort of people, and who deserve some regard, though of too still and composed tempers for you. . . . It is indeed a very unhappy way these people are in: they in a manner cut themselves out from all advantages of conversation, except that of being entertained with their own talk: their business in coming into company not being at all to be informed, to hear, to learn; but to display themselves; or rather to exert their faculty and talk without any design at all. And if we consider conversation as an entertainment, as somewhat to unbend the mind: as a diversion from the cares, the business, and the sorrows of life; it is of the very nature of it that the discourse be mutual. This, I say, is implied in the very notion of what we distinguish by conversation or being in company. Attention to the continued discourse of one alone grows more painful often than the cares and business we come to be diverted from. He therefore who imposes this upon us is guilty of a double offence; arbitrarily enjoining silence upon all the rest, and likewise obliging them to this painful attention.

JOSEPH BUTLER

In the Epistle of St. James we read, 'Be ye doers of the word, and not hearers only, deceiving your own selves. For if any be a hearer of the word, and not a doer, he is like unto a man beholding his natural face in a glass: for he beholdeth himself, and goeth his way, and straightway forgetteth what manner of man he was.'

What is required in order to look at oneself with true blessing in the mirror of the word?

The *first* requirement is that you do not look at the mirror, in order to inspect it, but that you look at yourself in the mirror. . . . If there were only a single passage in the Bible which you understood—well, that is your first concern. You need not sit down and ponder over the obscure passages. God's word is given in order that you may act according to it, not in order that you may practise the interpretation of what you find obscure. . . . The *second* requirement is that, in order to see yourself in the mirror when you read God's word, you must remember to be constantly saying to yourself, 'It is speaking to me; I am the one it is talking about.'. . . If God's word is only a doctrine to you, it is no mirror. It is just as impossible to be mirrored in a doctrine as in a wall. . . . No, when you read God's word, you must constantly be saying to yourself, 'It is talking to me, and about me.' *Finally*, if you desire to observe yourself in the mirror of the word with real blessing, you must not at once begin to forget how you looked. You must not be the forgetful hearer (or reader) of whom the apostle says that he carefully looked at his own face in a mirror and straightway forgot what manner of man he was. . . . The right thing to do is to say to yourself at once: 'I shall begin now to prevent myself from forgetting. Now, this very moment, I make this promise to myself and to God, even if it be but for the next hour or for today. For that length of time it shall be certain that I do not forget.'. . . Doing it this way is much better than taking too big a bite to begin with, and saying 'I shall never forget'. It is much better never to forget to remember immediately than immediately to say that you will never forget.

SÖREN KIERKEGAARD

THOSE faults that we do not perceive till after they are committed will not be cured by inquietude and vexation with ourselves; on the contrary, this fretfulness is only the impatience of pride at the view of its own downfall. The only use, then, to be made of such errors is to submit quietly to the humiliation they bring, for it is not being humble to resist humiliations. We must condemn our faults, lament them, repent of them, without seeking any palliation or excuse, viewing ourselves as in the presence of God, with all our imperfections upon our heads, and without any feeling of bitterness or discouragement, meekly improving our disgrace. Thus may we draw from the serpent a cure for the venom of the wound. . . .

Never let us be discouraged with ourselves; it is not when we are conscious of our faults that we are the most wicked; on the contrary we are then less so. We see by a brighter light; and let us remember for our consolation that we never perceive our sins till we begin to cure them. We must neither flatter nor be impatient with ourselves in the correction of our faults. Despondency is not a state of humility; on the contrary, it is the vexation and despair of a cowardly pride—nothing is worse; whether we stumble or whether we fall, we must think only of rising again and going on in our course. Our faults may be useful to us, if they cure us of a vain confidence in ourselves, and do not deprive us of a humble and salutary confidence in God. Let us bless God with as true thankfulness if He have enabled us to make any progress in virtue as if we had made it through our own strength, and let us not be troubled with the weak agitations of self-love; let them pass; do not think of them. God never makes us feel our weakness but that we may be led to seek strength from Him. What is involuntary should not trouble us; but the great thing is never to act against the light within us, and to desire to follow where God would lead us.

FÉNELON

THERE is a grace of kind listening, as well as a grace of kind speaking. Some men listen with an abstracted air, which shows that their thoughts are elsewhere. Or they seem to listen, but by wide answers and irrelevant questions show that they have been occupied with their own thoughts, as being more interesting, at least in their own estimation, than what you have been saying. Some listen with a kind of importunate ferocity which makes you feel that you are being put upon your trial, and that your auditor expects beforehand that you are going to tell him a lie, or to be inaccurate, or to say something which he will disapprove, and that you must mind your expressions. Some interrupt, and will not hear you to the end. Some hear you to the end, and then forthwith begin to talk to you about a similar experience which has befallen themselves, making your case only an illustration of their own. Some, meaning to be kind, listen with such a determined, lively, violent attention that you are at once made uncomfortable, and the charm of conversation is at an end. Many persons whose manners will stand the test of speaking, break down under the trial of listening. But all these things should be brought under the sweet influence of religion. Kind listening is often an act of the most delicate interior mortification, and is a great assistance towards kind speaking. Those who govern others must take care to be kind listeners, or else they will soon offend God and fall into secret sins.

FREDERICK WILLIAM FABER

WE need society, and we need solitude also, as we need summer and winter, day and night, exercise and rest. I thank heaven for a thousand pleasant and profitable conversations with acquaintances and friends; I thank heaven also, and not less gratefully, for thousands of sweet hours that have passed in solitary thought or labour, under the silent stars.

Society is necessary to give us our share and place in the collective life of humanity, but solitude is necessary to the maintenance of the individual life. Society is to the individual what travel and commerce are to a nation, during which it develops its especial originality and genius.

The life of the perfect hermit, and that of those persons who feel themselves nothing individually, and have no existence but what they receive from others, are alike imperfect lives. The perfect life is like that of a ship of war which has its own place in the fleet and can share in its strength and discipline, but can also go forth alone in the solitude of the infinite sea. We ought to belong to society, to have our place in it, and yet to be capable of a complete individual existence outside of it.

Which of the two is the grander, the ship in the disciplined fleet, arranged in order of battle, or the ship alone in the tempest, a thousand miles from land? The truest grandeur of the ship is in neither one nor the other, but in the capacity for both. What would that captain merit who either had not seamanship enough to work under the eye of the admiral, or else had not sufficient knowledge of navigation to be trusted out of range of signals.

I value society for the abundance of ideas that it brings before us, like carriages in a frequented street; but I value solitude for sincerity and peace, and for the better understanding of the thoughts that are truly ours.

PHILIP GILBERT HAMERTON

IT is thoughts of God's thinking which we need to set us right and, remember, they are not as our thoughts. A man cannot come to the great God and remain himself, little and mean and suspicious; he has to give up something, to clear his mind of something, to get another heart and other eyes. When a man does come to God, it is as if he looked from the other side of the sky, seeing the same things but from another standpoint. His fault which seemed excusable in a trivial earth is now serious and great; repentance, I suppose, is nothing else than the sight, for a moment, of sin as God sees it. And Jesus, the dim far-off figure, with a kind of idyllic charm and pathos about it, is seen with other eyes, seen now as God sees Him, in whom it pleased the Father that all fullness should dwell.

When my thoughts about life are put away that I may get God's thoughts, Christ becomes the gift of God's heart to me, a Deliverer in whom the power of my new life consists, an Enlightener from whom I learn how to think of God and man. 'If any man be in Christ', says Paul, 'he is a new creature: old things have passed away, behold they have become new.' His former judgements, his estimate of great and small, are changed; he finds himself in a new washen earth. It is no power of earth that can work a change like that, but the redeeming will of God, who is able also to subdue all things unto Himself.

W. M. MACGREGOR

THE acquisition of knowledge causes us to approach truth when it is a question of knowledge about something we love, and not in any other case.

Love of truth is not a correct form of expression. Truth is not an object of love. It is not an object at all. What one loves is something which exists, which one thinks on, and which may hence be an occasion for truth or error. A truth is always the truth with reference to something. Truth is the radiant manifestation of reality. Not truth but reality is the object of love. To desire truth is to desire contact with a piece of reality. To desire contact with a piece of reality is to love. We desire truth only in order to love in truth. We desire to know the truth about what we love. Instead of talking about love of truth, it would be better to talk about the spirit of truth in love.

Pure and genuine love always desires above all to dwell wholly in the truth whatever it may be, unconditionally. Every other sort of love desires before anything else means of satisfaction, and for this reason is a source of error and falsehood. Pure and genuine love is in itself spirit of truth. It is the Holy Spirit. The Greek word which is translated spirit means literally fiery breath, breath mingled with fire, and it represented, in antiquity, the notion which science represents today by the word energy. What we translate by 'spirit of truth' signifies the energy of truth, truth as an active force. Pure love is this active force, the love which will not at any price, under any condition, have anything to do with either falsehood or error.

For such a love as this to be able to be the motive of the savant in his exhausting task of research, he would have to have something to love. It would be necessary for the conception which he forms of the object of his studies to contain an aspect of the Good.

SIMONE WEIL

'THERE is nothing', says Plato, 'so delightful as the hearing or the speaking of truth.' For this reason there is no conversation so agreeable as that of the man of integrity, who hears without any intention to betray, and speaks without any intention to deceive.

Among all the accounts which are given of Cato, I do not remember one that more redounds to his honour than the following passage related by Plutarch. As an advocate was pleading the cause of his client before one of the praetors, he could only produce a single witness in a point where the law required the testimony of two persons; upon which the advocate insisted upon the integrity of that person whom he had produced; but the praetor told him, that where the law required two witnesses he would not accept of one, though it were Cato himself. Such a speech, from a person who sat at the head of a court of justice while Cato was still living, shows us, more than a thousand examples, the high reputation this great man had gained among his contemporaries upon the account of his sincerity.

When such an inflexible integrity is a little softened and qualified by the rules of conversation and good breeding, there is not a more shining virtue in the whole catalogue of social duties. A man however ought to take great care not to polish himself out of his veracity, nor to refine his behaviour to the prejudice of his virtue.

JOSEPH ADDISON

THE night is come, like to the day,
Depart not Thou, great God, away.
Let not my sins, black as the night,
Eclipse the lustre of Thy light:
Keep still in my horizon; for to me
The sun makes not the day, but Thee.
Thou, whose nature cannot sleep,
On my temples sentry keep;
Guard me 'gainst those watchful foes
Whose eyes are open while mine close.
Let no dreams my head infest;
But such as Jacob's temples blest.
While I do rest, my soul advance;
Make my sleep a holy trance;
That I may, my rest being wrought,
Awake into some holy thought;
And with as active vigour run
My course as doth the nimble sun.
Sleep is a death; O make me try,
By sleeping, what it is to die;
And as gently lay my head
On my grave, as now my bed.
Howe'er I rest, great God, let me
Awake again at last with Thee;
And thus assured, behold I lie
Securely, or to wake or die.
These are my drowsy days; in vain
I do now wake to sleep again:
O come that hour when I shall never
Sleep again, but wake for ever.

SIR THOMAS BROWNE

THERE is great importance even in the handling of infancy. If it is unchristian, it will beget unchristian states or impressions. If it is gentle, even patient and loving, it prepares a mood and temper like its own. There is scarcely room for doubt that all most crabbed, hateful, resentful, passionate, ill-natured characters; all most even, lovely, firm, and true, are prepared in a great degree by the handling of the nursery. To these and all such modes of feeling and treatment as make up the element of the infant's life, it is passive as wax to the seal. . . .

Let every Christian father and mother understand, when their child is three years old, that they have done more than half of all they will ever do for his character. What can be more strangely wide of all just apprehension than the immense efficacy imputed by most parents to the Christian ministry, compared with what they take to be the almost insignificant power conferred on them in their parental charge and duties? Why, if all preachers of Christ could have their hearers for whole months and years in their own will, as parents do their children, so as to move them by a look, a motion, a smile, a frown, and act their own sentiments over in them at pleasure; if also, a little further on, they had them in authority to command, direct, tell them whither to go, what to learn, what to do, regulate their hours, their books, their pleasures, their company, and call them to prayer over their own knees every night and morning, who could think it impossible, in the use of such a power, to produce almost any result? Should not such a ministry be expected to fashion all who come under it to newness of life? Let no parent, shifting off his duties to his children, in this manner think to have his defects made up, and the consequent damages mended afterwards, when they have come to their maturity, by the comparatively slender, always doubtful, efficacy of preaching and pulpit harangue.

                                        HORACE BUSHNELL

IT is a fond thing for a man to think to set bounds to himself in any thing that is bad, to resolve to sin in number, weight and measure, with great temperance and discretion and government of himself; that he will commit this sin and then give over, entertain but this one temptation, and after that he will shut the door and admit no more.

To sin in hopes that hereafter we shall repent is to do a thing in hopes that we shall one day be mightily ashamed of it, that we shall one time or other be heartily grieved and troubled that we have done it. It is to do a thing in hopes that we shall afterwards condemn ourselves for it, and wish a thousand times that we had never done it; in hopes that we shall be full of horror at the thoughts of what we have done, and shall treasure up so much guilt in our consciences as will make us a terror to ourselves, and be ready to drive us even to despair and destruction. . . . 'Tis just as if a man should be content to be ship-wracked, in hopes that he shall afterwards escape by a plank, and get safe to shore.

       *   *   *

On a death-bed the sinner is resolved against sin, just as a man that hath no stomach is resolved against meat; but if the fit were over, and death would but raise the siege, and remove his quarters a little farther from him, it is to be feared that his former appetite would soon return to him, and that he would sin with the same eagerness he did before. . . . It is much to be feared that the repentance of a dying sinner is usually but like the sorrow of a malefactor, when he is ready to be turned off:—he is not troubled that he hath offended the law, but he is troubled that he must die. . . .

Why should any man, for offering up to God the mere refuse and dregs of his life, and the days which himself hath no pleasure in, expect to receive the reward of eternal life and happiness at His hands?

JOHN TILLOTSON

As the times and seasons, so the ways and means of the approaches of death have especial trials which, unless we are prepared for them, will keep us under bondage with the fear of death itself. Long waiting, wearing consumptions, strong pains of the stone or the like, from within, or sword, fire, tortures, with shame and reproach from without, may be in the way of the access of death unto us. Some who have been wholly freed from all fears of death as a dissolution of nature, who have looked on it as amiable and desirable in itself, have yet had great exercise in their minds about these ways of its approach. They have earnestly desired that this peculiar bitterness of the cup might be taken away. To get above all perplexities on the account of these things is part of our wisdom in dying daily. And we are to have always in a readiness those graces and duties which are necessary thereunto. Such are a constant resignation of ourselves in all events unto the sovereign will, pleasure and disposal of God. May He not do what He will with His own? . . . Doth He not know what is best for us, and what conduceth most unto His own glory? So is it to live in the exercise of faith that if God calls us unto any of those things which are peculiarly dreadful unto our natures, He will give us such supplies of spiritual strength and patience as shall enable us to undergo them, if not with ease and joy, yet with peace and quietness beyond our expectation. Multitudes have had experience that those things which at a distance have had an aspect of overwhelming dread, have been far from unsupportable in their approach, when strength has been received from above to encounter with them. And moreover it is in this case required that we be frequent and steady in comparing these things with those which are eternal, both as unto the misery which we are freed from and that blessedness which is prepared for us.

JOHN OWEN

I SHOULD like to speak of God not on the borders of life but at its centre, not in weakness but in strength, not therefore in man's suffering and death but in his life and prosperity. On the borders it seems to me better to hold our peace and leave the problem unsolved. Belief in the Resurrection is not the solution of the problem of death. The 'beyond' of God is not the beyond of our perceptive faculties. The transcendence of theory based on perception has nothing to do with the transcendence of God. God is the 'beyond' in the midst of our life. The Church stands, not where human powers give out, on the borders, but in the centre of the village.

*   *   *

Weizsäcker's book on the world-view of physics is still keeping me busy. It has brought home to me how wrong it is to use God as a stop-gap for the incompleteness of our knowledge. For the frontiers of knowledge are inevitably being pushed back farther and farther, which means that you think of God only as a stop-gap. He also is being pushed back farther and farther, and is in more or less continuous retreat. We should find God in what we do know, not in what we don't; not in problems still outstanding, but in those we have already solved. . . . God cannot be used as a stop-gap. We must not wait until we are at the end of our tether: He must be found at the centre of life: in life, and not only in death; in health and vigour, and not only in suffering; in activity, and not only in sin. The ground for this lies in the revelation of God in Christ. Christ is the centre of life, and in no sense did He come to answer our unsolved problems. From the centre of life certain questions are seen to be wholly irrelevant, and so are the answers commonly given to them.

DIETRICH BONHOEFFER

MONEY never made any man rich, but his mind. He that can order himself to the law of nature is not only without the sense but the fear of poverty. O, but to strike blind the people with our wealth and pomp is the thing? What a wretchedness is this, to thrust all our riches outward and be beggars within; to contemplate nothing but the little, vile, and sordid things of the world; not the great, noble, and precious! We serve our avarice and, not content with the good of the earth that is offered to us, we search and dig for the evil that is hidden. God offered us those things, and placed them at hand and near us, that He knew were profitable for us, but the hurtful He laid deep and hid. Yet do we seek only the things whereby we may perish, and bring them forth when God and nature hath buried them. We covet superfluous things, when it were more honour for us if we could contemn necessary. What need hath nature of silver dishes, multitudes of waiters, delicate pages, perfumed napkins? She requires meat only, and hunger is not ambitious. Can we think no wealth enough but such a state for which a man may be brought into a praemunire, begged, proscribed, or poisoned? O, if a man could restrain the fury of his gullet and groin, and think how many fires, how many kitchens, cooks, pastures, and ploughed lands; what orchards, stews, ponds and parks, coops and garners, he could spare; what velvets, tissues, embroideries, laces, he could lack; and then how short and uncertain his life is; he were in a better way to happiness than to live the emperor of these delights, and be the dictator of fashions. But we make ourselves slaves to our pleasures, and we serve fame and ambition, which is an equal slavery. Have not I seen the pomp of a whole kingdom, and what a foreign king could bring hither, all to make himself gazed and wondered at, laid forth, as it were, to the show, and vanish all away in a day? And shall that which could not fill the expectation of few hours entertain and take up our whole lives, when even it appeared as superfluous to the possessors as to me that was a spectator? The bravery was shown, it was not possessed; while it boasted itself it perished. It is vile, and a poor thing, to place our happiness on these desires.

BEN JONSON

THE casuists of the Romish Church, who gain by confession great opportunities of knowing human nature, have generally determined that what it is a crime to do, it is a crime to think. Since by revolving with pleasure the facility, safety, or advantage of a wicked deed a man soon begins to find his constancy relax and his detestation soften, the happiness of success glistening before him withdraws his attention from the atrociousness of the guilt, and acts are at last confidently perpetrated, of which the first conception only crept into the mind, disguised in pleasing complications, and permitted rather than invited.

No man has ever been drawn to crimes, by love or jealousy, envy or hatred, but he can tell how easily he might at first have repelled the temptation; how readily his mind would have obeyed a call to any other object; and how weak his passion has been after some casual avocation till he has recalled it again to his heart and revived the viper by too warm a fondness.

Such, therefore, is the importance of keeping reason a constant guard over imagination that we have otherwise no security for our own virtue, but may corrupt our hearts in the most recluse solitude with more pernicious and tyrannical appetites and wishes than the commerce of the world will generally produce; for we are easily shocked by crimes which appear at once in their full magnitude; but the gradual growth of our own wickedness, endeared by interest, and palliated by all the artifices of self-deceit, gives us time to form distinctions in our own favour, and reason by degrees submits to absurdity, as the eye is in time accommodated to darkness.

In this disease of the soul it is of the utmost importance to apply remedies at the beginning.

SAMUEL JOHNSON

BUT art Thou come, dear Saviour? Hath Thy love
Thus made Thee stoop, and leave Thy throne above
The lofty heavens, and thus Thyself to dress
In dust to visit mortals? Could no less
A condescension serve? And after all,
The mean reception of a cratch and stall?
Dear Lord, I'll fetch Thee thence; I have a room.
'Tis poor, but 'tis my best, if Thou wilt come
Within so small a cell, where I would fain
Mine and the world's Redeemer entertain.
I mean my heart; 'tis sluttish, I confess,
And will not mend Thy lodging, Lord, unless
Thou send before Thy harbinger, I mean
Thy pure and purging grace, to make it clean
And sweep its nasty corners; then I'll try
To wash it also with a weeping eye;
And when 'tis swept and washed, I then will go
And, with thy leave, I'll fetch some flowers that grow
In Thine own garden, faith and love to Thee;
With those I'll dress it up; and these shall be
My rosemary and bays; yet when my best
Is done, the room's not fit for such a guest,
  But here's the cure; Thy presence, Lord, alone
  Will make a stall a court, a cratch a throne.

                                        SIR MATTHEW HALE

THE Christian is one who has forever given up the hope of being able to think of himself as a good man. He is forever a sinner for whom the Son of God had to die because by no other means could he be forgiven. In a sense we can say that he has given up the effort to be good. That is no longer his aim. He is seeking to do one thing and one thing only—to pay back something of the un-payable debt of gratitude to Christ who loved him as a sinner and gave Himself for him. And in this new and self-forgetting quest he finds that which—when he sought it directly—was forever bound to elude him, the good life.

No two motives could be more distinct from one another than these two, yet it is the commonest thing to find them confused. How ready we are to take Christ as our pattern and teacher only, using the words of the Gospel, and yet never allowing ourselves to face the experience of forgiveness at the foot of the Cross—the humiliating discovery that, so far from our being like Jesus, there is literally no hope for us at all except that He has forgiven us. There is a whole universe of moral and psychological difference between saying, 'Christ is my pattern, and if I try I can be like Him', and saying, 'I am so far from goodness that Christ had to die for me that I might be forgiven.' The one is still in the world of legalism, and its centre of attention is still the self. The other is in the world of grace, and its centre of attention is another to whose love it is our whole and only aim to give ourselves. The one must always lack what the other increasingly has, the spontaneity and whole-heartedness that come when there is the whole force of an emotionally integrated life behind action.

LESSLIE NEWBIGIN

As for that which is beyond your strength, be absolutely certain that our Lord loves you, devotedly and individually: loves you just as you are. How often that conviction is lacking even in those souls who are most devoted to God! They make repeated efforts to love Him, they experience the joy of loving, and yet how little they know, how little they realize, that God loves them incomparably more than they will ever know how to love Him. Think only of this and say to yourself, 'I am loved by God more than I can either conceive or understand.' Let this fill all your soul and all your prayers and never leave you. You will soon see that this is the way to find God. It contains the whole of St. John's teaching: 'As for us, we have believed in the love which God has for us. . . .' Accustom yourself to the wonderful thought that God loves you with a tenderness, a generosity, and an intimacy which surpasses all your dreams. Give yourself up with joy to a loving confidence in God and have courage to believe firmly that God's action towards you is a masterpiece of partiality and love. Rest tranquilly in this abiding conviction.

*   *   *

You want to compete with His affection before you have understood it; that is your mistake. You are like a child who wants to help his mother before allowing himself to be trained by her. You are like St. Peter; he wanted to wash his Master's feet, but refused to allow his Master to wash his feet. He did not understand. Our Lord showed him his mistake with the clear and decisive sharpness of a friend: 'Peter! if I do not do this, and if you will not let me do it, you have no part in me!' And St. John, who knew all the depth and tenderness of God's love, was constantly ravished by the thought, 'He loved us first!'

Come then! show a little deference to our Lord and allow Him to go first. Let Him love you a great deal long before you have succeeded in loving Him even a little as you would wish to love Him. That is all I ask of you, and all that our Lord asks of you.

HENRI DE TOURVILLE

ANOTHER branch of blessedness is a power of reposing ourselves and our concerns upon the Lord's faithfulness and care, and may be considered in two respects: a reliance upon Him that He will surely provide for us, guide us, protect us, be our help in trouble, our shield in danger, so that, however poor, weak, and defenceless in ourselves, we may rejoice in His all-sufficiency as our own; and further, in consequence of this, a peaceful, humble submission to His will under all events which, upon their first impression, are contrary to our own views and desires. Surely, in a world like this, where every thing is uncertain, where we are exposed to trials on every hand, and know not but a single hour may bring forth something painful, yea dreadful, to our natural sensations, there can be no blessedness but so far as we are thus enabled to entrust and resign all to the direction and faithfulness of the Lord our Shepherd. For want of more of this spirit multitudes of professing Christians perplex and wound themselves and dishonour their high calling by continual anxieties, alarms, and complaints. They think nothing safe under the Lord's keeping unless their own eye is likewise upon it, and are seldom satisfied with any of His dispensations: for though He gratify their desires in nine instances, a refusal in the tenth spoils the relish of all, and they show the truths of the Gospel can afford them little comfort, if self is crossed. But blessed is the man who trusteth in the Lord, and whose hope the Lord is. He shall not be afraid of evil tidings: he shall be kept in perfect peace, though the earth be moved, and the mountains cast into the midst of the sea.

JOHN NEWTON

WHEREVER a man hath been made a partaker of the divine nature, in him is fulfilled the best and noblest life, and the worthiest in God's eyes, that hath been or can be. And of that eternal love which loveth Goodness as Goodness and for the sake of Goodness, a true, noble, Christ-like life is so greatly beloved that it will never be forsaken or cast off. Where a man hath tasted this life, it is impossible for him ever to part with it . . .; and if he could exchange it for an angel's life, he would not.

This is our answer to the question, 'If a man, by putting on Christ's life, can get nothing more than he hath already, and serve no end, what good will it do him?' This life is not chosen in order to serve any end, or to get anything by it, but for the love of its nobleness, and because God loveth and esteemeth it so greatly. And whoever saith that he hath had enough of it, and may now lay it aside, hath never tasted nor known it; for he who hath truly felt or tasted it can never give it up again. And he who hath put on the life of Christ with the intent to win or deserve aught thereby, hath taken it up as an hireling and not for love, and is altogether without it. For he who doth not take it up for love, hath none of it at all; he may dream indeed that he hath put it on, but he is deceived. Christ did not lead such a life as His for the sake of reward, but out of love; and love maketh such a life light and taketh away all its hardships, so that it becometh sweet and is gladly endured. But to him who hath not put it on from love but, as he dreameth, for the sake of reward, it is utterly bitter and a weariness, and he would fain be quit of it. And it is a sure token of an hireling that he wisheth his work were at an end. But he who truly loveth it is not offended at its toil nor suffering, nor the length of time it lasteth.

THEOLOGIA GERMANICA

IT is just that we should thank and praise God; because He has created us as reasonable creatures, and has ordained and destined heaven and earth and the angels to our service; and because He became man for our sins, and taught us, and lived for our sake, and showed us the way; and because He has ministered to us in humble raiment, and suffered an ignominious death for the love of us, and promised us His eternal kingdom and Himself also for our reward and for our wage. And He has spared us in our sins, and has forgiven us or will forgive us; and has poured His grace and His love into our souls, and will dwell and remain with us, and in us, throughout all eternity. And He has visited us and will visit us all the days of our lives with His noble sacraments, according to the need of each, and has left us His flesh and His blood for food and drink, according to the desire and hunger of each; and has set before us nature and the Scriptures and all creatures, as examples, and as a mirror, that therein we may look and learn how we may turn all our deeds to works of virtue; and has given us health and strength and power, and sometimes for our own good has sent us sickness; and in outward need has established inward peace and happiness in us; and has caused us to be called by Christian names and to have been born of Christian parents. For all these things we should thank God here on earth, that hereafter we may thank Him in eternity.

✳   ✳   ✳

He who does not praise God while here on earth shall in eternity be dumb.

JOHN OF RUYSBROECK

THE man to whom any good in this world is given by another man is often wont so fervently to love him who hath given him this good, and so continually to give himself to his service, that if the cause of his benefactor required it, oftentimes he would not fear to meet even death for him; and yet anything which ever man in this world can have, or which one man can give to another, none is so devoid of understanding as not to perceive that he cannot retain it for ever, but must give up either before his end come, or if not before, at least then, when his end has come.

But what God giveth to man in this world is either such as he can never lose, and none can ever take from him, or such that even though man lose it, yet by it he may obtain that, when this present life is ended, he may be ever with his Creator in a life of bliss. God giveth to man oftentimes in this life to live according to reason, and as He hath commanded, and as is right, to love his Creator; and in all things, without any contradiction, to obey His commandments; and this good no man, except he himself of his own will let it go, can take from him. This world's riches, whether he will or no, he must needs give up; but while he hath them, if he bestow them as his God hath commanded, he may so be able to attain to everlasting life.

O immeasurable goodness of our Creator! O inestimable mercy! Himself in nothing ever needing man, yet of His goodness alone He created man; creating, He adorned him with reason, that he might be able to be partaker of His happiness and His eternity, and so with Him possess for ever joy and gladness.

Still further, while man in many things is contrary to Him, knowingly and wilfully doeth many things although they are displeasing to Him, yet He warneth him to return, to seek again the mercy of his Creator, nor for any sin, however grievous, presume to despair. For He is the fountain of loving-kindness and mercy, and all, with whatever stain of sin they are defiled, He longeth to cleanse; cleansed, to give them the joy of everlasting life.

ST. ANSELM

IF reverence for the inner personality of others was a matter of course with me from my childhood up, I had on the other hand much trouble in answering the question how far in our ordinary intercourse with others we should hold ourselves back, and how far we should freely give ourselves. The two tendencies struggled within me, but up to the last year of my time at the Gymnasium the former was the stronger. My shyness held me back from showing as much interest in others as I really felt, and from giving them as much help and service as inward impulse bade; and in this habit of mind I was strengthened by my aunt's bringing up at Mülhausen. She impressed me deeply with the idea that reserve is of the essence of good breeding. Every kind of 'forwardness' I ought (she said) to learn to regard as a very serious fault, and I did make genuine efforts to avoid it. As time went on, however, I ventured to emancipate myself somewhat from these rules about well-bred reserve. They seemed to me to be like the rules of harmony which are indeed universally valid, but are often swept aside by the living stream of music. I realized more and more clearly how many opportunities of doing good we miss, if we let ourselves be slavishly hemmed in by the reserve which the conventional rules of social intercourse expect us to practice.

We must, indeed, take care to be tactful, and not mix ourselves up uninvited in other people's business. On the other hand we must not forget the danger lurking in the reserve which our practical life daily forces on us. We cannot possibly let ourselves get frozen into regarding everyone we do not know as an absolute stranger.

ALBERT SCHWEITZER

THE church is catholic, universal, as are all her actions; all that she does belongs to all. When she baptizes a child, that action concerns me; for that child is thereby connected to that head which is my head too, and ingrafted into that body whereof I am a member. And when she buries a man, that action concerns me: all mankind is of one another, and is one volume. . . . No man is an island, entire of itself, every man is a piece of the continent, a part of the main. If a clod be washed away by the sea, Europe is the less, as well as if a promontory were, as well as if a manor of thy friend's or of thine own were; any man's death diminishes me, because I am involved in mankind; and therefore never send to know for whom the bell tolls; it tolls for thee. Neither can we call this a begging of misery, or a borrowing of misery, as though we were not miserable enough of ourselves, but must fetch in more from the next house, in taking upon us the misery of our neighbours. Truly it were an excusable covetousness if we did, for affliction is a treasure, and scarce any man has enough of it. No man hath affliction enough that is not matured and ripened by it, and made fit for God by that affliction. If a man carry treasure in bullion, or in a wedge of gold, and have none coined into current money, his treasure will not defray him as he travels. Tribulation is treasure in the nature of it, but it is not current money in the use of it, except as we get nearer and nearer our home, heaven, by it. Another man may be sick too, and sick to death, and this affliction may lie in his bowels, as gold in a mine, and be of no use to him; but this bell, that tells me of his affliction, digs out and applies that gold to me: if by this consideration of another's danger I take mine own into contemplation, and so secure myself, by making my recourse to my God, who is our only security.

JOHN DONNE

THAT which I am now going to persuade you to (namely, the not excusing of yourselves) causeth a great confusion in me, being a very perfect quality and of great merit, for I ought to practise what I tell you concerning this virtue. But I confess myself very little improved in it; for methinks I never want reason to conceive it more virtue in me to make an excuse. Now, it being sometimes lawful to do and ill to omit it, I have not the discretion or, to say better, the humility to do it when it is fit. For indeed it is a sign of great humility to see oneself condemned without cause and conceal it, and it is a noble imitation of that Lord who took away all our offences. . . . I conceive that it imports much to accustom oneself to this virtue, or to endeavour to obtain of our Lord true humility; for hence it must come, since one truly humble ought to desire indeed to be disesteemed and persecuted and condemned, though having given no cause. If one would imitate our Lord, wherein can he better than in this? Here no corporal strength is necessary, nor any one's assistance, save only God's. These excellent virtues I would have to be our study and our penance; as for other great and excessive penances you know already that I restrain you because they may hurt your health if done without discretion. In those other ye need not fear, because the interior virtues, how great soever, destroy not the body's strength required for observing religion, but fortify the soul; and persons may accustom themselves by very little matters to get the victory in great. But how well is this written, and how ill practised by me! Indeed I could never make this trial in matters of consequence, because I never heard any speak ill of me but I saw plainly it came short of what was true; for though not in those very particulars, I have offended God in many others; and methought they favoured me much in omitting them, for I am ever more glad they should report of me what is not, than what is, true.

SANTA TERESA

THE man who believes in the peculiar doctrines will readily bow to the peculiar demands of Christianity. When he is told to love God supremely, this may startle another; but it will not startle him to whom God has been revealed in peace and in pardon and in all the freeness of an offered reconciliation. When told to shut out the world from his heart, this may be impossible with him who has nothing to replace it—but not impossible with him who has found in God a sure and a satisfying portion. When told to withdraw his affections from the things that are beneath, this were laying an order of self-extinction upon the man who knows not another quarter in the whole sphere of his contemplation to which he could transfer them—but it were not grievous to him whose view has been opened up to the loveliness and glory of the things that are above, and can there find for every feeling of his soul a most ample and delighted occupation. When told to look not to the things that are seen and temporal, this were blotting out the light of all that is visible from the prospect of him in whose eye there is a wall of partition between guilty nature and the joys of eternity—but he who believes that Christ hath broken down this wall finds a gathering radiance upon his soul, as he looks onwards in faith to the things that are unseen and eternal. Tell a man to be holy—and how can he compass such a performance when his only fellowship with holiness is a fellowship of despair? It is the atonement of the Cross reconciling the holiness of the lawgiver with the safety of the offender that hath opened the way for a sanctifying influence into the sinner's heart; and he can take a kindred impression from the character of God now brought nigh and now at peace with him. Separate the demand from the doctrine; and you have either a system of righteousness that is impracticable or a barren orthodoxy. Bring the demand and the doctrine together—and the true disciple of Christ is able to do the one through the other strengthening him.

THOMAS CHALMERS

TRUE, there were excuses for him; for whom are there none? He was poor and struggling; and it is much more difficult (as Becky Sharp, I think, pathetically observed) to be good when one is poor than when one is rich. It is (and all rich people should consider the fact) much more easy, if not to go to heaven, at least to think one is going thither, on three thousand a year than on three hundred. Not only is respectability more easy, as is proved by the broad fact that it is the poor people who fill the jails, and not the rich ones; but virtue and religion—of the popular sort. It is undeniably more easy to be resigned to the will of heaven, when that will seems tending just as we would have it; much more easy to have faith in the goodness of providence, when that goodness seems safe in one's pocket in the form of bank-notes; and to believe that one's children are under the protection of omnipotence, when one can hire for them in half an hour the best medical advice in London. One need only look into one's own heart to understand the disciples' astonishment at the news that 'How hardly shall they that have riches enter into the kingdom of heaven.'

'Who then can be saved?' asked they, being poor men, accustomed to see the wealthy Pharisees in possession of 'the highest religious privileges and means of grace'. Who indeed, if not the rich? If the noblemen, and the bankers, and the dowagers, and the young ladies who go to church, and read good books, and have been supplied from youth with the very best religious articles which money can procure, and have time for all manner of good works, and give their hundreds to charities, and head reformatory movements, and build churches, and work altar-cloths, and can taste all the preachers and father-confessors round London, one after another, as you would taste wines, till they find the spiritual panacea which exactly suits their complaint—if they are not sure of salvation, who can be saved?

Without further comment, the fact is left for the consideration of all readers. . . .

CHARLES KINGSLEY

The Passion not Passive

IF we look at the Gospel story of the Passion as a whole and do not isolate the Cross from its context, one of the most impressive and revealing things in it is the air of strong deliberation and mastery which characterizes Jesus throughout those last days. He is so manifestly not in the least a straw on the stream of events. His enemies are not manipulating Him so much as He is manipulating them, not in any wrong way, but in the way in which God does lay hold of the wrath and sin of man and make them subserve His infinite purpose of love. To the end He could have escaped the Cross by the simple expedient of going somewhere else; but He did not do so. He deliberately directs His steps to it. There is an atmosphere of mastery all about Him as He steadfastly sets His face towards Jerusalem. Standing before the council, or before Pilate, there is no suggestion of fumbling or hesitancy. Nor on the other hand is there any suggestion of a merely excited and fanatical confidence. It is the other people who are excited, not He. And it is always the excited people who are the weak people. He says almost regally, 'No man taketh my life from me; I lay it down of myself.' He says—very plainly, quietly, with the direct steadiness of clear-sighted conviction— 'Hereafter ye shall see the Son of man seated at the right hand of power.' The hereafter refers to their seeing. He Himself sees now. He is conscious of being in a very real sense at the right hand of power now. He is with God now; the victory is His now.

H. H. FARMER

NOR do I so forget God as to adore the name of Nature; which I define not, with the Schools, to be the principle of motion and rest, but that streight and regular line, that settled and constant course the Wisdom of God hath ordained for the actions of His creatures, according to their several kinds. . . . And thus I call the effects of Nature the works of God, whose hand and instrument she only is; and therefore to ascribe His actions unto her is to devolve the honour of the principal agent upon the instrument; which if with reason we may do, then let our hammers rise up and boast they have built our houses, and our pens receive the honour of our writings. I hold there is a general beauty in the works of God, and therefore no deformity in any kind or species of creature whatsoever. I cannot tell by what Logick we call a Toad, a Bear, or an Elephant ugly; they being created in those outward shapes and figures which best express the actions of their inward forms, and having past that general Visitation of God, who saw that all that He made was good, that is, conformable to His Will, which abhors deformity, and is the rule of order and beauty. There is no deformity but in Monstrosity; wherein, notwithstanding, there is a kind of Beauty; Nature so ingeniously contriving the irregular parts, as they become sometimes more remarkable than the principal Fabrick. To speak yet more narrowly, there was never anything ugly or mis-shapen but the Chaos; wherein, notwithstanding (to speak strictly), there was no deformity, because no form; nor was it yet impregnant by the voice of God. Now nature is not at variance with Art, nor Art with Nature, they being both servants of His providence. Art is the perfection of Nature. Were the World now as it was the sixth day, there were yet a Chaos. Nature hath made one World, and Art another. In brief, all things are artificial; for Nature is the Art of God.

SIR THOMAS BROWNE

'FOR we, in spirit, wait for the hope of righteousness through faith' (Gal. v. 5). Brother, thou desirest to have a sensible feeling of thy justification; that is, thou wouldst have such a feeling of God's favour as thou hast of thine own sin. But that will not be. Yet thy righteousness ought to surmount all feeling of sin; that is to say, thy righteousness or justification, whereupon thou holdest, standeth not upon thine own feeling, but upon thy hoping that it shall be revealed when it pleaseth the Lord. Wherefore thou must not judge according to the feeling of sin which troubleth and terrifieth thee, but according to the promise and doctrine of faith, whereby Christ is promised unto thee, who is thy perfect and everlasting righteousness. Thus the hope of the afflicted, consisting in the inward affection, is stirred up by faith in the midst of all terrors and feeling of sin, to hope that he is righteous. Moreover, if hope be here taken for the thing which is hoped for, it is thus to be understood—that that which a man now seeth not, he hopeth in time shall be made perfect and clearly revealed.

Either sense may stand; but the first, touching the inward desire and affection of hoping, bringeth more plentiful consolation: for my righteousness is not yet perfect, it cannot yet be felt; yet I do not despair; for faith showeth unto me Christ in whom I trust; and when I have laid hold of Him by faith, I wrestle against the fiery darts of the devil, and I take good heart through hope against the feeling of sin, assuring myself that I have a perfect righteousness prepared for me in heaven. So both these sayings are true, that I am made righteous already by that righteousness which is begun in me; and also I am raised up on the same hope against sin, and wait for the full consummation of perfect righteousness in heaven. These things are not rightly understood, but when they be put in practice.

MARTIN LUTHER

GOD cannot prove His existence in any other sense than He can swear; He has nothing higher to swear by.

*   *   *

The real trap in which to catch the sceptic is ethics. Since Descartes they have all maintained that during the period in which they doubted they might not make any definite statement with regard to knowledge, but that they might act, because in that respect one could be satisfied with probability. What a tremendous contradiction! As though it were not far more terrible to do something about which one was doubtful (for one thereby assumes a responsibility) than make a statement.

*   *   *

It is so impossible for the world to exist without God that if God should *forget* it, it would immediately cease to be.

*   *   *

God creates out of *nothing*. Wonderful, you say. Yes, to be sure, but He does what is still more wonderful: He makes saints out of sinners.

*   *   *

People say that faith rests upon authority, and think that they have thereby excluded dialectics, but that is not so. For dialectics begins by asking how it is that one abandons oneself to this authority, whether one cannot understand why one chose it, whether it was chance; for in that case the authority is not authority, not even for the believer, if he knows that it was chance.

SÖREN KIERKEGAARD

SCRIPTURE is full of Christ. From Genesis to Revelation everything breathes of Him, not every letter of every sentence, but the spirit of every chapter. It is full of Christ, but not in the way that some suppose; for there is nothing more miserable, as specimens of perverted ingenuity, than the attempts of certain commentators and preachers, to find remote, and recondite, and intended, allusions to Christ everywhere. For example, they chance to find in the construction of the temple the fusion of two metals, and this they conceive is meant to show the union of divinity with humanity in Christ. If they read of coverings to the tabernacle, they find implied the doctrine of imputed righteousness. If it chance that one of the curtains of the tabernacle be red, they see in that a prophecy of the blood of Christ. If they are told that the Kingdom of Heaven is a pearl of great price, they will see in it the allusion that, as a pearl is the production of animal suffering, so the Kingdom of Heaven is produced by the sufferings of the Redeemer. I mention this perverted mode of comment because it is not merely harmless, idle and useless; it is positively dangerous. This is to make the Holy Spirit speak riddles and conundrums, and the interpretation of Scripture but clever riddle-guessing. Putting aside all this childishness, we say that the Bible is full of Christ. Every unfulfilled aspiration of humanity in the past; all partial representation of perfect character; all sacrifices, nay even those of idolatry, point to the fulfilment of what we want, the answer to every longing—the type of perfect Humanity, the Lord Jesus Christ.

F. W. ROBERTSON

TRUTH does not, and cannot, come from ourselves. In all that is spiritual it comes from God, or from those spirits, the friends of God, on whom His light has shone; in what is material, from the things where God has placed it. Therefore in all that is spiritual we must first take counsel of God, then of the wise, and lastly of our own souls; and in all that is material we must search things to their depths.

*　　　*　　　*

Study the sciences in the light of truth, that is—as before God; for their business is to show the truth, that is to say, God everywhere. Write nothing, say nothing, think nothing that you cannot believe to be true before God.

*　　　*　　　*

We love repose of the mind so well that we are arrested by anything which has even the appearance of truth; and so we fall asleep on clouds.

*　　　*　　　*

What is true in the lamplight is not always true in the sunlight.

*　　　*　　　*

Time and truth are friends, although there are many moments hostile to truth.

*　　　*　　　*

The most useful knowledge is to know that we have been deceived, and the most delightful discovery is to find out that we have been mistaken. 'Capable of forsaking an error'—this is fine praise, and a fine quality.

*　　　*　　　*

Those who never retract love themselves better than the truth.

*　　　*　　　*

Simple and sincere minds are never more than half mistaken.

JOSEPH JOUBERT

GIVE me my scallop-shell of quiet,
My staff of faith to walk upon,
My scrip of joy, immortal diet,
My bottle of salvation,
My gown of glory, hope's true gage;
And thus I'll take my pilgrimage.

Blood must be my body's balmer,
   No other balm will there be given;
Whilst my soul, like quiet palmer,
   Travelleth towards the land of heaven;
Over the silver mountains,
Where spring the nectar fountains;
   There will I kiss
   The bowl of bliss,
And drink mine everlasting fill
Upon every milken hill.
My soul will be a-dry before,
But after, it will thirst no more.

       *   *   *

From thence to heaven's bribeless hall,
Where no corrupted voices brawl,
No conscience molten into gold,
No forged accuser bought or sold,
No cause deferred, no rain-spent journey;
For there Christ is the King's Attorney,
Who pleads for all without degrees,
And He hath angels, but no fees;
And when the grand twelve-million jury
Of our sins, with direful fury,
Against our souls black verdicts give,
Christ pleads His death, and then we live.

                              SIR WALTER RALEIGH

NEVER talk of religion but when you think seriously of it; not to betray the want of it by one's discourse of it, which should be decent, grave, sober, prudent.

That our discourse of religion be practical rather than notional, or disputing, that it be devout, edifying after a hearty and affectionate manner.

That it be seasonable; that is, when men are like to be the better for it. Not in promiscuous company, not mixed with sports, hurry, business, nor with drink.

And that we join a good life to our religious conversation; and never contradict our tongue by our deeds.

'As He sat at meat, He took bread, and blessed it, and brake, and gave to them, and their eyes were opened.' We may know religious persons, not only in the exercise of religious actions, but even in the most common actions of life, which they convert into holy actions by the manner of doing them, the holiness of their dispositions, by prayer, thanksgiving, &c.

We always do good or harm to others by the manner of our conversation; we either confirm them in sin or awaken them to piety. . . .

'Refrain not to speak when there is an occasion to do good.' It is an extraordinary talent to be able to improve conversation to the advantage of religion, by taking some fit occasion to say something that is edifying and beneficial.

The great subject of a Christian's discourse should be about the true way of attaining the grace of God, through the blood of Christ, and by the assistance of the Holy Spirit. But then they must say no more than what they are sure of, lest they should lead men to error.

THOMAS WILSON

THERE are great drynesses even in the way of *meditation*; the bread of prayer is often without taste; the most beautiful thoughts often leave nothing affective in the soul, and sometimes the drynesses pass into powerlessness to meditate. But the soul, in spite of the dryness which has come to it, does not leave its meditation; it strains itself, it goes over and over its material for meditation, and when it can no longer do anything it resolves to suffer without inquietude, this cross being of greater merit than affections or thoughts. Neither does the contemplative soul abandon its *contemplation* on account of dryness; its nothingness suffices it in the presence of God, and dryness is, after all, in greater conformity with its state of abnegation than consolations and sweetnesses. The faith which upholds it is verily a dry ground, but it is a solid ground on which one can build firmer foundations than on ground wet with rain or dew, in which one's feet sometimes sink down and bring back nothing but mud. Dryness deprives one of thought, but it does not deprive one of the presence of God, even though it can deprive one of the feeling of His presence. Faith is never really lost even in the greatest tribulations, and in consequence the presence of God, which nourishes it, endures for ever. If nature becomes weary, it is an imperfection natural to it, and it is right and proper that grace should allow it to become wearied. 'Ah, nature!' said a soul, 'thou wilt not remain one hour in prayer, and I would thou couldst remain two!' When the contemplative dryness continues to battle with the senses, it suffers wearisome dryness till it has thoroughly stripped itself; but when the senses are once thoroughly mortified, the dryness will be wholly spiritual. The soul will no longer have anything, and it will not desire anything, but the good pleasure of God.

FRANÇOIS MALAVAL

ON Tuesday, 26 July, I found Mr. Johnson alone. It was a very wet day, and I again complained of the disagreeable effects of such weather. JOHNSON. 'Sir, this is all imagination, which physicians encourage; for man lives in air, as a fish lives in water; so that if the atmosphere press heavy from above, there is an equal resistance from below. To be sure, bad weather is hard upon people who are obliged to be abroad; and men cannot labour so well in the open air in bad weather, as in good: but, Sir, a smith or a taylor, whose work is within doors, will surely do as much in rainy weather, as in fair. Some very delicate frames, indeed, may be affected by wet weather; but not common constitutions.'

We talked of the education of children; and I asked him what he thought was best to teach them first. JOHNSON. 'Sir, it is no matter what you teach them first, any more than what leg you shall put into your breeches first. Sir, you may stand disputing which is best to put in first, but in the mean time your breech is bare. Sir, while you are considering which of two things you should teach your child first, another boy has learnt them both. . . . '

The conversation then took a philosophical turn. JOHNSON. 'Human experience, which is constantly contradicting theory, is the great test of truth. A system, built upon the discoveries of a great many minds, is always of more strength than what is produced by the mere workings of any one mind. There is not so poor a book in the world that would not be a prodigious effort were it wrought out entirely by a single mind, without the aid of prior investigators. . . .'

'As to the Christian religion, Sir, besides the strong evidence which we have for it, there is a balance in its favour from the number of great men who have been convinced of its truth, after a serious consideration of the question.'

JAMES BOSWELL

RELIGION is essentially social *horizontally*; in the sense that each several soul is *therefore* unique because intended to realize just *this* post, function, joy, effect, within the total organism of all souls. Hence no soul is expected to be a 'jack-of-all-trades', but only to develop fully its own special gifts and *attraits* within and through and for that larger organism of the human family, in which other souls are as fully to develop their own differing gifts and *attraits* as so many supplements and compensations to the others. The striving of any one soul can thus be peaceful, since limited in range to what this particular soul, at its best, most really wants and loves.

And religion is essentially social *vertically*—indeed here is its deepest root. It is unchangeably a faith in God, a love of God, an intercourse with God; and though the soul cannot abidingly abstract itself from its fellows, it can and ought frequently to re-collect itself in a simple sense of God's presence. Such moments of direct preoccupation with God alone bring a deep refreshment and simplification to the soul.

And religion, in its fullest development, essentially requires not only this our little span of earthly years but a life beyond. Neither an eternal life that is already fully achieved here below, nor an eternal life to be begun and known solely in the beyond, satisfies these requirements. But only an eternal life already begun and truly known in part here, though fully to be achieved and completely to be understood hereafter, corresponds to the deepest longings of man's spirit as touched by the prevenient Spirit, God.

                        BARON FRIEDRICH VON HÜGEL

THE complaints you make of what passes *within* encourage me under what I feel myself. Indeed, if those whom I have reason to believe are more spiritual and humble than I am, did not give some testimony that they find their hearts made of the same materials as mine is, I should be sometimes hard put to it to believe that I have any part or lot in the matter, or any real knowledge of the life of faith. But this concurrent testimony of many witnesses confirms me in what I think the Scripture plainly teaches—that the soil of human nature, though many spots are certainly better weeded, planted, and manured than others, is everywhere the same, universally bad; so bad that it cannot be worse, and of itself is only capable of producing noxious weeds and nourishing venomous creatures. We often see the effects of culture, skill, and expense will make a garden where all was desert before. When Jesus, the good husbandman, encloses a soil, and separates it from the waste of the world, to make it a residence for Himself, a change presently takes place; it is planted and watered from above, and visited with beams infinitely more cheering and fertilizing than those of the material sun. But its natural propensity to bring forth weeds still continues, and one-half of His dispensations may be compared to a company of weeders, whom He sends forth into His garden to pluck up all which He has not planted with His own hand and which, if left to grow, would quickly overpower and overtop the rest. But alas! the ground is so impregnated with evil seeds, and they shoot in such quick succession, that if this weeding work were not constantly repeated, all former labour would be lost. *Hinc illae lacrymae.* Hence arises the necessity of daily crosses and disappointments, daily changes of frame, and such multiplied convictions that we are nothing and can do nothing of ourselves; all are needful and barely sufficient to prevent our hearts from being overrun with pride, self-dependence and security.

JOHN NEWTON

COULD we see a miracle from God, how would our thoughts be affected with a holy awe and veneration of His Presence! But if we consider everything as God's doing, either by order or permission, we shall then be affected with common things as they would be who saw a miracle. For as there is nothing to affect you in a miracle but as it is the action of God and bespeaks His Presence, so when you consider God as acting in all things and all events, then all things will become venerable to you like miracles, and fill you with the same awful sentiments of the divine Presence. Now, you must not reserve the exercise of this pious temper to any particular times or occasions, or fancy how resigned you will be to God if such or such trials should happen. For this is amusing yourself with the notion or idea of resignation instead of the virtue itself. Do not, therefore, please yourself with thinking how piously you would act and submit to God in a plague, a famine, or persecution, but be intent upon the perfection of the present day, and be assured that the best way of showing a true zeal is to make little things the occasion of great piety. Begin therefore in the smallest matters and most ordinary occasions, and accustom your mind to the daily exercise of this pious temper in the lowest occurrences of life. And when a contempt, an affront, a little injury, loss, or disappointment, or the smallest events of every day, continually raise your mind to God, then you may justly hope that you will be numbered amongst those that are resigned and thankful to God in the greatest trials and afflictions.

WILLIAM LAW

BUT there are hours, and they come to us all at some period of life or other, when the hand of Mystery seems to be heavy on the soul—when some life-shock scatters existence, leaves it a blank and dreary waste henceforth for ever, and there appears nothing of hope in all the expanse which stretches out, except that merciful gate of death which opens at the end—hours when the sense of misplaced or ill-requited affection, the feeling of personal worthlessness, the uncertainty and meanness of all human aims, and a doubt of all human goodness, unfix the soul from all its old moorings—and leave it drifting—drifting over the vast Infinitude, with an awful sense of solitariness. Then the man whose faith rested on outward authority and not on inward life will find it give way: the authority of the priest: the authority of the Church: or merely the authority of a document proved by miracles and backed by prophecy: the soul—conscious life hereafter—God—will be an awful desolate Perhaps. Well! in such moments you doubt all—whether Christianity be true: whether Christ was man or God or a beautiful fable. You ask bitterly, like Pontius Pilate, What is Truth? In such an hour what remains? I reply, Obedience. Leave those thoughts for the present. Act—be merciful and gentle—honest: force yourself to abound in little services: try to do good to others: be true to the Duty that you know. *That* must be right whatever else is uncertain. And by all the laws of the human heart, by the word of God, you shall not be left in doubt. Do that much of the will of God which is plain to you, and 'you shall know of the doctrine, whether it be of God.'

F. W. ROBERTSON

IF we look upon the unworthy contest betwixt God's mercies and most men's ingratitude, and but reflect upon the small return of love that the greatest disbursements of His do usually bring home, we cannot but acknowledge that our loving God for His favours is one of the greatest favours that we love Him for. So unrequitable is God's love, and so insolvent are we, that that love vastly improves the benefit by which alone we might have pretended to some ability of retribution; and so unlimited is this impotence of ours to recompense or repay God's dilection that it extends to and fetters our very wishes. For God enjoys an affluence of felicity so perfect and entire that even our wishes can aim at nothing for Him worthy of Him, unless instituted by what He already actually possesses. . . . It grieves us sensibly to see ourselves reduced to be only passive, and the receivers in this commerce. We would fain contribute something, and cannot always refrain from devoting our wishes to increase His happiness to whom we owe all ours. And some holy persons (particularly St. Austin) have, by the exuberance of their gratitude and devotion, been transported to make wishes, and use expressions, wherein their affections had a greater share than their reason, and which argued them much better to apprehend how much God deserved of them than how little He needed them. But upon second thoughts we shall find that the cause of our grief ought to turn it into our joy, since the desires we would frame, aiming at God's being infinitely happy, are all fulfilled before they are conceived, and that in the most advantageous and noblest way; for could God's happiness admit accession by our accomplished wishes, there were then a possibility of His wanting something to render it complete. And sure it is a more supreme felicity to be by nature transcendently above all increase of blessedness than to receive the greatest that men can wish.

ROBERT BOYLE

THE conversation of Christ with His disciples, when He took His leave of them at His last supper, was most sweet, loving and friendly, talking with them lovingly, as a father with his children when he must depart from them. He took their weakness in good part and bore with them, though now and then their discourse was very full of simplicity, as when Philip said, 'Shew us the Father', &c.; and Thomas, 'We know not the way', &c.; and Peter, 'I will go with Thee unto death'; each freely showing the thoughts of his heart. Never since the world began was a more precious, sweet and amiable conversation!

*　　　*　　　*

Is it not a shame that we are always afraid of Christ, whereas there was never in heaven or earth a more loving, familiar, or milder man, in words, works and demeanour, especially towards poor, sorrowful and tormented consciences?

*　　　*　　　*

I expect more goodness from Kate my wife, from Philip Melanchthon, and from other friends, than from my sweet and blessed Saviour Christ Jesus; and yet I know for certain that neither she nor any other person on earth will or can suffer that for me which He has suffered. Why then should I be afraid of Him? This my foolish weakness grieves me very much. We plainly see in the Gospel how mild and gentle He showed Himself towards His disciples; how kindly He passed over their weakness, their presumption, yea, their foolishness. He checked their unbelief and in all gentleness admonished them. . . . Fie on our unbelieving hearts that we should be afraid of this man who is more loving, friendly, gentle, and compassionate towards us than are our own kindred, our brothers and sisters—yea, than parents towards their own children.

MARTIN LUTHER

I MUST now state, in all diffidence, what I conceive to be the essential character of the religious spirit.

Religion is the vision of something which stands beyond, behind, and within the passing flux of immediate things; something which is real, and yet waiting to be realized; something which is a remote possibility, and yet the greatest of present facts; something that gives meaning to all that passes, and yet eludes apprehension; something whose possession is the final good, and yet is beyond all reach; something which is the ultimate ideal, and the hopeless quest.

The immediate reaction of human nature to the religious vision is worship. . . . The vision claims nothing but worship; and worship is a surrender to the claim for assimilation, urged with the motive force of mutual love. The vision never overrules. It is always there, and it has the power of love presenting the one purpose whose fulfilment is eternal harmony. Such order as we find in nature is never force—it presents itself as the one harmonious adjustment of complex detail. Evil is the brute motive force of fragmentary purpose, disregarding the eternal vision. Evil is overruling, retarding, hurting. The power of God is the worship He inspires. That religion is strong which in its ritual and its modes of thought evokes an apprehension of the commanding vision. The worship of God is not a rule of safety—it is an adventure of the spirit, a flight after the unattainable. The death of religion comes with the repression of the high hope of adventure.

                                                    A. N. WHITEHEAD

FIRST keep thyself in peace and then shalt thou be able to pacify others. A peaceable man doth more good than he that is well learned. . . . He that is well in peace is not suspicious of any. But he that is discontented and troubled is tossed with divers suspicions: he is neither quiet himself nor suffereth others to be quiet. . . . He considereth what others are bound to do, and neglecteth that which he is bound to himself. First therefore have a careful zeal over thyself, and then thou mayest justly show thyself zealous also of thy neighbour's good.

Thou knowest well how to excuse and colour thine own deeds, but thou art not willing to receive the excuses of others. It were more just that thou shouldest accuse thyself and excuse thy brother. . . . It is no great matter to associate with the good and gentle; for this is naturally pleasing to all, and everyone willingly enjoyeth peace and loveth those best that agree with him. But to be able to live peaceably with hard and perverse persons, or with the disorderly or with such as go contrary to us, is a great grace, and a most commendable and manly thing.

*　　　　*　　　　*

We cannot trust too much to ourselves, because grace oftentimes is wanting to us, and understanding also. There is but little light in us, and that which we have we quickly lose by our negligence. Oftentimes too we do not perceive our own inward blindness, how great it is. We often do evil, and excuse it worse. We are sometimes moved with passion, and we think it to be zeal. We reprehend small things in others, and pass over greater matters in ourselves. We quickly enough feel and weigh what we suffer at the hands of others; but we mind not what others suffer from us. He that well and rightly considereth his own works will find little cause to judge hardly of another.

THOMAS A KEMPIS

ONE degree higher than the Judaical Christians I would place those who, when they pray, have no object in view but their salvation, and are moreover less concerned with the idea of gaining Paradise than with that of avoiding Hell.

Here again it is self-love that prompts and directs devotion. This is not wicked, assuredly, but it is very imperfect. They know they have sinned, but they do not know whether they have been forgiven by God. . . . Thence arise excessive fears and anxieties: all their thoughts converge on this point. In their religious exercises they have no idea but the expiation of their sins; they see in God only His offended justice, and because it alarms them, they think only of appeasing it. If they attend Mass, they offer the Holy Sacrifice for the expiation of their sins; . . . they recite the rosary and certain special prayers, too, merely in the hope of gaining indulgences; they approach the Holy Table with the same object. . . ; and if they perform good works and practise mortifications their intention is the same.

All this is good, no doubt, and I have no wish to express disapproval of it. It is a holy and salutary thought that leads us, even when the motive is our own eternal interest, to detest and expiate our past sins, and resolve to keep ourselves from sin in the future. But it is certainly a matter for disapproval that a person's mind should be entirely concentrated on this object, and that the eyes should never be raised above self and fixed upon God. Penitence is undeniably necessary; but we should find our principal motives for it in the goodness of God, which we have outraged; . . . in His holiness which we have insulted and to which we owe reparation; . . . in Jesus Christ, whom we have crucified afresh. . . . These are the chief reasons that should move us to grief and repentance. . . . They should surely be more effectual in making us truly contrite, in appeasing the divine wrath, and gaining pardon for our sins than the fear of being lost or the desire to be saved. One thing is certain: as long as you only pray to God for yourselves, your prayers will not be as perfect as He wishes them to be.   JEAN NICOLAS GROU

HE that can equally despise riches when he hath them and when he hath them not; that is not sadder if they lie in his neighbour's trunks, nor more brag if they shine round about his own walls; he that is neither moved with good fortune coming to him nor going from him; that can look upon another man's lands evenly and pleasedly, as if they were his own, and yet look upon his own, and use them too, just as if they were another man's; that neither spends his goods prodigally and like a fool, nor yet keeps them avariciously and like a wretch; that weighs not benefits by weight and number, but by the mind and circumstances of him that gives them; that never thinks his charity expensive, if a worthy person be the receiver; he that doth nothing for opinion sake, but every thing for conscience, being as curious of his thoughts as of his actings in markets and theatres, and is as much in awe of himself as of a whole assembly: he that knows God looks on, and contrives his secret affairs as in the presence of God and his holy angels; that eats and drinks because he needs it, not that he may serve a lust or load his belly: he that is bountiful and cheerful to his friends, and charitable and apt to forgive his enemies; that loves his country, and obeys his prince, and desires and endeavours nothing more than that he may do honour to God: this person may reckon his life to be the life of a man, and compute his months, not by the course of the sun, but the zodiac and circle of his virtues; because these are such things which fools and children, and birds and beasts, cannot have; these are therefore the actions of life, because they are the seeds of immortality. That day in which we have done some excellent thing, we may as truly reckon to be added to our life as were the fifteen years to the days of Hezekiah.

JEREMY TAYLOR

WE acknowledge that there are broken lives, pieces of lives which began in this world, to be completed, as we believe, in another state of being. And some of them have been like fragments of ancient art, which we prize not for their completeness but for their quality, and because they seem to give us a type of something which we can hardly see anywhere upon earth. Of such lives we must judge, not by what the person said or wrote or did in the short span of human existence, but by what they were: if they exercised some peculiar influence on society and on friends, if they had some rare grace of humility, or simplicity, or resignation, or love of truth, or self-devotion, which was not to be met with in others. God does not measure men's lives only by the amount of work which is accomplished in them. He who gave the power to work may also withhold the power. And some of these broken lives may have a value in His sight which no bustle or activity of ordinary goodness could have attained. There have been persons confined to a bed of sickness, blind, palsied, tormented with pain and want, who yet may be said to have led an almost perfect life. Such persons afford examples to us, not indeed of a work carried out to the end (for their circumstances did not admit of this), but of a work, whether finished or unfinished, which at any moment is acceptable to God. And we desire to learn of them, and to have an end like theirs when the active work of life is over and we sit patiently waiting for the will of God.

BENJAMIN JOWETT

IF thou art not in heaven in this life, thou wilt never be in heaven in the life to come. At death, says the wise man, each thing returns into its own element, into the ground of its life; the light into the light, and the darkness into the darkness. As the tree falls, so it lies. My friends, you who call yourselves enlightened Christian folk, do you suppose that you can lead a mean, worldly, covetous, spiteful life here, and then, the moment your soul leaves the body, that you are to be changed into the very opposite character, into angels and saints, as fairy tales tell of beasts changed into men? If a beast can be changed into a man, then death can change the sinner into a saint—but not else. If a beast would enjoy being a man, then a sinner would enjoy being in heaven—but not else. A sinful, worldly man enjoy being in heaven? Does a fish enjoy being on dry land? The sinner would long to be back in this world again. Why, what is the employment of spirits in heaven according to the Bible? What but glorifying God? Not *trying* only to do everything to God's glory, but actually succeeding in *doing* it— basking in the sunshine of His smile, delighting to feel themselves as nothing before His glorious majesty, meditating on the beauty of His love, filling themselves with the sight of His power, search- ing out the treasures of His wisdom, and finding God in all and all in God—their whole eternity one act of worship, one hymn of praise. Are there not some among us who will have had but little practice at that work? Those who have done nothing for God's glory here, how do they expect to be able to do everything for God's glory hereafter? Those who will not take the trouble of merely standing up at the psalms, like the rest of their neighbours, even if they cannot sing with their voices God's praises in this church, how will they like singing God's praises through eternity?

CHARLES KINGSLEY

GOD directs the tongues of His ministers as He doth His showers of rain: they fall upon the face of a large compass of earth, when as all that earth did not need that rain. . . . [But] for the refreshing of one span of ground God lets fall a whole shower of rain; for the rectifying of one soul God pours out the meditations of the preacher into such a subject as perchance doth little concern the rest of the congregation. St. Matthew relates Christ's Sermon at large, and St. Luke but briefly, and yet St. Luke remembers some things that St. Matthew had left out. If thou remember not all that was presented to thy faith, all the citations of places of Scripture, nor all that was presented to thy reason, all the deducements, and inferences of the Schools, nor all that was presented to thy spiritual delight, all the sentences of ornament produced out of the Fathers, yet if thou remember that which concerned thy sin, and thy soul, if thou meditate upon that, apply that, thou hast brought away all the sermon, all that was intended by the Holy Ghost to be preached to thee. And if thou have done so, as at a donative at a Coronation, or other solemnity, when money is thrown among the people, though thou light but upon one shilling of that money, thou canst not think that all the rest is lost, but that some others are the richer for it, though thou beest not; so if thou remember, or apply, or understand but one part of the sermon, do not think all the rest to have been idly, or unnecessarily, or impertinently spoken, for thou broughtest a fever and hast had thy juleps, another brought a fainting and a diffident spirit and must have his cordials.

JOHN DONNE

WE must not forget that if earthly love has in the vulgar mind been often degraded into mere animal passion, it still remains in its purest sense the highest mystery of our existence, the most perfect blessing and delight on earth, and at the same time the truest pledge of our more than human nature.

*　　　*　　　*

Would not the carrying out of one single commandment of Christ, 'Love one another', change the whole aspect of the world, and sweep away prisons and workhouses, and envying and strife, and all the strongholds of the devil? Two thousand years have nearly passed, and people have not yet understood that one single command of Christ, 'Love one another'!

*　　　*　　　*

If we do a thing because we think it is our duty, we generally fail; that is the old law which makes slaves of us. The real spring of our life, and of our work in life, must be love—true, deep love—not love of this or that person, or for this or that reason, but deep human love, devotion of soul to soul, love of God realised where alone it can be—in love of those whom He loves. Everything else is weak, passes away; that love alone supports us, makes life tolerable, binds the present together with the past and future, and is, we may trust, imperishable.

*　　　*　　　*

How selfish we are even in our love! Here we live for a short season, and we know we must part sooner or later. We wish to go first, and to leave those whom we love behind us, and we sorrow because they went first and left us behind. As soon as one looks beyond this life, it seems so short; yet there was a time when it seemed endless.

*　　　*　　　*

The past is ours, and there we have all who loved us, and whom we love as much as ever, ay, more than ever.

MAX MÜLLER

JOB had a custom to offer burnt-offerings according to the number of his sons; for he said, It may be that my sons in their feasting have sinned, and cursed God in their hearts. It may be, not it must be, he was not certain, but suspected it. But now, what if his sons had not sinned? Was Job's labour lost, and his sacrifice of none effect? Oh no! only their property was altered; in case his sons were found faulty, his sacrifices for them were propitiatory and through Christ obtained their pardon: in case they were innocent, his offerings were eucharistical, returning thanks to God's restraining grace for keeping his sons from such sins, which otherwise they would have committed.

I see in all doubtful matters of devotion it is wisest to be on the surest side, better both lock and bolt and bar it than leave the least door of danger open. Hast thou done what is disputable whether it be well done? Is it a measuring cast whether it be lawful or no? So that thy conscience may seem in a manner to stand neuter, sue a conditional pardon out of the court of heaven, the rather because our self-love is more prone to flatter, than our godly jealousy to suspect, ourselves without a cause; with such humility heaven is well pleased. For suppose thyself over-cautious, needing no forgiveness in that particular, God will interpret the pardon thou prayest for to be the praises presented unto Him.

THOMAS FULLER

Now as they were going along and talking, they espied a boy feeding his father's sheep. The boy was in very mean clothes, but of a very fresh and well-favoured countenance, and as he sate by himself he sang. Hark, said Mr. Greatheart, to what the shepherd's boy saith. So they hearkened, and he said:

> He that is down needs fear no fall,
>   He that is low no pride:
> He that is humble ever shall
>   Have God to be his guide.
>
> I am content with what I have,
>   Little be it or much:
> And, Lord, contentment still I crave,
>   Because thou savest such.
>
> Fullness to such a burden is
>   That go on pilgrimage:
> Here little, and hereafter bliss,
>   Is best from age to age.

Then said their guide, Do you hear him? I will dare to say that this boy lives a merrier life, and wears more of that herb called hearts-ease in his bosom, than he that is clad in silk and velvet.

JOHN BUNYAN

IF I Him but have,
   If He be but mine,
If my heart, hence to the grave,
   Ne'er forgets His love divine—
Know I nought of sadness,
Feel I nought but worship, love, and gladness.

If I Him but have,
   Pleased from all I part;
Follow, on my pilgrim staff,
   None but Him, with honest heart;
Let the rest, nought saying,
On broad, bright and crowded streets go straying.

If I Him but have,
   Glad to sleep I sink;
From His heart the flood He gave
   Shall to me be food and drink;
And—oh, soft compelling!—
All shall mollify with deep indwelling.

If I Him but have,
   Mine the world I hail;
Happy, like a cherub grave
   Holding back the Virgin's veil;
I deep sunk in gazing,
Earth's distastes are lost in heavenly praising.

Where I have but Him,
   Is my fatherland,
Where all favours to me come
   As a portion from His hand:
Brothers long deplored—
Lo, in His disciples all restored!

NOVALIS

THE day now approaching whereon she was to depart this life (which day Thou well knewest, though we knew it not), it came to pass, Thyself, as I believe, so ordering it, that she and I stood alone, leaning in a certain window which looked into the garden of the house where we now lay at Ostia; where, removed from the din of men, we were recruiting from the fatigues of a long journey for the voyage by sea. We were discoursing then together alone, very sweetly....

We were saying then: If to any the tumult of the flesh were hushed, hushed the images of earth and waters and air, hushed also the poles of heaven, yea the very soul be hushed to herself, and by not thinking on self surmount self, hushed all dreams and imaginary revelations, every tongue and every sign, and whatsoever exists only in transition, since if any could hear, all these say, 'We made not ourselves, but He made us who abideth for ever'— If then having uttered this, they too should be hushed, having raised only our ears to Him who made them, and He alone speak, not by them but by Himself, that we might hear His Word, not through any tongue of flesh, nor angel's voice, nor sound of thunder, nor in the dark riddle of a similitude, but might hear Whom in these things we love, might hear His very self without these (as we two now strained ourselves, and in swift thought touched on that Eternal Wisdom which abideth over all); could this be continued on, and other visions of kind far unlike be withdrawn, and this one ravish and absorb and wrap up its beholder amid these inward joys, so that life might be for ever like that one moment which now we sighed after; were not this 'Enter into the joy of thy Lord'? And when shall that be? When 'we shall all rise again', though we 'shall not all be changed'.

ST. AUGUSTINE

THE SOURCES

DAY 1   Baron F. von Hügel, *Selected Letters* (1927), p. 229.

DAY 2   Dated by Coleridge from Highgate on 13 July 1834—twelve days before his death.

DAY 3   Père Jean Nicolas Grou, *The School of Jesus Christ* (c. 1794), English translation (1932), pp. 237 f.

DAY 4   Dora Greenwell (1821–82).

DAY 5   François de la Mothe Fénelon, Archbishop of Cambrai (1651–1715), *Letters to Madame de Maintenon*, ix.

DAY 6   Thomas à Kempis (1379–1471), *The Imitation of Christ*, III. lix.

DAY 7   Simone Weil (1909–43), *Waiting on God*, English translation (1951), pp. 77 f.

DAY 8   J. Rendel Harris, *Memoranda Sacra* (1892), pp. 82–84.

DAY 9   Father R. H. J. Steuart, S.J., *The Inward Vision* (1930), pp. 130–2.

DAY 10   D. S. Cairns, *The Faith That Rebels* (1928), pp. 211 f.

DAY 11   Baron F. von Hügel, *Selected Letters* (1927), pp. 286 f.

DAY 12   John Henry, Cardinal Newman, *Apologia pro Vita Sua* (1865), chap. v.

DAY 13   George Herbert (1593–1633).

DAY 14   St. Francis de Sales (1567–1622), *On the Love of God*, Knox Little's translation, book viii, chap. ii.

DAY 15   Lady Julian of Norwich, *Revelations* (1373), transcribed by Harford.

DAY 16   Alexander Whyte (1836–1921), *Lord, Teach us to Pray*, vii.

DAY 17   St. Athanasius (293–373), *De Incarnatione Verbi Dei*, Robertson's translation (1884), xliii.

DAY 18   William James, *The Principles of Psychology* (1890), vol. i, chap. iv.

DAY 19   W. R. Inge, *Personal Religion and the Life of Devotion* (1924), pp. 60 ff.

DAY 20   Richard Baxter (1615–91), *The Saints' Everlasting Rest*, chap. xiii.

DAY 21   Sören Kierkegaard (1813–55), *Journals*, Alexander Dru's translation (1938), §§ 974, 248.

DAY 45   Albert Schweitzer, *Memories of Childhood and Youth*, English translation (1925), pp. 86–88.

DAY 46   John Owen (1616–83), *On the Glory of Christ*, xii.

DAY 47   Archibald C. Craig, *University Sermons* (N.D.), pp. 36 f.

DAY 48   Sir Henry Wotton (1568–1639).

DAY 49   William Law, *A Practical Treatise upon Christian Perfection* (1726).

DAY 50   Thomas Fuller, *Good Thoughts in Worse Times* (1647), Personal Meditations, vi.

DAY 51   Archbishop William Temple, *Personal Religion and the Life of Fellowship* (1926), p. 79.

DAY 52   Samuel Taylor Coleridge, *Aids to Reflection* (1825).

DAY 53   Paul Tillich, *The Shaking of the Foundations* (1948), pp. 93 f.

DAY 54   Alfred, Lord Tennyson, *In Memoriam* (1850), xxxi, xxxii.

DAY 55   Richard Baxter, *The Saints' Everlasting Rest* (1650), chap. xii. 6.

DAY 56   St. Bernard of Clairvaux (1091–1153), *De diligendo Deo*, English translation (1950), pp. 49–52.

DAY 57   Emil Brunner in a statement quoted by William Paton, *The Church and the New Order* (1941), pp. 63 f.

DAY 58   Francis Bacon (1561–1626), *Essays*, xxi.

DAY 59   Augustus and J. C. Hare, *Guesses at Truth* (1827).

DAY 60   François de la Mothe Fénelon (1651–1715), *Letters and Reflections*, English translation (1906), pp. 127 f.

DAY 61   H.-F. Amiel, *Journal intime*, Mrs. Humphry Ward's translation: entry for 29 April 1874.

DAY 62   George Tyrrell, *Oil and Wine* (1907), xii.

DAY 63   John Bunyan, *Grace Abounding to the Chief of Sinners* (1666).

DAY 64   Gregory Dix, *The Shape of the Liturgy* (1945), pp. 744 f.

DAY 65   Thomas Fuller, *Good Thoughts in Bad Times* (1645), Historical Applications, ii.

DAY 66   R. D. Blackmore (1825–1900).

DAY 67   Herbert Butterfield, *History and Human Relations* (1951), pp. 61–63.

DAY 68   William Law, *A Serious Call to a Devout and Holy Life* (1728).

DAY 69   John Foster, *Essays* (1806), II. iv.

DAY 70   Archbishop William Temple, *Personal Religion and the Life of Fellowship* (1926), p. 46.

DAY 71 John Ruskin, *Sesame and Lilies* (1865), Lecture i.

DAY 72 Andrew Marvell (1621–78).

DAY 73 John Wesley, *Journal*: entry for 24 May 1738.

DAY 74 F. J. A. Hort, *The Way, the Truth, the Life* (1893), p. 168.

DAY 75 Christina Rossetti, *Time Flies* (1885), pp. 113 f.

DAY 76 C. H. Robinson, *Studies in the Resurrection of Christ* (1909), pp. 46–48.

DAY 77 Père Jean Nicolas Grou (1731–1803), *The Hidden Life of the Soul*, English translation, p. 244.

DAY 78 J. P. de Caussade (1675–1751), *Self-Abandonment to Divine Providence*, English translation (1933), pp. 25 f.

DAY 79 John W. Taylor, *The Doorkeeper and Other Poems*.

DAY 80 W. M. Macgregor, *Jesus Christ the Son of God* (1917), pp. 121–3.

DAY 81 Richard Jefferies, *The Story of My Heart* (1883), chap. vi.

DAY 82 Frederick W. Robertson of Brighton, Sermon preached 12 August 1849.

DAY 83 William Penn, *Some Fruits of Solitude* (1693), §§ 32–40.

DAY 84 John Bunyan (1628–88), *The Pilgrim's Progress*, Second Part.

DAY 85 Richard Rothe (1799–1867), *Still Hours*, English translation (1886), pp. 253–5.

DAY 86 Francis Thompson (1860–1907), *Works*, vol. iii (1913), pp. 81 f.

DAY 87 Henry Scougal, *The Life of God in the Soul of Man* (1677).

DAY 88 Percy Bysshe Shelley (1792–1822), 'Ozymandias': 'Adonais'.

DAY 89 St. Bernard of Clairvaux (1091–1153), *De diligendo Deo*, English translation (1950), pp. 40–42.

DAY 90 A. R. Vidler, *God's Demand and Man's Response* (1938), pp. 101 f.

DAY 91 Count Nicolas Zinzendorf, *Nine Public Discourses* (1747), English translation of 1748, pp. 160–2.

DAY 92 H.-F. Amiel, *Journal intime*, Mrs. Humphry Ward's translation; entry for 6 January 1853.

DAY 93 Reinhold Niebuhr, *The Nature and Destiny of Man*, vol. i (1941), pp. 196 f.

DAY 94 St. Augustine (354–430), *Confessions*, book viii, E. B. Pusey's translation, slightly amended.

DAY 95 Albert Schweitzer, *Memories of Childhood and Youth*, English translation (1925), pp. 89–91.

DAY 96 Thomas Fuller, *Good Thoughts in Worse Times* (1647), Occasional Meditations, v.

DAY 97 Jeremy Taylor (1613–67), *Holy Living*, iv. 10.

DAY 98 Samuel Taylor Coleridge, *Aids to Reflection* (1825).

DAY 99 Christina Rossetti (1830–94).

DAY 100 François de la Mothe Fénelon (1651–1715), *Letters and Reflections*, English translation (1906), pp. 95 f.

DAY 101 John Donne, *Devotions upon Emergent Occasions* (1624), vii.

DAY 102 Brother Lawrence (Nicholas Herman of Lorraine, 1611–91), *The Practice of the Presence of God*; English translation by H. C.

DAY 103 Dietrich Bonhoeffer, *Nachfolge* (1937); English translation, *The Cost of Discipleship*, pp. 112 f.

DAY 104 *Theologia Germanica* (c. 1350), chap. l; Susanna Winkworth's translation, slightly amended.

DAY 105 Sören Kierkegaard (1813–55), *Journals*, English translation (1938), §§ 762, 786; *Concluding Unscientific Postscript*; English translation (1941), p. 348 n.

DAY 106 James Boswell, *Life of Johnson*; report of conversation of 29 May 1783.

DAY 107 *The Times*, London, Weekly Edition, 3 July 1924; David Pye, *George Leigh Mallory: A Memoir* (1927), *ad fin.*

DAY 108 *Spiritual Letters of Father Congreve* (1928), pp. 125 f. Letter dated 22 May 1899.

DAY 109 William Cowper (1731–1800).

DAY 110 Bishop Francis Paget, *The Spirit of Discipline* (1891).

DAY 111 John Henry, Cardinal Newman (1801–90), *Parochial and Plain Sermons.*

DAY 112 Phillips Brooks, *The Candle of the Lord* (1881), *ad fin.*

DAY 113 Thomas Carlyle, *Sartor Resartus* (1834), book ii, chap. ix.

DAY 114 George Macdonald (1824–1905), *Unspoken Sermons*, Third Series, pp. 65–67.

DAY 115 Thomas Erskine of Linlathen (1788–1870), *Letters*, one-volume edition (1878), pp. 484 f.

DAY 116 Sir Tom Taylor in *University of Edinburgh Journal*, vol. xvi, no. 2 (1952), p. 96.

DAY 117 William Paton, *The Church and the New Order* (1941), pp. 152 f.

DAY 118 William Penn, *Some Fruits of Solitude* (1693), §§ 117–26.

DAY 142 Brother Lawrence (Nicholas Herman of Lorraine, 1611–91), *The Practice of the Presence of God*; translated by H. C.

DAY 143 John Bunyan (1628–88), *The Pilgrim's Progress*, Second Part.

DAY 144 W. M. Macgregor, *Jesus Christ the Son of God* (1907), pp. 77 f.

DAY 145 George Tyrrell, *Oil and Wine* (1907), li.

DAY 146 James Boswell, *Life of Johnson*, Dec. 1784; quoting Dr. Brocklesby's account.

DAY 147 Jeremy Taylor (1613–67), *Holy Living*, ii. 6.

DAY 148 Richard Rothe (1799–1867), *Still Hours*; English translation (1886), pp. 246–9.

DAY 149 Francis Thompson (1860–1907), *A Fallen Yew* (in *Selected Poems*, 1908).

DAY 150 Frederick W. Robertson, Sermon preached at the Autumn Assizes at Lewes, 1852.

DAY 151 Augustus and Julius Charles Hare, *Guesses at Truth* (1827).

DAY 152 St. Augustine (354–430) *Confessions*, book x; E. B. Pusey's translation.

DAY 153 John Henry, Cardinal Newman (1801–90), sermon on 'The Invisible World'.

DAY 154 Mechthild of Magdeburg (1210–97) *Revelations*, translated by Lucy Menzies (1953), pp. 211 ff.

DAY 155 Izaak Walton, *The Compleat Angler* (1663), chap. xxi.

DAY 156 Thomas Fuller, *Good Thoughts in Worse Times* (1647); Occasional Meditations, v.

DAY 157 Reinhold Niebuhr, *Reflections on the End of an Era* (1934), pp. 284 f.

DAY 158 H.-F. Amiel, *Journal intime*, Mrs. Humphry Ward's translation; entry for 2 May 1852.

DAY 159 John Bunyan (1628–88), *The Pilgrim's Progress*.

DAY 160 Richard Jefferies (1848–87), *Greene Ferne Farm*.

DAY 161 Henry Scougal, *The Life of God in the Soul of Man* (1677).

DAY 162 Baron F. von Hügel (1852–1925), *Selected Letters* (1927), pp. 180, 227, 228.

DAY 163 George Macdonald, *Unspoken Sermons*, First Series (1867), pp. 214 f.

DAY 164 Bishop Francis Paget, *The Spirit of Discipline* (1891).

DAY 187 R. W. Barbour, *Thoughts* (1900), pp. 134, 135, 105, 61, 100, 107.

DAY 188 John Woolman, *Journal* (1774); a letter appended to chap. iii.

DAY 189 John Donne, *Fifty Sermons* (1649), xlix.

DAY 190 Thomas à Kempis (1379–1471), *The Imitation of Christ*, II. xi, xii.

DAY 191 St. Augustine (354–430), *Confessions*, book x; E. B. Pusey's translation, amended.

DAY 192 Charles Kingsley, *Two Years Ago* (1857), chap. xxvi.

DAY 193 Jonathan Edwards (1703–58), *Works*, 1844 edition, pp. 7–9.

DAY 194 Emily Brontë (1818–48).

DAY 195 Thomas Fuller, *Good Thoughts in Bad Times* (1645), Historical Applications, xiii.

DAY 196 John Bunyan (1628–88), *The Pilgrim's Progress*, Second Part.

DAY 197 William Law, *A Serious Call to a Devout and Holy Life* (1728).

DAY 198 William Temple, Archbishop of Canterbury, *Personal Religion and the Life of Fellowship* (1926), p. 81.

DAY 199 John Donne, *Fifty Sermons* (1649), xiv.

DAY 200 John Bunyan (1628–88), *Grace Abounding to the Chief of Sinners*, The Conclusion.

DAY 201 John Tillotson (1630–94), Archbishop of Canterbury; Maxims and Discourses, as arranged by Laurence Echard (1719), pp. 61 ff.

DAY 202 Bishop Thomas Wilson (1663–1755), *Works*, vol. iii, Sermon xcvi.

DAY 203 Joseph Joubert (1754–1824), *Pensées*; Katherine Lyttelton's translated selection (1898), pp. 48 ff.

DAY 204 Thomas Chalmers, *Astronomical Discourses* (1817), vii.

DAY 205 *Life and Letters of F. W. Robertson*, vol. i, pp. 258 f.; letter of October 1849.

DAY 206 John Ker (1819–86), *Thoughts for Heart and Life*, pp. 107–14.

DAY 207 Edward Taylor (1644–1729).

DAY 208 Samuel Johnson (1709–84), *The Rambler*, no. 79; Tuesday, 18 December 1750.

DAY 209 Horace Bushnell, *Christian Nurture* (1847), part i, chap. iii.

DAY 210 Alexander Whyte, *The Walk, Conversation and Character of Jesus Christ our Lord* (1905) [now entitled *Jesus Christ our Lord*], pp. 244 ff.

DAY 211 The Marquis de Vauvenargues (1715–47), *Reflections and Maxims*, nos. 12, 27, 28, 45, 65, 66, 106, 160, 165, 172, 173; English translation (1940).

DAY 212 Reinhold Niebuhr, *The Children of Light and the Children of Darkness* (1944), pp. 188 f.

DAY 213 John Keble (1792–1866), *Letters of Spiritual Counsel*, xiv.

DAY 214 Lorenzo Scupoli, *The Spiritual Combat* (1589), E. B. Pusey's translation; 'Of Inward Peace', chap. vii.

DAY 215 Henry Drummond, *The Programme of Christianity* (1882).

DAY 216 Ben Jonson (1573–1637), *Discoveries*, i, xvi, lx.

DAY 217 St. Francis de Sales (1567–1622), *Introduction to the Devout Life*, iv. 14. English translation (1875).

DAY 218 Bishop Lesslie Newbigin, *Christian Freedom in the Modern World* (1937), pp. 84 f.

DAY 219 Edmund Spenser, *An Hymne of Heavenly Love* (1596).

DAY 220 Jonathan Edwards (1703–58), *A Treatise Concerning the Religious Affections* (1746), part iii. 10.

DAY 221 John of Ruysbroeck (1293–1381), *The Adornment of the Spiritual Marriage*, English translation (1916), pp. 25 f.

DAY 222 St. Anselm (1033–1109), *Meditations*; E. B. Pusey's translation (1856), Meditation ix.

DAY 223 *Theologia Germanica* (c. 1350), chap. x; Susanna Winkworth's translation.

DAY 224 John Henry, Cardinal Newman (1801–90), sermon on 'Warfare the Condition of Life'.

DAY 225 James Denney, *The Way Everlasting* (1911), pp. 219–21.

DAY 226 G. A. Studdert Kennedy, *The New Man in Christ* (1932), pp. 214, 225.

DAY 227 Johann Tauler (c. 1300–61), *Thirty-Seven Sermons for Festivals*, v; A. W. Hutton's translation.

DAY 228 Baron F. von Hügel, *Selected Letters*: 1896–1924, pp. 353 f.

DAY 229 H. H. Farmer, *The Healing Cross* (1938), pp. 55 f.

DAY 230 Samuel Johnson, *The Vanity of Human Wishes* (1749), *ad fin.*

DAY 231 St. Adamnan (624–704), *Life of St. Columba*, book iii, chap. xxiii, Huyshe's translation (1905).

DAY 232 Benjamin Whichcote, *Moral and Religious Aphorisms* (1753), ii and iii.

DAY 233 Frederick William Faber, *Spiritual Conferences* (1859), pp. 162–7.

DAY 234 Prebendary Robert South (1634–1716), Sermon i.

DAY 235 John Donne, *Sermons* (1640), ii.

DAY 236 From *The Little Flowers of St. Francis* (13th century); English translation of 1863.

DAY 237 C. S. Lewis, *The Problem of Pain* (1940), pp. 141 f.

DAY 238 Archibald C. Craig, *University Sermons* (N.D.), pp. 53–55.

DAY 239 Dietrich Bonhoeffer (died 1945), *Widerstand und Ergebung* (1951); English translation, *Letters and Papers from Prison* (1953), p. 24 f.

DAY 240 Lionel Johnson (1867–1902).

DAY 241 Sir Thomas Browne, *Religio Medici* (1642), The First Part.

DAY 242 Nicholas Berdyaev, *The End of the Renaissance* (1919); English translation (1933), pp. 54–56.

DAY 243 W. R. Matthews, Dean of St. Paul's, *Strangers and Pilgrims* (1945), pp. 61 ff.

DAY 244 Father John Iliyitch Sergieff (born 1829), *Thoughts and Counsels* (1899), pp. 305 f.

DAY 245 John Flavel, *Husbandry Spiritualized* (1699), Occasional Meditations, vii.

DAY 246 James Martineau, *Endeavours after the Christian Life* (1843), xviii.

DAY 247 St. John of the Cross (1542–91), *Spiritual Sentences and Maxims; Complete Works*, translated by E. Allison Pears (1935), vol. iii, pp. 241 f.

DAY 248 Freya Stark, *Beyond Euphrates* (1951), pp. 44, 40.

DAY 249 Bishop Joseph Hall (1574–1656), *The Christian*.

DAY 250 Bishop John Coleridge Patteson, Letter to his sister dated Advent 1870; from Charlotte M. Yonge's *Life* (1873). Patteson was killed by natives of the Santa Cruz Islands on 20 September 1871.

DAY 251 Hugh Miller, *My Schools and Schoolmasters* (1854), chap. xvii.

DAY 252 Henry Vaughan, *Silex Scintillans* (1650).

DAY 253 John Woolman, *Journal* (1744), chap. i.

DAY 254 Mrs. Pearsall Smith, *The Unselfishness of God* (1903), pp. 16–18.

DAY 255 Thomas Arnold of Rugby, letter to J. C. Platt dated 4 February 1837; quoted in Stanley's *Life*.

DAY 256 William Cowper, Letter to William Unwin dated 7 September 1783.

DAY 257 Herbert Butterfield, *Christianity and History* (1949); the closing paragraph.

DAY 258 Samuel Rutherford, letter to the Laird of Carleton, dated from Aberdeen (where he was living in banishment) 10 May 1637.

DAY 259 Stopford A. Brooke, *Religion in Literature and Religion in Life* (1900), pp. 62–65.

DAY 260 Sir Arthur Eddington, *Science and the Unseen World* (1929), pp. 42 f.

DAY 261 William Guthrie of Fenwick, *The Christian's Great Interest* (1658), part i, chap. vi.

DAY 262 Forbes Robinson (1867–1904), *Letters to His Friends* (1904), pp. 99 f.

DAY 263 James Shirley, *The Contention of Ajax and Ulysses* (1659).

DAY 264 Archbishop Robert Leighton (1611–84), *Commentary on 1 Peter*.

DAY 265 Sir Thomas Browne (1605–82), *Christian Morals*, x, xi, xv.

DAY 266 *Spiritual Letters of Father Congreve* (1928), pp. 11 f. Letter dated St. Matthew's Day, 1884.

DAY 267 Frederick W. Robertson of Brighton (1816–53), *Sermons*, vol. iv, pp. 276 f.

DAY 268 François Malaval, *A Simple Method of Raising the Soul to Contemplation* (1669); English translation (1931), pp. 80 f.

DAY 269 Charles Kingsley (1819–75), *True Words for Brave Men* (posthumously published), pp. 65 f.

DAY 270 Edward Meyrick Goulburn, Dean of Norwich, *Thoughts on Personal Religion* (1861), part iii, chap. iv.

DAY 271 Principal John Caird, *University Sermons: preached before the University of Glasgow 1873–1898*, pp. 336 f.

DAY 272 Arthur Clutton-Brock, *Studies in Christianity* (1918), pp. 152–4.

DAY 273 Alexander Whyte, *Thomas Shepard, Pilgrim Father and Founder of Harvard* (1909), pp. 73 f.

DAY 274 From *The New Fioretti* by John R. H. Moorman (1946), pp. 67–69, where the references are given.

DAY 275 J. H. Oldham, *Life is Commitment* (1953), pp. 79 f.

DAY 276 Francis Thompson (1860–1907), *A Judgement in Heaven*.

DAY 277 A. E. Taylor, *The Faith of a Moralist* (1930), vol. i, pp. 137 f.

DAY 278 Heinrich Suso (1300–66), *Das Büchlein der einigen Wahrheit*, chap. xxi; Richard Raby's translation (1886).

DAY 279 Sir Thomas Browne, *Religio Medici* (1642), the Second Part.

DAY 280 Bishop Thomas Wilson (1663–1755), *Private Thoughts* in *Works*, vol. vii.

DAY 281 Joseph Joubert (1754–1824), *Pensées*; Katherine Lyttelton's translated selection (1898), pp. 13 ff.

DAY 282 Bishop Hugh Latimer (*c.* 1490–1555), *Sermons on the Card*, ii.

DAY 283 Desiderius Erasmus (1466–1536), *Encheiridion*, xii.

DAY 284 John Donne, *Eighty Sermons* (1640), ii; *Fifty Sermons* (1649), xxxii.

DAY 285 Richard Hooker (1594–1662), *Of the Laws of Ecclesiastical Polity*, book v, chap. xxxvii.

DAY 286 John Ker (1819–86), *Thoughts for Heart and Life*, pp. 211 f.

DAY 287 John Bunyan (1628–88), *The Pilgrim's Progress* (1678).

DAY 288 Richard Rothe (1799–1867), *Still Hours*; English translation (1886), pp. 45–49.

DAY 289 Henry Smith (1550?–91), Sermon on 'The Betraying of Christ'.

DAY 290 Sir John Davies, Queen Elizabeth's Attorney-General for Ireland, *Nosce Teipsum* (1599), *ad fin.*

DAY 291 Samuel Johnson, *The Rambler*, no. 184, 21 December 1751.

DAY 292 Juan de Valdes (*c.* 1500–41), *One Hundred and Ten Considerations*, 74: Nicholas Ferrar's translation of 1638.

DAY 293 James Denney, *The Way Everlasting* (1911), pp. 173 f.

DAY 294 William Law, *A Serious Call to a Devout and Holy Life* (1728).

DAY 295 John Henry, Cardinal Newman (1801–90), *Parochial and Plain Sermons*.

DAY 296 John Ker (1819–86), *Thoughts for Heart and Life*, pp. 62 f.

DAY 297 Francis Bacon, *Essays* (Final edition, 1625), xi.

DAY 298 Bishop Joseph Butler, *Sermons* (1729), vii.

DAY 323 Dietrich Bonhoeffer, *Widerstand und Ergebung* (1951); English translation, *Letters and Papers from Prison* (1953); Letters of 30 April 1944 and 25 May 1944.

DAY 324 Ben Jonson (1573–1637), *Discourses*, ci.

DAY 325 Samuel Johnson, *The Rambler*, no. 8; Saturday, 4 April 1750.

DAY 326 Sir Matthew Hale (1609–76), Lord Chief Justice of England.

DAY 327 Bishop Lesslie Newbigin, *Christian Freedom in the Modern World* (1937), pp. 84 f.

DAY 328 Abbé Henri de Tourville (1842–1903), *Letters of Direction*, English translation by Lucy Menzies (1939), pp. 78 ff.

DAY 329 John Newton, *Cardiphonia* (1781), Letters to a Nobleman, xxiii.

DAY 330 *Theologia Germanica* (*c.* 1350), chap. xxxviii; Susanna Winkworth's translation.

DAY 331 John of Ruysbroeck (1293–1381), *The Adornment of the Spiritual Marriage*; English translation (1916), pp. 64 f.

DAY 332 St. Anselm (1033–1109), *Meditations*: E. B. Pusey's translation (1856), Meditation xv.

DAY 333 Albert Schweitzer, *Memories of Childhood and Youth*; English translation (1925), pp. 94 f.

DAY 334 John Donne (1573–1631), Dean of St. Paul's, *Devotions upon Emergent Occasions*, xvii.

DAY 335 St. Teresa, *The Way of Perfection* (1564), chap. xv; translation of Abraham Woodhead (1671).

DAY 336 Thomas Chalmers, *Commercial Discourses* (1820), ix.

DAY 337 Charles Kingsley, *Two Years Ago* (1857), chap. xi.

DAY 338 H. H. Farmer, *The Healing Cross* (1938), pp. 170–2.

DAY 339 Sir Thomas Browne, *Religio Medici* (1642), The First Part.

DAY 340 Martin Luther (1483–1546), *Commentary on the Epistle to the Galatians*; English translation of 1575.

DAY 341 Sören Kierkegaard (1813–35), *Journals*; Alexander Dru's translation (1938), §§ 268, 443, 129, 209, 482.

DAY 342 F. W. Robertson of Brighton (1816–53), *Sermons*, vol. iv, pp. 305 f.

DAY 343 Joseph Joubert (1754–1824); Katherine Lyttelton's translated selection (1898), pp. 77 ff.

INDEX

OF AUTHORS AND SOURCES